MALAYSIAN
WORLD-VIEW

The **Southeast Asian Studies Program** (SEASP) was established in December 1976 by a group of scholars from Southeast Asia. It aims at promoting comparative research and writing on Southeast Asia by social science and humanities scholars of the region. It is directed by a committee composed of representatives of various countries in the region, but it is based at and formally affiliated with the Institute of Southeast Asian Studies.

The **Institute of Southeast Asian Studies** was established as an autonomous organization in May 1968. It is a regional research centre for scholars and other specialists concerned with modern Southeast Asia, particularly the multi-faceted problems of stability and security, economic development, and political and social change.

The Institute is governed by a twenty-one member Board of Trustees comprising nominees from the Singapore Government, the National University of Singapore, the various Chambers of Commerce, and professional and civic organizations. A ten-man Executive Committee oversees day-to-day operations; it is chaired by the Director, the Institute's chief academic and administrative officer.

MALAYSIAN WORLD-VIEW

EDITED BY

MOHD. TAIB OSMAN

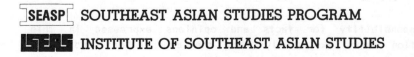
SOUTHEAST ASIAN STUDIES PROGRAM

INSTITUTE OF SOUTHEAST ASIAN STUDIES

MALAYSIAN
WORLD-VIEW

EDITED BY

MOHD. TAIB OSMAN

Published by
Institute of Southeast Asian Studies
Heng Mui Keng Terrace
Pasir Panjang
Singapore 0511

ISBN 9971-988-12-7

The responsibility for facts and opinions expressed in this
publication rests exclusively with the contributors and their
interpretations do not necessarily reflect the views or the policy
of the Institute or its supporters.

The Southeast Asian Studies Program (SEASP) was established in 1976 in response to a need to promote comparative research and writing on Southeast Asia by scholars in the Social Sciences and Humanities. Of particular concern was the lack of appropriate tertiary level teaching and reference materials pertaining to the region and written from local, though not necessarily nationalistic, perspectives.

Towards this end, SEASP launched three projects: one focused on the preparation of a series of country-specific volumes on Politics and Government, the second on History, and the third on World-View.

The project on World-View initially comprised the production of a volume each on Indonesia, Malaysia, the Philippines, Singapore and Thailand, but was finally scaled down to those involving Malaysia, the Philippines and Thailand only. As the work involved almost thirty scholars and the project was complicated, it became increasingly evident that the task was going to take much longer than originally envisaged. Each manuscript had to undergo a process of review by two independent referees - one from within and one from outside the region - to ensure the desired quality. The first volume of the series was published in Thailand in June this year. We are delighted to see the second volume of the series, Malaysia World-View, in print and look forward to the publication of the Philippine volume in due course.

Needless to say, the project on World-View could not have been completed without the co-operation of the individual contributors, the editor, and the co-ordinator involved. In the case of Malaysia, we are especially thankful to Prof Mohd. Taib Osman, who in addition to being the editor, was the coordinator of the project as a whole. We would also like to express our appreciation to the Ford Foundation for its generous financial support to SEASP and its various projects, including that on World-View.

In thanking all our benefactors and contributors, as well as others who have in one way or another helped to make this publication possible, it is clearly understood that the responsibility for the facts and opinions expressed in Malaysia World-View rests with the individual authors and editor, and their interpretations do not necessarily reflect the views and policies of SEASP or its supporters.

THE EXECUTIVE COMMITTEE
SOUTHEAST ASIAN STUDIES PROGRAM

CONTENTS

ACKNOWLEDGEMENTS

I wish to acknowledge the invaluable assistance given by the Southeast Asian Studies Program (SEASP) in making it possible to bring out the present volume on <u>Malaysia World-View</u>. A special word of thanks must go to the former and present co-ordinators of the program, namely, Dr Wilfredo F. Arce and Dr Jesucita L. Sodusta respectively, without whose patience and gentle handling, the whole project would have collapsed. To them is due the credit that the present volume finally sees daylight.

Gratitude is also due to the scholars who kindly agreed to participate in a seminar to discuss the concept of the project at the beginning. Needless to say, the responsibility for the contents and views expounded in this book remains with the respective authors themselves.

Kuala Lumpur
September 1985

Mohd. Taib Osman
Editor

Asmah Haji Omar is Professor of Malay Linguistics in the Department of Malay Studies, University of Malaya. She has a number of books and papers dealing with Malay linguistics to her credit.

Lee Poh Ping is a Political Scientist teaching at the Faculty of Economics and Public Administration, University of Malaya.

Md. Salleh Yaspar is Lecturer in the Universiti Sains Malaysia. He obtained his Masters degree from the University of the Philippines in the field of folklore and oral tradition. Presently, he is reading for his Ph.D. in Temple University, USA.

Mohd. Nor Ngah is Lecturer in the Department of Islamic Studies, University of Malaya. His field of specialization is Islamic Thought as manifested in the writings of religious scholars in the Malay area.

Mohd. Taib Osman is Professor of Malay Studies, University of Malaya. He has been involved with UNESCO, SEASP and other international bodies dealing with Southeast Asian cultures.

R. Rajoo is Lecturer in the Department of Indian Studies, University of Malaya. He teaches courses which deal with the local Indian community and culture.

Yap Beng Liang is Lecturer in the Department of Malay Studies. She teaches subjects such as kinship, social stratification and ethnography on Sabah where she did her field-work for her Masters degree.

INTRODUCTION

MOHD. TAIB OSMAN

The essays collected in this volume arise from the need to introduce the world-view of the peoples of Southeast Asia to the outside world as much as to the Southeast Asians themselves. It is a myth that Southeast Asians know themselves or about each other, for after the experience of thousands of years of history, and being truncated into many states and kingdoms over the past hundreds of years, and further subjected to various colonial rules and Western influence in recent times, the peoples of Southeast Asia are as varied in their background as ever in spite of the efforts to bring them together with the formation of ASEAN. It is to foster better understanding between the Southeast Asian nations, whose creations were very much a colonial legacy in the region, that the project to describe and discuss the world-view of each people or nation was envisaged.

Malaysia gained its independence from the British in 1963, as a result of the unification of three colonial territories -- British North Borneo, Sarawak and Singapore -- and the independent states of the Federation of Malaya. In 1965, Singapore left Malaysia, thus leaving the eleven states in the Malay Peninsula and the territories of Sabah (North Borneo) and Sarawak to forge a new nation. There are many factors that make Malaysia a viable nation, an important factor being that more than half of the people are indigenous and most of them adhere to Islam as a religion. Because of the background of the nine Malay

1

states which formed the backbone of the new nation and which had Islam as their official religion, the Federation of Malaysia adopted Islam as the official religion of the state, although it does not make Malaysia a Muslim state.

Bearing this fact in mind, the first essay presented here deals with the Islamic world-view of man, society and nature among the Malays of Malaysia. In it, one finds an exposition of how a universal religion like Islam finds expression in the books of kitabs as written by Malay scholars in the past. Although Islam provides the inviolable tenets through Allah's revelation to Holy Prophet Muhammad (peace be unto him) as found in the Qur'an, Islam has encouraged man to enquire and research further, to seek the truth of His word. The Malay scholars during the Islamic period had written a great number of works dealing with the teachings of Islam, and this "kitab literature" as it is known amongst scholars, has influenced the Malay mind over the last 500 years. It is not in keeping with reality therefore to ignore Islam from the Malay's world-view, for it forms the very essence of his personality. Thus, Mohd. Nor Ngah's essay is placed first in the present volume.

However much the Malay is imbued with Islam, he has as part of his cultural heritage, the traditions he had with him before he was converted to Islam. To-day, although Islam provides him with the foundation of his life, as a human being he still has his cultural roots to contend with. In reality, many facets of his life are still dictated by his pre-Islamic past, a combination of his indigenous and Hindu heritage. Realising the importance of this, the second essay by Mohd. Taib Osman attempts to deal with the traditional Malay socio-political world-view. As stated in the essay, the unifying factor in the constitution of Malaysia, the Yang Di Pertuan Agong, was born out of a contemporary political necessity, yet the institution is an old one, going way back to the early history of the Malays. Besides

2

that, the structure of the Malay state and that of the village, especially the world-view pertaining to them, are important to the understanding of the nation's viability as a political entity. It throws light on how the Malays are facing meaningfully the situation of change. It is imperative to realise that today in Malaysia, the Malays and other indigenous groups still form the definitive backbone of the Malaysian society.

With this in mind, two essays were set for Sabah and Sarawak. Unfortunately, the one on the Sarawak world-view was not forthcoming as the writer had gone to Australia to pursue a higher degree. However, the essay on the Sabah world-view was received from Yap Beng Liang, whose field-work was carried out among a remote Bajau community in that state. However, for the purpose of this volume, she has cast her net wider so as to include other groups besides the Bajau. She has utilised both the published sources and primary data to enable the reader to get an overall perspective of the world-view of the main groups in Sabah.

The Chinese who make up more than 30 per cent of Malaysia's population come from different dialect groups, depending on the original districts of China they hail from. However, in the early history of their immigration to Malaysia, they must have had some kind of world-view with regard to their sense of belonging or sense of togetherness, for otherwise they would not have prospered, let alone survived, in the hostile and unfamiliar environment. A lot of credit must be given to the role of secret societies, the clans and dialect-group associations in initially fostering a sense of social belonging among the Chinese. The essay by Lee Poh Ping attempts at outlining this factor in Malaysian history, especially in the nineteenth century, when the British first colonised the Malay states. Similarly, the Indians who form about 10 per cent of the Malaysian population, had the same problem. Although the Indian population is mixed, with some of the urban Tamils hailing from Ceylon, yet the majority of the Indian labourers imported by the British to work in the rubber estates and plantations were Tamils from South India. R. Rajoo has written an essay covering the period 1900-57 showing the world-view among the estate Tamils regarding social belongings. It is undeniable that many of the Tamils at the time regarded Malaya as a place to earn money before returning to India to retire. And it cannot be gainsaid that many still retain the ties with the mother-country, although they now hold Malaysian citizenship. Whatever it is, it is interesting to perceive how the world-view of the Indians or Tamils in this country is developing: from entertaining the idea of Malaya being a place of transit to Malaysia being a place of permanent residence.

It was unfortunate that a paper showing the world-view with regard to belonging to Malaysia among the various races had to be left out, as the writer was too busy, for otherwise we would have a complete picture encompassing all ethnic groups. As part of this volume, however, we have the world-view as expressed in the language, folk-tales and the arts in Malaysia. The essay by Asmah Haji Omar deals with the language of the Kedah peasantry, thus showing how the world-view of the traditional padi-planters is expressed in their language. It is an example of how rich and how expressive a language can be, and how the varied world-view of the people who live close to nature can be elicited from their language. It is important to know the richness of the dialect, for in the endeavour to build up a national vocabulary, the expressiveness of a dialect should not be ignored. The last essay deals with the world-view as gleaned from traditional folk-tales. The background is the same as the essay on language, that is, the Malay peasantry. Here the essay deals with content analysis. The essay by Salleh Jaafar tries to analyse the culture of the Malay folk-tale and folk drama. Besides emphasizing the points highlighted by the tales and dramas, which

4

show deep concern of the peasants, it also deals with the perception and aspiration of the people. And these can be gathered from the concept of distances, either physically or socially, as revealed by the tale or drama, or by the symbolism used. Salleh Jaafar tries to cover as much ground as possible, but a subject like this, to be really exhaustive, would warrant a book. Although the original plan included discussions of the world-view as evidenced by modern literature and the arts (like painting or sculpture), this had to be abandoned finally as the writers were too engrossed in other aspects of the world-view. Thus, only seven essays form this volume of work on the world-view.

ISLAMIC WORLD-VIEW OF MAN, SOCIETY AND NATURE AMONG THE MALAYS IN MALAYSIA

MOHD. NOR BIN NGAH

Before the coming of Islam, the Malays were animists and loose adherents of the Hindu faith, but with the coming of Islam, the Hindu faith was abandoned and the Islamic faith was adopted instead. Although all the Malays are Muslims today, most of them do not understand the Arabic language. Therefore, their understanding of Islam is mainly based on religious books written in the Malay language using the Arabic alphabet. These books are known as Kitab Jawi. This study, therefore, is based on a collection of Kitab Jawi which reflects the world-view of the Malays in Malaysia with regard to the Islamic interpretation of man, society and nature.

Definition of Kitab Jawi

Literally, kitab means "book", Jawi means "people of Jawa" which also means "Malays" as the Arabs in the past referred to all the people in the Malay Archipelago as Javanese. Therefore, Malay writing using the Arabic alphabet is called Jawi writing. Kitab Jawi are widely read in mosques, surau (prayer places) and pondok.[1] A kitab entitled Matla' alBadrain is used as a text book in the government religious schools of Johore. Kitab Jawi were written mostly between the seventeenth and the early twentieth centuries.

One of the earliest and most notable authors of Kitab Jawi is Nuruddin b. 'Ali Hasanji b. Muhammad Hamid al-Raniri who wrote Kitab Bad' Khalq al-Samawat wa al-Ard (The Creation of the Heavens and the Earth) on the request of Sultan Iskandar Thani who reigned in Acheh between 1636 and 1641. This book contains stories pertaining to the creation of man, angels, jinn and all things in the universe, based on the Qur'an, Hadith (Traditions of the Prophet) and stories from old texts. In the Fiqh (Islamic Law) section, he wrote Sirat al-Mustaqim (The Straight Path) in 1054 A.H., basing the book on a number of other works, such as Minhaj al-Talibin by Nawawi, Minhaj al-Tullab and Fath al-Wahhab by Shiekh al-Islam Zakariya Ansari, and many more Fiqh books of the Shafi'ite school. Al-Raniri also wrote more than 23 books on several branches of Islamic knowledge, including Tauhid, Sufism and Hadith.

In the eighteenth century, Muhammad Arshad b. Abdullah al-Banjari wrote a thick Fiqh book named Sabil al-Muhtadin (The Way of the Guided). He completed this work in 1195 A.H. (1780 A.D.) at the request of Sultan Tahmidullah ibn Sultan Tamjidullah. According to the author, Nuruddin al-Raniri's Sirat al-Mustaqim contained many Achinese words which were not fully understood by many people, so he wrote his own book based on Zakariya Ansari's Sharh Minhaj, Sharbini's Mughni, Ibn Hajar al-Haitami's Tuhfah, al-Ramli's Nihayah and other Arabic books of the Shafi'ite school.

Then came one of the most productive authors of Kitab Jawi, Daud b. Abdullah al-Fatani, who wrote in the nineteenth century. His total works include more than twenty books, his greatest book being Furu' al-Masa'il, written in 1254 A.H., based on al-Ramli's Fatawa and al-Mahalli's Kashf al-Litham. Besides writing on Islamic law, he also wrote on Tauhid or Theology.

Yet another author, Abd. al-Samad al-Falembani wrote a book

7

on Sufism entitled Hidayat al-Salikin in 1192 A.H. Although it was actually a translation of al-Ghazzali's Bidayat al-Hidayah, he added some of his personal views. Besides that, he also wrote Sair al-Salikin which was actually an adaptation of al-Ghazzali's Ihya'.

Two other books written by Ibn 'Ata'ullah al-Iskandari, namely Hikam and Taj al-'Arus, were also translated into the Malay language; the former was translated anonymously while the latter was translated by 'Uthman al-Funtiani.

The writers of Kitab Jawi came from every corner of the Malay Archipelago and their places of origin are identifiable from their names which normally indicate the names of their hometowns, for example, Daud al-Fatani (that is, Daud from Patani). However, some of them, being very pious, preferred to remain anonymous, claiming that they wrote for the sake of Allah (God), not for worldly purposes.

The Features and Contents of Kitab Jawi

Many of the Kitab Jawi are translations of Arabic texts, but they contain, in addition, their respective authors' views and ideas with regard to the original books. On language structure the Kitab Jawi are greatly influenced by Arabic structure as evidenced by the many Arabic words that are used. The spelling is more brief than modern Jawi writing.

Many branches of Islamic knowledge, for instance, Tauhid, Hadith, Fiqh and Sufism, are found in the Kitab Jawi, but an interpretation or commentary of the Qur'an is rarely written. The Malay scholars only interpret the Qur'an when it is relevant to their discussions. At the pondok the Arabic interpretation of al-Suyuti's al-Jalalyn[2] is usually used.

Most of the Kitab Jawi were published and printed by Sulayman Mar'ie of Singapore, Penang and Surabaya, but some were published in Mecca and Cairo. Generally, the absence of copyright laws means that anyone can freely print or publish Kitab Jawi without fear of prosecution just as it is being done nowadays. Usually, a small kitab is combined with another bigger one with the contents of the smaller kitab written in the margin of the bigger kitab.

The Tauhid section of the Kitab Jawi expounds the Sunni doctrine while the Fiqh section expounds the Shafi'ie school of thought, Sufism, and the teachings of al-Ghazzali. Teachings of Naqshabandi and other tariqah teachings are included in Tariqah (Sufi order). Nearly all Sufi orders trace their origin to the first and sixth Shi'ah Imam, namely 'Ali ibn Abi Talib and Ja'far al-Sadiq respectively.

Almost all the titles of the Kitab Jawi are in Arabic, perhaps to attract the readers, but their contents are written in Malay. For several centuries, the Malays relied on the Kitab Jawi to understand the teachings of Islam. However, in the past 25 years some Islamic texts have been written in the romanized script.

The Origin of Man

According to the literature of the Kitab Jawi, man was created from Nur Muhammad (The Light of Muhammad). This belief is to be seen in a number of Malay classical literary works such as Hikayat Nur Muhammad and Hikayat Ali Hanafiah. It was said that the Light was in the form of a peacock made from a very white jewel. Then Allah created a tree called al-Muttaqin and placed the peacock on the tree. It praised Allah for about 70,000

9

years. Then Allah created a mirror in front of it and when it saw its reflection in the mirror, it was ashamed and began to perspire. The drops of sweat became the souls of the Prophets, companions of the Prophet Muhammad, such as Abu Bakr Umar, Uthman and Ali, and all things in the Universe. The Light then prostrated five times and this is believed to be the origin of the five daily prayers for the Muslims.[3]

The above story sounds like a myth. It is not supported by any Qur'anic verse.[4] However, the authors of the Kitab Jawi have related several Hadith (Traditions of the Holy Prophet) concerning the subject to support their claim. According to one version, the Prophet said to Jabir, his companion, "The first thing Allah created was the light of your Prophet, O Jabir, then He created other things and you are one of them".[5] According to another version, the Prophet also said, "I came from Allah and the believers from me". There are also other sayings such as: "Allah created the soul of Prophet Muhammad from His Divine Essence and created everything in the universe from the light of Muhammad" or "O Jabir! Allah created before everything else the light of your Prophet which came from His light".[6] What Allah said in the Qur'an is: "Of a surety, there hath come unto you from Allah a light and a Book luminous".[7] The light refers to the Prophet Muhammad.[8] Another saying attributed to Prophet Muhammad is: "I am the father of all souls and Adam was the father of all bodies".[9] But Ahmad Khatib al-Minangkabawi opposed this view and said that the first thing created by Allah was Qalam (Pen); when it started to write, all creations began.[10] However, what is found in the Qur'an is: "Allah is the light of the heavens and the earth...".[11] The interpretation and commentary of this verse was made in detail by al-Ghazzali in his book Mishkat al-Anwar. He concluded that the light meant the faculty of intelligence which was considered a source of enlightenment,[12] and not a source of creation.

10

The Creation of Adam and Eve

It is widely stated in the Kitab Jawi that Adam was created from clay taken from several places on earth. The clay was in different colours and as such the skins of Adam's children were also of different colours.[13] Then Allah created Eve from the left rib of Adam.[14] Thus, the Malays believe that woman is the companion of man; she is not a rival to him but a life partner. Her role in life is complementary to the man's role. The manifestations of this belief can be seen in the everyday life of the Malays, especially in rural areas where men and women work together in the rice fields or rubber plantations. Women can own and inherit property and their status is never discussed because it is taken as understood.

The Soul of Man

Allah created Adam and breathed into him a spirit or soul which spread in his body. Then Adam stood up quickly,[15] and Allah gave him beautiful clothes and all things he desired except the wish to go near a forbidden tree in Paradise. But after Adam committed sin by eating the forbidden fruit, the beauty of his body disappeared. The fair colour of his skin remained only on the tip of his fingers -- his nails -- to remind his children how beautiful his skin was during his stay in Paradise.[16] Adam died at the age of 930 years, because "Every soul shall have a taste of death."[17] Death takes place when men have reached the age which Allah has appointed for them, not sooner nor later.[18] Hence, suicide cases are very rare among the Malays because they believe that only Allah has the right to take their souls.

The way death comes to man is decribed in a vivid manner by the Kitab Jawi. Death comes when the soul is separated from the

body by 'Izrail, the Angel of Death. He and his assistants draw
the soul up to a man's throat, where it is pierced by a poisonous
lance which detaches it completely from the body. 'Izrail then
seizes the soul as is explained by the Qur'an, "The Angel of
Death, put in charge of you, will take your souls. Then shall ye
be brought back to your Lord."[19] The dying man should be taught
to recite shahadah: "La ilaha ill-Allah" ("There is no god but
Allah") because he is in Sakarat al-maut (intoxication of death).
Reading Surah Ya Sin[20] and Surah al-Ra'd[21] is believed to help
the soul to separate quickly from the body and ease the pain.[22]
Such notions have influenced the behaviour of the Malays in
circumstances surrounding death in the family. For example, the
Malays do not generally wish their sick relatives to die in
hospital, as the last rites cannot be performed there. If they
think that the sick person has no hope of recovering, they will
take him home and read the verses from the Qur'an to him to make
his soul leave his body painlessly. When death finally takes
place, they will not wail or cry loudly as such an act is not
only forbidden but regarded as contrary to the will of the
Almighty. According to the Kitab Jawi, Allah and the angels
curse people who cry loudly over the dead.[23] However, silent
crying is allowed to show fortitude and patience in facing such a
misfortune.

After burial, and after the relatives of the dead leave the
grave, it is popularly believed that two large black frightful
angels will visit the dead man in his grave to determine whether
he is an infidel, a hypocrite, or a believer. They hold enormous
iron hammers of such weight that if they were to let them fall
down on a mountain they would grind it to powder.[24] The soul
after death enters the state or interval called Barzakh; that is,
the intervening state between death and the day of
Resurrection.[25] In order that this examination of the dead may
take place, Allah makes the spirit of the dead person return to
its body with all its senses and memory.[26] Thus, the Malays read

12

the Talqin[27] over the grave of the dead at the conclusion of the burial rituals supposedly to instruct and to remind the dead to answer the questions posed by the two angels correctly. The following questions illustrate this point: Who is your Lord? What is your religion? Who is your Prophet? Who is your Imam?...etc. If the dead person answers correctly, that "Allah is my Lord, Islam is my religion, Muhammad is my Prophet, Qur'an is my Imam," a beautiful angel will then approach him to assure him of the mercy of Allah and the delights of Paradise.[28] If he fails to provide the right answers, the two angels will beat him between his eyes with the iron hammers till he screams so loudly in anguish that his cries will be heard by all creatures except man and jinn.

The belief in life after death, torment and suffering in the grave is even reflected in Malay songs such as Selimut putih (white death shroud) and Rukun Islam. The words, like the Kitab Jawi, remind man of life after death, but the songs go further to exhort and remind man that torment and suffering await him in the after-life unless he conducts himself in the present life like a good and exemplary Muslim. Some Malays try to ease the punishment of the dead by reading the Qur'an over the grave in a ceremony called Tunggu kubur (guarding the grave). This ritual is performed the day after the funeral, continuing for several days -- usually three, seven or forty days, depending on the wealth of the deceased. If he is rich, his family can employ more than one Qur'an reader to recite the verses over a longer period over his grave, and if the family is not well-off, the reading will last only a few days.[29] At the house of the deceased, several religious feasts called Kenduri arwah may be held during the days that follow. These feasts generally held on the third, seventh, fortieth and hundredth day after the death, are occasions when prayers and dhikr (recitation of the name of Allah) are recited to benefit the soul of the deceased.[30]

13

Life in Paradise

Paradise described in the Kitab Jawi clearly notes that its
blessed people are dressed in clothes of the finest green silk
and brocade.[31] This view is consistent with the Qur'anic verse:
"For them there will be Gardens of Eternity; beneath them rivers
will flow, they will be adorned therein, with bracelets of gold,
and they will wear green garments of fine silk and heavy
brocade...".[32] Perhaps in emulating the inhabitants of Paradise,
members of a Malay religious group called al-Arqam wear green
robes and turbans, in the hope of being included among the
blessed in Paradise. They conscientiously attempt to form a
society similar to the society in Madinah during the days of the
Prophet. Green is generally considered by the Malays as a symbol
of Islam. For example, the symbol of the Pan Malaysian Islamic
Party is a white moon on a green background. The flags and
symbols of other Islamic associations are also green in colour.
Apart from green being the predominant "heavenly" colour,
Paradise is pictured as an idyllic world attainable only by men
who are pious and moral in the present life. Such is the reward
awaiting people of this category but the opposite, purgatory or
hell, awaits the wicked and the unbelieving.

Man and God

Allah is the creator of all things in existence and He has twenty
attributes. Almost all the Kitab Jawi explain the attributes of
Allah in great detail with very convincing dalil (proofs). The
proofs are of two kinds: namely, dalil naqli (proof from the
Qur'an and Hadith) and dalil 'aqli (proof of reason). An example
of dalil 'aqli: Allah is Self Existence; the sign of His
Existence is this world because this world is new; therefore it
is created. Proof that the world is new is provided as follows:
It is ever-changing because it is situated in space and time.

The belief in <u>Allah</u>, His oneness and His eternal attributes is called <u>Usul al-Din</u> (Principle of Religion).[33] Therefore, all Muslims, in fact those Malays who have adopted the Islamic religion, must know <u>Sifat Dua Puluh</u> (The Twenty Attributes of <u>Allah</u>) before anything else.[34] This belief is reflected in almost every Malay village in Malaysia where villagers are taught the <u>Sifat Dua Puluh</u> first by religious teachers in <u>surau</u> (prayer places) and mosques before they receive instructions on Islamic religious law and rituals.[35] Besides the 20 attributes, <u>Allah</u> also has 99 beautiful names called <u>Asma' al-Husna</u>. Examples of His names are <u>al-Rahim</u> which means "Merciful", <u>al-Ghafur</u> which means "All-forgiving" and <u>al-Wadud</u> which means "Loving-kindness". But in <u>Fiqh</u> or the Islamic law section, the <u>Kitab Jawi</u> depict <u>Allah</u> as an Avenger who wrecks vengeance on sinners.[36] The authors tend to focus more on the kinds of punishments one will suffer after death, providng minimal information about rewards and pleasures one may get in Paradise. Examples of this rather biased <u>Kitab Jawi</u> interpretation can be seen in <u>Kitab al-Yawaqit wa al-Jawahir</u>.[37] Ten out of the twelve chapters of the book dwell on the multifarious punishments, that is, punishments for those who neglect their daily prayers; those who behave unkindly towards their parents; those who consume liquor or engage in adultery or homosexuality; those who accept interest or practise usury; those who wail over the dead; those who fail to pay <u>zakat</u>; and those Muslims who destroy relationships among the faithful. The sinners will be called upon to suffer the punishments and hardship on the Day of Resurrection. <u>Tanbih al-Ghafilin</u> and many <u>Kitab Jawi</u> reveal a strong tendency to stress on the punishments for wrong-doing and ignore the rewards of doing what is right.

In fact, according to true Islamic teachings, there are both punishments and rewards, Hell and Paradise. The Prophet was sent to give good news and warning to man as explained in the Qur'an, "O Prophet, truly We have sent thee as a witness, a bearer of glad tidings and a warner...".[38] The one-sided teaching of the

15

Kitab Jawi is reflected only in the attitude of the Muslim Malays towards Allah. They tend to fear Allah more than love Him. In the weekly Friday sermon, the Khatib (preacher) always says "Fear Allah" when he translates the Arabic word "Ittaqullah". In fact, the word does not mean only to fear but to love Allah and be faithful to Him. It was only recently that the translation was corrected in some mosques. Nevertheless, almost all the Kitab Jawi translate the word as "Fear Allah". However, there is a good side to this attitude. Generally, the Malays are afraid or reluctant to commit sins especially when they are abroad or when they are staying in a non-Muslim society. Such an attitude is best exemplified by the Malay community in Capetown, South Africa, who are pictured as follows, "The Malays of the Cape have long been regarded as a most law-abiding, industrious and peaceful community, strict in their adherence to the practice of Islam. So far, little scientific value has been published to give their compatriots an understanding of the ideas which motivate their actions, the precepts which determine their behaviour or the beliefs which instil their way of life".[39] It is difficult to deny that it is the fear of Allah which motivates the community's actions and determines its behaviour.

Communication with Allah

Man stands at the centre of the universe, in the sense that he can communicate directly with Allah without the aid of an intermediary body, because Allah is very close to man, closer than his jugular vein.[40] But some Malays say that they use wasilah or an intermediary in approaching Allah. By this they mean that they pray to Allah in the name of the Prophet, saints and other people who happen to possess barakah or karamah (blessing) from Allah.[41] This belief is also reflected in the popular practice of some ignorant Malays who visit shrines or

16

tombs of saints to pray and to seek the blessing and intercession of the holy persons buried there. By and by, these places become sacred in the eyes of the worshippers and they eventually become the places where vows are made and offerings given. The tomb of Habib Buh in Singapore and numerous other graves and edifices are still visited and worshipped by Malays although Muslim scholars have spoken frequently and vigorously against such a practice. And from time to time, a man who claims himself to be a wali or a saint would soon procure a number of followers who believe in his magic. Saint-worship is often known as keramat in Malay, and some Kitab Jawi seem to contribute to this popular but erroneous practice in Islam.[42]

The Freedom of Man

The Malays believe in Allah's decree and predestination, both of good and evil or, in other words, believe in al-Qada' wa al-Qadar because it is the sixth article of faith (Rukun Iman). It means that Allah has, from eternity, predetermined and decreed everything, good as well as bad, believers and unbelievers, and everything that has been or will be depends entirely on His fore-knowledge and sovereign will.[43] Hence, some Malays are inclined to rely on fate rather than on their own efforts. They are easily contented and if anything happens, good or bad, they always say it is a taqdir or measure of Allah. The belief in al-Qada' wa al-Qadar, however, should motivate man to work hard without fear because everything is in the power of Allah, but many Malays misinterpret it by not working hard.[44]

The Malays are Sunni Muslims who follow the school of Ash'ari, a school peculiar to Southeast Asia. According to Ash'arite doctrine, man has no influence whatsoever on his voluntary actions; these are the result of Allah's power alone.

But though each individual action is foreordained, the individual "acquires" (Iktisab) it by identifying himself with it in action, and so becomes responsible for it as explained by the Qur'an.[45] However, the Malays tend to forget about effort and initiative which is stressed in Ash'arite doctrine. They are more inclined towards the school of Jabariyah which says that man is necessarily and inevitably compelled to act by the force of Allah's immutable decree. Man, like a feather in the air moving about at will, has neither power nor will nor choice. He is not more than an inanimate agent, with no control of his actions and consequently, he has no initiative. The inclination of the Malays towards the Jabariyah school of thought is caused by the complicated theory of Ash'ari which says that man's action is powerless, although he has the initiative and Ikhtiyar (free choice).[46] It means that man has no effective power; thus, this theory is almost identical with Jabariyah's theory. It is little wonder that even Sunnit critics of Ash'arism called this theory "compulsion" (jabr) theory. The Mu'tazilah school, on the other hand, is more easily understood by the layman. According to this school, man has power which is given by God and with this he is free to act whether in a good or bad way, that is to say, man is a free agent. But the Kitab Jawi consider the Mu'tazilites heretics, and states that Allah's curse will be on them.[47]

This trend of thought, that is, leaving things to fate, as held by the Malays is manifested in their proverb "Rezeki secupak takkan jadi segantang",[48] (what Allah has given cannot be increased by man). Of course, there is truth in the proverb, but man should not stop working because he does not know how much Allah will give him. Some Malays use this as a reason not to work, but it is not correct to think along such lines as no man has a right to question the work of Allah. The economic backwardness of the Malays in rural areas is one of the manifestations of their thought and perception of life. They misinterpret the theory of the Ash'ari school which says that man has no power or influence over his actions.[49]

18

In fact, several verses of the Qur'an explain that man's action is important. For example, the Qur'an says, "Verily, Allah will change not the condition of a folk until they (first) change that which is in their heart...".[50] There are also other verses which explain that man's fate has been predetermined by Allah. For example, the Qur'an says, "Say nothing will overfall us save what Allah has written for us. He is our patron, so let the believers put their trust in Allah".[51] Therefore, man should rely on Allah for his rewards only after working hard and not before that, because he does not know what Allah has decreed for him. In short, the opinions of Mu'tazillah, Jabariyah and Sunni are all correct, but they must be used only at such time and place that are appropriate and relevant. To the ordinary Malay, the popular notion of the question forms an important part of his world-view in everyday behaviour.

The Shi'ah followers, however, have a better solution; their Imam, Ja'far al-Sadiq said, "Discussion about al-Qada' wa al-Qadar (The Decree of Allah) is forbidden because Amir al-Mu'minin 'Ali said: "It is a deep sea, venture not into". As such, they have no trouble dealing with al-Qada' wa al-Qadar as it becomes a non-issue with them.

The Purpose of the Creation of Man

Man is created because Allah wants His creatures to know Him, as is explained by a Hadith qudsi (sacred Hadith). The Prophet said, "Allah said: I was a hidden treasure, then I liked to be known, therefore I created the creatures, so that they may know Me."[52] In the Qur'an Allah said, "I created the jinn and humankind only that they might worship Me".[53] Therefore, the most important thing in the writing of the Kitab Jawi is Ma'rifatullah (knowing Allah) and worshipping Him.

19

The Angels

The Angels form an important part of the world-view of the Malay Muslims. As explained in the Kitab Jawi, they are creatures of Allah, created from light. Being asexual, they neither eat nor drink; they can transform themselves into different shapes and they obey the law of Allah all the time. There are four Archangels (leaders of the angels) whom all Muslims must know, namely, Jibril, Israfil, Mikail and 'Izrail. The number of other angels is countless; there is an angel representing every drop of rain.[54] Besides the Archangels, there are Guardian Angels who continually attend to man to guard him from danger.[55] Consequently, the rural Malays are reluctant to take their baths naked even in fully closed bathrooms because they believe that the Guardian Angels and the Angels of Mercy will go away when a man is undressed. There are also Recording Angels who constantly observe and take note of man's actions.[56] Every man has two of them, one standing on the right, to write down his good actions, the other on his left to note his bad actions. They are constantly watching (raqib) and are always present (a'tid).[57]

The Jinn

The jinn plays a crucial role in the beliefs of the Malays, both as propounded in the religious literature as well as in legends and tales. According to religion, they are creatures of Allah, created from fire as explained by the Qur'an, "And He created jinn from fire free of smoke".[58] The Iblis or Satan was formerly a kind of jinn, but when he disobeyed Allah's commands he became Iblis,[59] as explained by the Qur'an, "...they bowed down except Iblis; he was one of the jinn and he broke the command of his Lord...".[60] Some jinn are Muslims and some are not. They are of different kinds and shapes.[61] The Malays believe that man can

20

befriend a _jinn_, and as a result the Malay _Bomoh_ (medicine man) sometimes seeks the help of the _jinn_ to cure the sick. Such a notion originates from the folklore of the people. Some _jinn_ eat and drink while some do not. It is said that they eat bones and, therefore, the _Fuqaha'_ (Muslim jurists) disapprove _(makruh)_ of the use of bones as instruments to clean _najis_.[62]

Society

How the Malay Muslims view the nature of society is attributable to the _Kitab Jawi_. All believers of Islam are supposed to possess equal rights and duties in the community to which they may be admitted regardless of sex, class, office, or position. In Islam, all men are equal; there is no racial discrimination, no distinction, save that of piety,[63] as explained by the Qur'an "Verily, the most honoured of you in the sight of _Allah_ is the most righteous of you. _Allah_ is Knower, Aware".[64] The Malays tend to stick to this Qur'anic structure of society. In Malay society, there are no discussions or questions about colour or race. This belief is reflected in their everyday life where inter-marriage with non-Malay Muslims, especially with Arabs and Indian Muslims is common. Descendants from such inter-marriages live mostly in cosmopolitan cities like Penang and Singapore. Arab-Malay descendants usually bear the titles _Sheikh_ or _Syed_ before their names signifying, in the instance of the latter, that they are descended from the family of the Holy Prophet.

Generally, the Malays are broad-minded Muslims in spite of the fact that they can be fanatical in their religious beliefs especially when the truth of their faith is questioned. Towards the other Muslim sects or schools of law, they are amenable and would accept certain interpretations under special circumstances. The Indian Muslims tend to be the followers of the sect of

21

Hanafi, while the Malays are the followers of the Shafie school, but they agree on many aspects as according to the Kitab Jawi all four schools (Maliki, Hanafi, Shafi'ie and Hanbali) are recognized as belonging to orthodox Islam. The Malays readily take Hanafi law instead of Shafi'ie in some cases. For instance, in the paying of Zakat al-Fitr[65] which according to Shafi'ie law must be paid in kind (in this case a measure of the best rice or wheat), the Malays tend to follow the Hanafi law. According to Hanafi law, it is better to pay in cash or money, or in kind. Thus, the Malays pay their Zakat al-Fitr in cash because it is easier and more practical.

From the Shi'ah sect, the Malays also receive some influences; for example, many Malay Hikayat (stories) such as Hikayat Ali Hanafiah[66] and Hikayat Nur Muhammad, are influenced by Shi'ah ideas. During the Islamic revolution in Iran, the Malays in Malaysia, especially the younger generation, supported the leadership of Ayatullah Khumaini although he and his followers are Shi'ah Muslims. This is another reflection of their belief and perception about Muslim brotherhood, solidarity and international community.

The Malays are very sensitive about religion. They feel very hurt if they are not considered Muslims although some of them do not perform their religious duties regularly. To a certain extent, this is reflected in every general election campaign in the rural areas, when the Malays from one party accuse the Malays in another party of being infidels because the latter's party espouse policies which are perceived as not following the strict tenets of Islam. Such accusations usually lead to quarrels and boycotts among the villagers. The adherence of the Malays to Islam is reflected in the word "Malay" itself which sometimes is taken to mean "Muslim" in Malaysia. Therefore, converts to Islam sometimes say that they have become Malays, meaning Muslims. In the Constitution of Malaysia, a

Malay is defined as a Muslim who speaks the Malay language habitually and conforms to the Malay custom.

Kitab Jawi emphasize the importance of solidarity in society; Qat' al-arham or severing relationships with other Muslims or relatives is a grave sin. As a Hadith explained, if a person left his society and then died without repentance, he would have died an unbeliever.[67] The Prophet said, "A Muslim who does not speak to his fellow Muslims for more than three days, and then dies, will go to Hell."[68] Hence, the Malays do not believe in an individualistic social system and this is manifested in their everyday life. The Malay saying "kera sumbang" (single monkey) is aimed at a person who has no social contacts with others. The teaching of Islam itself compels the Malays to work together. From the cradle to the grave, a Malay must live together and co-operate with other members of his society. For example, if a man dies, it is fardu kifayah to attend his funeral.[69] The dead must be buried quickly for according to a Hadith, he who dies in the early morning ought not to rest at midday anywhere but in his grave.[70] Thus, urgent work like this must be done in co-operation with the members of the society, otherwise it cannot be accomplished.

The prayer of Jama'ah[71] or prayer in congregation is also fardu kifayah; the whole community in a village will be guilty of sin if its members do not offer prayer in congregation in surau or mosques. Furthermore, the reward of the prayer is twenty-seven times more than that of ordinary prayers.[72] Such a world-view so dominates Malay life that every village has a surau or mosque for the villagers to pray together, especially the Friday noon prayer. The reason for the emphasis on prayer in congregation is to unite Muslim society, as explained by the Qur'an, "And hold fast all of you together, to the rope of Allah and do not separate...".[73] The prayer in congregation can be offered during the usual daily prayers, that is, five times a day

23

-- at dawn, at noon, in the afternoon, at sunset and at nightfall. All Muslims must say their prayers in a definite way, bowing and prostrating in the direction of Ka'bah. Washing is strictly necessary before prayer; that is why there are tanks of water outside all surau and mosques in Malaysia, so that those going to prayer can make sure that they carry out their ablutions.[74]

Friday noon prayer is the ultimate prayer for the unity of the Muslims. It rests on direct command.[75] It is fardu 'ain (the bounden duty) of every Muslim to attend this public noon prayer personally with the congregation at the mosque. Any person who does not perform this prayer three times consecutively will be regarded as a bad Muslim[76]. The importance of this prayer is enforced in the Muslim law of several states in Malaysia, which stipulates that a man can be fined for not attending Friday prayer three times consecutively without reason. It is important to note here that it is not the law that gives rise to behaviour but rather it is the religious injunction which gives rise to the world-view and it, in turn, because of its high value, is thought fit to be enshrined in law.

The Hajj or pilgrimage to Mecca is the fifth foundation on which Islam stands. The performance of this pilgrimage, at least once in a person's life-time is obligatory for every Muslim, male or female, who is able to do it.[77] Muslims from different corners of the globe converge at Mecca on their Hajj or Annual Pilgrimage. It is the aim of every Malay to go to Mecca. Those who have been to Mecca can be distinguished by the title Haji (for men) or Hajah (for women). This can be used as a prefix before their names and will win them their society's respect. The title is a reflection of how much the Malays appreciate the Hajj performance, but their eagerness to go to Mecca sometimes makes them irrational. For instance, some Malays sell their lands and properties to get money for the journey. As a result

24

they get poorer materially, although they feel happy at having fulfilled the spiritual requirement. This can be attributed to the world-view they hold with regard to spiritual duties. To cope with this problem, a pilgrimage fund has been established in Malaysia to enable any Muslim to visit Mecca when he has adequate savings in the fund.

Besides the institution of Hajj, the payment of Zakat (alms) is another duty that continually reminds the Muslims that "The believers are brothers".[78] In conclusion, the nature of worship and ritual in Islam is related to the unity of Muslims; thus, it contributes to the solidarity and unity of the Malay society in Malaysia.

Value System: Seeking of Knowledge

The emphasis by the Kitab Jawi on the pursuit of knowledge is manifested in Malay society. Every Malay sends his children to learn to read the Qur'an; therefore illiteracy in the Arabic alphabet is very low. Abdullah Munshi observes in his Hikayat Abdullah that "It is the custom in all Malay countries, that the people do not study their own language, but from childhood they begin to read the Qur'an without really understanding it".[79] Of course, Abdullah did not agree with the idea of teaching the Qur'an before anything else. According to N.J. Ryan, there is little doubt that this emphasis on the Qur'an and little else caused a deterioration in Malay education in the seventeenth and eighteenth centuries.[80] However, that is the world-view of the Malay society; the Malays appreciate knowledge, and what knowledge is better than the Qur'an, the Holy Book of Allah?

According to the Kitab Jawi, acquisition of knowledge is obligatory to all believers, male or female.[81] In fact, Islam,

25

more than any other religion, stresses the importance of learning. The first revelation to the Prophet was in praise of learning:

Read! In the name of thy Lord and Cherisher who created -- created man out of mere clot of congealed blood. Read! And thy Lord is most bountiful. He who taught the use of the pen - taught men that which he knew not.[82]

Some of the Kitab Jawi confine their discussions to the importance of knowledge and its value; for instance Kitab Hidayat al-Mukhtar provides commentaries and explanations of 40 Hadith pertaining to the value of knowledge.[83] However, most the Kitab Jawi define knowledge as "Islamic knowledge" only. Therefore, it is obligatory for every Muslim to learn the Shari'ah or Islamic law and know the essence of Allah and His attributes.[84] Only Hidayat al-Salikin explains that any knowledge which benefits mankind should be learned. Going out of his house in the early morning to study in a quest for knowledge is better for a man than one thousand years of prayer, but this is on condition that he must be sincere in his study for the sake of Allah and not for the sake of money or any worldly purpose.[85]

Thus, although the pursuit of knowledge is encouraged in Malay society, it is confined mostly to Islamic knowledge. Religious education has always been respected by the Malays as well as by the ulama or religious scholars. The Malays value the Qur'an as a primary source of Islamic law. Although most of them do not understand Arabic, they find the translations and commentaries made by Muslim scholars reliable.[86] Additionally, they learn to read it correctly believing that Allah will reward them if they read even a verse of it. Every year a Qur'an reading competition is held in Malaysia to raise the standard of Qur'an reading. The emphasis on Qur'an reading is evidenced in

Malay customs and ceremonies; for example, at a wedding ceremony, khatam Qur'an, or reading of the Qur'an, is usually observed. A gathering is held at which a number of religious men are present and the bride then reads portions of the Qur'an. After this, a feast is held and the benedictions (do'a selamat) are read.

The main reason why the Portugese, the Dutch and the British failed to convert the Malays to Christianity, although promotion of Christianity was one of the objectives of these colonial powers, is the fact that, in the world-view of the Malays, knowledge is synonymous with the teachings of Islam.

Material Value

Very few Kitab Jawi speak about the material welfare of man, whether as an individual or as a group or both. Many of the Kitab moreover denounce material life or worldly pleasures. Below are some examples of statements found in them which very much influence the world-view of the Malays towards life:

"The Prophet said: The world is a dirty corpse".[87]

"The Prophet said: Live in this world as if you are a foreigner or a traveller, and consider yourself as an inhabitant of the grave".[88]

"The Prophet said: This world is a prison for the believers and a Paradise for the unbelievers".[89]

"Umar ibn al-Khattab said: Do not enter the houses of the rich because the wrath of Allah is on them".[90]

"Poverty is one of the treasures of Allah and one of the blessings of Him".[91]

27

Many more Kitab Jawi denounce the abuse of worldly life. Only in a few of them are there discussions on world economic affairs. The rest deal mainly with Ibadat, that is, worship in Muslim law. Kitab Perukunan is the most widely used in the teaching of basic Ibadat. The Hadith which denounce worldly life as explained in the Kitab Jawi should be interpreted correctly. The word Dunya (world) in Arabic also means "near"; therefore, if one's money and wealth is used for the purpose of the near future without thought of the hereafter, or the wrath of Allah on the Day of Resurrection, one is capable of all kinds of immoral actions. But if one's money or property is used wisely, this is not forbidden at all.

This one-sided explanation of Islamic teaching is reflected in Malay society. Generally, the Malays are not very keen to acquire material wealth believing that they have another better and permanent world to live in. For them, this world is not very important being transitory as revealed in their pantun: "Dunia ini pinjam-pinjaman, Akhirat juga akan sungguhnya" (This world is temporary, the hereafter is the real world). Probably, this is one of the reasons why Malay society is backward materially but rich in spiritual and traditional values. Economic planners in Malaysia failing to understand that the world-view of the Malays, especially those in the rural areas, was not inclined towards gaining material wealth, therefore had a difficult task in uplifting the economic position of the Malay peasants. Islam forbids a person to deny his body its natural needs. In an attempt to refine the spirit, the joys of life should thus not harm the body and soul. The philosophy that "man does not live by bread alone" is true only in a society which has already solved the problems of bread, not in one in which man is struggling hard for survival.

The majority of the Malays live in rural areas and economically, theirs is a peasant society. There is a Hadith pertaining to agriculture. According to the Prophet, if the produce of a tree or crop is eaten by bird, man or beast, the reward will be given to the planter.[92] This Hadith encourages the Muslims to work hard believing their efforts will be rewarded and will not be in vain. It also implies that agriculture is important for the economy of every country. Unfortunately, only one Kitab Jawi, that is, al-Jauhar al-Mauhub, emphasizes this Hadith, even though it is very important in the context of the Malay peasant society.[93] On the importance of trade and commerce, only one or two Kitab Jawi relate a Hadith transmitted by al-Tirmidhi: "The honest merchant will be with the Prophets, the believers and martyrs in the world to come".[94] Perhaps the absence of such encouragement explains the backwardness of the Malays in commerce.

Woman and Society

In Malay society, a woman is respected and considered a companion who shares a man's sorrows, joys and burdens. When she is a little girl, it is obligatory for her father to support and look after her until she gets married. After marriage, the obligation is transferred to her husband, and if she becomes a widow, her children are obliged to support her. If she has no children her brothers will have to bear the burden.

From the cradle to the grave, a woman in Malay society is supported and looked after by her father, brother, husband and children. It is not imperative for a woman in traditional Malay society to earn a living, as the usually large family circle ensures her a special place in it, offering a welcome refuge from social and economic pressures, even if she has no father or husband. Therefore, the inheritance share of a female heir is half of that allotted to a male.[95] An exception, however, is to

29

be found in the matriarchal society of Negeri Sembilan which gives the customary lands to the female descendants only. Thus, the man bears all the economic responsibilities; it is his duty to support his family completely even if his wife is rich and economically independent. That is why he gets a double share according to the Islamic law of inheritance.

Many Kitab Jawi explain the responsibilities of a woman towards her husband; some of the Kitab merely confine their text to the responsibilities of husband and wife. Kitab Muhimmah and 'Uqud al-Lajjayn are two examples of Kitab Jawi which attempt to provide some guidelines. However, most of the discussions and explanations spell out punishments meted out to women who are unfaithful to their husbands. Once again the Kitab Jawi give one-sided explanations. Nearly all the chapters of the books discuss the responsibilities of a woman, with only a few pages on the responsibilities of a man. Below are some examples of the contents of Kitab Jawi:

> The Prophet said, "If a human being can prostrate to another human being, I shall ask every woman to prostrate to her husband".[96]

> Disobedience to one's husband is among the great sins. Going out of the house without getting permission from one's husband is called disobedience and it is forbidden.[97]

And here is a portrait of the typical woman depicted by Kitab Jawi:

> The Prophet said, "A Muslim cannot obtain (after righteousness) anything better than a well-disposed, beautiful wife: such a wife, when ordered by her husband to do anything, obeys; and if her husband looks

at her, is happy; and if her husband swears by her to do a thing, she does it to make his oath true; and if he be absent from her, she wishes him well in her own person by guarding herself from inchastity, and takes care of his property".[98]

This teaching forms an important part of the world-view of Malay women who seek their husbands' permission to go out of their own homes. There are no women liberation movements in Malay society although there are some voices of protest from the urban Malay women asking for equal rights. From the Islamic point of view, the question of the equality of men and women is meaningless. It is like discussing the equality of a rose and a jasmine. Each has its own perfume, colour, shape and beauty. Men and women are not the same; each has particular features and characteristics. Women are not equal to men. But then neither are men equal to women. Islam envisages their roles in society not as competing roles but as complementary ones. Each has certain duties and functions in accordance with his or her nature and constitution.[99]

Of the many instructional information in the Kitab Jawi, some guidance in choosing one's bride is also provided. The Prophet said, "A woman may be married on account of qualifications: one on account of her money; another, on account of the nobility of her pedigree; another, on account of her beauty; a fourth, on account of her faith; therefore look out for religious women, you will be rich".[100] Thus, in Malay society, religion is one of the criteria for judging the value of a woman. After marriage, Malay women retain their maiden names, and thus unlike women in the West, they retain their identity. The false notion that a Muslim woman is inferior to man arises from the misinterpretation of the teachings of Islam.

31

Parent-Child Relationship

Given in detail in the Kitab Jawi are the duties of parents towards a child and the duties of a child towards his parents, for example:

> The Prophet said, "Verily, for a man to teach his child manners is better for him than to give one bushel of grain in alms".

> "No father has given his child anything better than good manners".[101]

> The Prophet said, "Say to a good child: Do as you like, you will not go to Hell, and say to the bad child: do as you like, you will not enter Paradise".

> The Prophet said, "The consent of Allah is in the consent of parents and the wrath of Allah is in the wrath of parents".[102]

Therefore, parental obligations are generally observed in Malay society to be consonant with these teachings. There is a Hadith which explains that everybody is responsible to the society and to the family:

> The Prophet said, "Everyone of you is a ruler and everyone of you shall be questioned about those under your rule; the king is a ruler and he shall be questioned about his subjects; and the man is a ruler in his family and he shall be questioned about those under his care; and a woman is a ruler in the house of her husband and she shall be questioned about those under her care; and the servant is a ruler so far as the property of his master is concerned and he shall be questioned about that which is entrusted to him".[103]

32

Thus parent-child relationship is very close in Malay society. There is no generation gap between the old and the young because everybody is expected to know his role in the family and society.

Political World-View

When Islam came to Malaya, the Malays subtituted the Sultanate for the Hindu Kingdom and in doing so, continued the concentration of political and religious authority in one person, that is, the Sultan. However, the Sultan must be supported by the ulama (religious scholars) as religion is both inseparable from politics and the basis of authority. According to the Kitab Jawi, the installation of the Sultan or King is fardu kifayah. The election of the King is valid if it is conducted by qualified persons such as the ulama and other important persons, or by will, as in the case of Abu Bakr who appointed 'Umar as his successor, or by the force of the King to appoint his son.[104]

In Islam, the supreme commander of the Muslim community after the death of the Prophet was called Imam or Caliph.[105] But after the power of the Caliph in Baghdad declined, the provinces of the Caliphate were ruled by independent governors who called themselves "Sultans". In his own dominion, every Sultan was an absolute ruler with unlimited powers over matters both spiritual and temporal. During this time, Islam came to the Malay Archipelago, and consequently the Malays called their supreme commander "Sultan".

Kitab Jawi support the Sultan by regarding him as the shadow of Allah upon the earth. Disobedience is only permissible in the event of the ruler's decisions being manifestly contrary to the Qur'an and the Sunnah or Hadith, as stated by Muniyat al-Musalli:

33

The Prophet said, "Respect the Sultan and honour him, because he is the honour of Allah and the shadow of Him upon the earth if he is a just Sultan".[106] Although the Kitab Jawi and the Malay scholars support the institution of Sultan, they always warn the ruler against ruling unjustly. From Ma'qil ibn Yasar, we are told that if a ruler rules unjustly he will not have a place in paradise.[107] In the context of political affairs, the Kitab Jawi provide a fairer account, that is, they support the Sultan but simultaneously issue stern warnings to him. Below is one of the verses quoted from the Kitab Jawi:

For the wrong-doers (unjust rulers) we have prepared a fire whose (smoke and flames) like the wall and roof of a tent, will hem them in.[108]

The ruler is also reminded that the prayer of the oppressed is usually accepted by Allah because there is no veil between him and Allah.[109] Imam al-Ghazzali advocated that it is wrong for anyone to pray for an unjust ruler, for in so doing, he is proclaiming that he likes the wickedness and sins on earth.[110] Evidence of this view is seen in this Malay saying: "Raja adil raja disembah, raja zalim raja disanggah" (The good king will be honoured, the bad king will be opposed). It can also be seen in Hikayat Hang Tuah where Hang Jebat, a Malay warrior, defied the power of the Sultan because the latter had transgressed the ethics of a just king. The world-view that the Sultan wields authority to rule is seen to-day in the position of the Malay Sultan who doubles as the Head of Religion in his state.

Nature

According to the Kitab Jawi, nature is the creation of Allah. The Qur'an refers constantly to the phenomena of nature as signs of Allah to be contemplated by the believers:

In the creation of the heavens and the earth and in the alternation of the night and the day there are indeed signs for people of understanding.[111]

Abdullah ibn 'Abbas said, "A group of men think about the Essence of Allah, therefore the Prophet says to them: You must think about the creations of Allah and think not of his Essence because the intelligence of man cannot reach that stage."[112]

Allah created the universe in six stages or processes, and subjected it to a pattern of physical laws which it must follow perfectly, inevitably and blindly:

Lo! your Lord is Allah Who created the heavens and the earth in six days, then mounted He the Throne...[113]

In other words, he has created everything in the universe and fixed for each a measure, a taqdir or a law of nature. Destruction of nature and natural beauty is forbidden, for the Kitab Jawi explain that killing animals unnecessarily is unlawful. This may be seen in the following Hadith:

The Prophet said, "There is no man who kills a sparrow without cause but Allah will question him for it".[114]

Thus, the Malays are nature lovers, and they do not destroy nature and natural resources unnecessarily. They believe that man is the guardian and custodian of nature and this forms part of their world-view of nature.

Conclusion

The Islamic world-view of the Malays is identical with the world-view of other Muslims in principle. In some cases, the Malays have their own interpretations and perceptions in line with the teachings they receive from the Malay ulama especially the Kitab Jawi that they write. The subjects dealt with by these kitab or religious texts are numerous, but basically they deal with moral questions affecting the individual as well as the communal lives of the Malays. Thus, a study of the Malay world-view must highlight the Kitab Jawi.

NOTES

1. Literally, it means "hut". It is usually built near the teacher's house and the students reside in the pondok where they receive instruction in a wide range of Islamic studies including Tafsir, Hadith, Tauhid, Arabic grammar and Tasawwuf.

2. According to HAMKA, an interpretation of the Qur'an has been written in Malay by Shaikh Aminuddin Abdurrauf bin Ali al-Fansuri in the middle of the seventeenth century. See H.B. Jassin, Pengantar Qur'an al-Karim (Jakarta, 1977), p. 7.

3. Daqa'iq al-Akhbar, pp. 2-3; Kashf al-Ghaibiyah, p. 3; Bad' Khalq, pp. 4-5.

4. The Qur'an explains that man was created from clay. See XII: 5. But the Kitab Jawi explains the origin of all things besides that of man.

5. Durr al-Nafis, p. 21.

6. Ibid., p. 22. All the above Hadith are not from the famous six collections of Hadith, viz. the collections of Bukhari, Muslim, Tirmidhi, Abu Daud, Nisa'i and Ibn Majah, which were most revered by Muslims. Thus, the stories told were not based on any strong foundation. The stories were usually told by Wahb I Munabbih, a Persian Muslim, as well as by Abdullah Ibn Salam and Ka'b al-Ahbar, Jews who became Muslims.

7. The Qur'an, V:15.

8. Durr al-Nafis, p. 22.

9. Ibid.

10. Al-Shumus al-Lami'ah, p. 25.

11. The Qur'an, XXIV: 35.

12. Abdullah Yusuf Ali, The Holy Qur'an, 3rd edition, pp. 920-922; Miftah al-Jannah, p. 5.

13. Kashf al-Ghaibiyah, p. 9.

14. This view is supported by a Hadith narrated by Bukhari that women was created from a bent rib and that man should be very careful not to hurt her feelings; he should not be too lenient nor too harsh in dealing with woman. As in the case of a bent rib, if we want to straighten it forcefully, it will break, and if we let it alone, it will stay bent in shape. The best way to deal with woman is to be gentle and patient. See Ibn Hajar, Fath al-Bari, Cairo, 1325 A.H., Vol. VI, pp. 231-232.

15. For this reason Allah said in the Qur'an, "For man is given to hast (deed)". XVII: 11.

16. Daqa'iq al-Akhbar, p. 5.

17. The Qur'an, III:185.

18. The Qur'an, VII:34.

19. The Qur'an, XXXII: 11; Daqa'iq al-Akhbar, p. 16.

20. Chapter 36.

21. Chapter 13.

22. Matla' al-Badrain, p. 51; al-Yawaqit wa al-Jawahir, pp. 20-22; Tanbih
    al-Ghafilin, p. 9.

23. Daqa'iq al-Akhbar, p. 15; Kash al-Ghaibiyah, pp. 27-28; Kitab al-Lubab, pp.
    140-145.

24. Daqa'iq al-Akhbar, p. 16; Kashf al-Ghaibiyah, p. 34.

25. The Qur'an, XXIII:100.

26. Jauharah al-Tauhid, p. 45.

27. Durr al-Thamin, pp. 70-71 explains how to perform Talqin. But the use of
    Talqin is widely debated because there is a Hadith which says, "From Abu
    Hurairah, the Prophet said, "When a man died, his deeds come to an end
    except for three things: Sadaqah jariah (charity that still benefit the
    people), or knowledge that is useful for other man, or a good child who
    prays for him." Sahih Muslim, Cairo 1955, III, p. 1255. It is understood
    from the said Hadith that nothing can help the dead man except the three
    sources which actually come from his own efforts - giving charity, teaching
    people, and giving good education to his children. However, it obviously
    benefits the living to hear the Talqin which is very instructive and make
    them conscious of their own earthly conduct.

28. Actually the good deeds of man will help to answer the questions because all
    good deeds during his life help him in his grave.

29. The practice is rare nowadays.

30. The validity of the practice is widely discussed and debated from time to
    time since 30 years ago. Like the Talqin, It is doubtful whether the
    rewards can be transferred or given to the dead because the Hadith which was
    referred to earlier clearly explains that only three sources of reward can
    be obtained by a dead man.

31. Al-Yawaqit wa al-Jawahir, p. 48.

32. The Qur'an, XVIII: 31.

33. Some Kitab Jawi discuss only the twenty attributes of Allah and nothing else
    like Kitab Sifat Dua Puluh, Matn Jauharah al-Tauhid and others.

34. *Matn Jauharah al-Tauhid*, p. 9; *Aqidah al-Najin*, p. 13; *Sharh Usul al-Tahqiq*, p. 2.

35. So much stress on monotheism sometimes causes young Malays to resort to emotional and extreme actions by damaging idols belonging even to other religions. In 1978 four Malay youths were killed and one was sentenced to six months jail on 16 March 1979 for damaging idols in a Hindu temple in Kerling, Selangor.

36. This is based on the saying of the Qur'an which says: "...then to those who is transgressed, We meted out retribution..." (XXX:47). But He is also most forgiving and merciful as explained by other verses.

37. By Muhammad Ali b. Abd. al-Rashid b. Abdullah al-Jawi al-Qadi al-Sambawi (a translation from Arabic text).

38. XXXIII:45. Although the Prophet is referred to as a warner, *Allah* also uses the words *Bashir* and *Mubashshir* (Messenger of Good Tidings) 32 times as reference to the Prophet Muhammad in the Qur'an.

39. Mia Brandel-Syrier, *The Religious Duties of Islam as taught and explained by Abu Bakr Effendi* (Leiden, 1960), p. vii, preface.

40. See the Qur'an, L:16.

41. This shows that they misunderstand the word *wasilah* which in the Qur'an means the way to bring oneself closer to *Allah,* as decreed by Him, "O, ye who believe, Do your duty to *Allah,* seek the means *(wasilah)* of approach unto Him..." (V:35). This question was explained in detail by the *al-Arqam* magazine, No. 9 (Kuala Lumpur 1398 A.H.), pp. 5-10.

42. For an account of saint-worship, see Mohd. Taib Osman, "Indigenous, Hindu and Islamic Elements in Malay Folk Belief" (Ph.D. diss., Indiana University, 1967).

43. *Usul al-Tauhid*, p. 26; *Matn Jauharat al-Tauhid*, p. 29.

44. The Malays are normally not superstitious; for example, they do not believe that number thirteen is unlucky.

45. "What happens to thee of good things is from *Allah,* and that happens to thee of evil is of thyself" (IV: 81).

46. *Matn Jauharat al-Tauhid*, p. 27.

47. Ibid.

48. *Cupak* is a measure of capacity, equal to a half of a coconut shellful or a quarter of a *gantang.* If *Allah* gives only a *cupak* of food, man cannot increase it to a *gantang.*

49. Many Islamic scholars have explained this issue in the Malaysian mass media

encouraging the Malays to work hard and not to rely on fate alone, because Ash'ari also said that man must work hard as he is genuinely responsible for his acts.

50. The Qur'an, XIII: 11.

51. The Qur'an, IX: 51.

52. Bad' Khalq, p. 3.

53. The Qur'an, LI: 56.

54. Jawahir al-Saniyah, pp. 18-19; Usul al-Tahqiq, p. 24; Bad' Khalq, pp. 11-14.

55. The Qur'an, VI: 61.

56. The Qur'an, XLIII: 80.

57. Jauharat al-Tauhid, p. 42.

58. The Qur'an, LV: 15.

59. Iblis is the father of Satan, 'Aqidat al-Najin, p. 138.

60. The Qur'an, XVIII: 50.

61. Qisas al-Anbiya', p. 4; Bad' Khalq, p. 17.

62. Najis is polluted objects or pollution, Kashf al-Litham, p. 6; Wishah al-Afrah, p. 12; Bad' Khalq, p. 18.

63. Uns al-Muttaqin, p. 31.

64. The Qur'an, XLIX: 13.

65. Alms-giving at the festival of the breaking of the fast.

66. Ali Hanafiyah is Muhammad ibn al-Hanafiyah, named after his mother to distinguish him from Hasan and Husain, sons of 'Ali through Fatimah.

67. Sharh Usul al-Tahqiq, p. 31.

68. 'Uqud al-Lajjayn, pp. 47-48.

69. Irshad al-Ibad, p. 14; Fardu kifayah means a duty which is not obligatory on every individual of the Muslim community; if only a few fulfil it, that is sufficient, but if none fulfil it the whole community is guilty of sin.

70. Kashf al-Ghammah, I, pp. 91-92.

71. The prayer must be performed in a group with at least one Imam (leader) and one ma'mum (follower).

72. Fur' al-Masa'il, pp. 97-110; Muniyat al-Musalli, p. 20.

40

73. The Qur'an, III: 102; Muniyat al-Musalli, p. 20.

74. Some Kitab Jawi centre on the questions of prayer, like Muniyat al-Musalli, Mau'zah li al-Nas and others.

75. The Qur'an, LXXII: 8.

76. Muniyat al-Musalli, p. 21; Sirat al-Mustaqim, p. 220.

77. The Qur'an, XXII: 27; Sirat al-Mustaqim, pp. 154-158.

78. The Qur'an, XLIX: 10; Sabil al-Muhtadin, pp. 95-108.

79. Hikayat Abdullah, translated by A.H. Hill, Journal of the Malayan Branch of the Royal Asiatic Society (June 1955), p. 76.

80. N.J. Ryan, The Cultural Heritage of Malaya (Kuala Lumpur: Longman, 1975), p. 50.

81. Uns al-Muttaqin, p. 26.

82. The Qur'an, XCVI: 1-5.

83. Hidayat al-Mukhtar by Wan Hasan b. Sheikh Tuan Allah Fatani.

84. Usul al-Tauhid, pp. 4-10.

85. Hidayat al-Salikin, p. 5.

86. Some Malay newspapers translate a verse of the Qur'an in every issue of their publication.

87. Jauharat al-Tauhid, p. 42; Aqidat al-Najin, p. 80; al-Mawa'iz.

88. Fath al-Mutafakirin, p. 45.

89. Ibid.

90. Uns al-Muttaqin, p. 31.

91. Ibid., p. 32; Kitab al-Lubab, p. 88.

92. Sahih al Bukhari, Kitab al-Muzara'ah.

93. However this Hadith is included in the syllabus of Islamic Religious Knowledge for the Lower Certificate of Education students in Malaysia.

94. Fath al-Mutafakkirin, p. 19.

95. See the Qur'an, IV: 11-12.

96. Muhimmah, p. 21.

97. 'Uqud al-Lajjayn, p. 3.

98. Ibid., pp. 16-17.

99. Seyyed Hossein Nasr, Ideals and Realities of Islam (London, 1975), p. 112.

100. 'Uqud al-Lajjayn, pp. 16-17.

101. Kitab al-Lubab, pp. 109-110.

102. Ibid., pp. 106-107. The fate of the ungrateful child is reflected in Hikayat Si Tanggang where a son and his family were transformed into stones after he was cursed by his mother.

103. Tanwir al-Qulub, p. 24; al-Yawaqit wa al-Jawahir, p. 33.

104. Kashf al-Litham, ii. p. 362.

105. The word Imam means primarily an example, head, or leader who is followed by the people. Caliph (Ar. Khalifah) means successor, that is, successor of the Prophet. See Ibn Manzur, Lisan al-'Arab (Beirut, 1955) xiii, pp. 24-25; ix, p. 83.

106. Miniyat al-Musalli, p. 31. However this Hadith is not sahih (sound). The word "Sultan" here means supreme leader, not king.

107. Muniyat al-Musalli, p. 31; This Hadith is sahih, transmitted by Muslim; see Sahih Muslim, Kitab al-Iman, Hadith no. 261.

108. The Qur'an, XVIII: 29; Muniyat al-Musalli, p. 35.

109. Muniyat al-Musalli, p. 36.

110. Sair al-Salikin, ii, p. 85.

111. III: 190; Fath al-Mutafakkirin, p. 5.

112. Fath al-Mutafakkirin, p. 5.

113. The Qur'an, VII: 54; Bad' Khalq, p. 18.

114. Al-Yawaqit was al-Jawahir, p. 30; Tanbih al-Ghafilin, p. 11.

REFERENCES

Kitab Jawi

Abdullah b. Abd al-Mubin, Tanbih al-Ghafilin, Egypt, 1938.

Abdullah b. Abd al-Rahim, Fatani, Muhimmah pada Ilmu Hadith, Penang (n.d.).

Abd al-Rashid Banjar, Kitab Perukunan, Da'irat al-Mu'arif Penang (n.d.).

Abd Ra'uf Fansuri, al-Mawa'iz al-Badi'ah, Sulaiman Mar'ie affiliated to
Muhimmah), Penang (n.d.).

Abd al-Samad al-Falembani, Hidayat al-Salikin, Sulaiman Mar'ie,
Singapore (n.d.).

Abd al-Samad al-Falembani, Sair al-Salikin, Sulaiman Mar'ie, Singapore, 1350 A.H.

Ahmad Khatib b. Abd al-Ghaffar, Fath al-'Arifin, Dar al-Tiba'ah al-Misriyah,
Singapore (n.d.).

Ahmad Khatib b. Abd al-Latif al-Minangkabawi, al-Shumus al-Lami'ah, Singapore,
1357 A.H.

Ahmad b. Muhammad Yunus Langka, Daqa'iq al-Akhbar, al-Mu'arif, Penang (n.d.).

Ali b. Abd al-Rahman, al-Kelantani, al-Jauhar al-Mauhub, Singapore (n.d.).

Daud b. Abdullah al-Fatani, Durr al-Thamin, Sulaiman Mar'ie. Written in 1252
A.H., Singapore (n.d.).

_____.   Kifayat al-Muhtaj.

_____.   Jawahir al-Saniyah, Singapore (n.d.).

_____.   Furu' al-Masa'il, Singapore (n.d.).

_____.   Kashf al-Ghammah (with Furu' al-Masa'il), Singapore (n.d.).

_____.   Baghiyat al-Tullab, Vol. I, Singapore (n.d.).

_____.   Muniyat al-Musalli, written in 1259 A.H. 'Isa Al-Halabi, Egypt (n.d.).

Husayn b. Muhammad, Uns al-Muttaqin, Dar al-Taba'ah al-Misriyah, (affiliated to
Tanbih al-Ghafilin), Egypt 1938.

Husayn Nasir b. Muhammad Tayyib al-Mas'udi al-Banjari, Usul al-Tauhid, Taiping,
Perak, 1953.

Mawa'iz li al-Nas, anonymous (affiliated to Miftah al-Jannah).

Muhammad Ali b. Abd al-Rashid al-Sambawai, al-Yawaqit wa al-Jawahir, Singapore
(n.d.).

Muhammad Arshad b. Abudllah al-Banjari, Sabil al-Muhtadin, written 1195 A.H./1780
A.D. (publisher unknown)

Muhammad b. Ismail Daud Fatani, Matla' al-Badrain, Singapore, 1303 A.H.

43

_____. Wishah al-Afrah, Cairo (n.d.).

Muhammad Nafis b. Idris al-Banjari, al-Durr al-Nafis, Singapore, 1347 A.H.

Muhammad Taib b. Mas'ud, al-Banjari, Miftah al-Jannah, Penang (n.d.).

Nuruddin b. Ali Hasanji b. Muhammad Hamid al-Raniri, Bad' Khalq al-Samawat wa
     al-Ard, Mekkah, 1328 A.H.

_____. Sirat al-Mustaqim (affiliated to Sabil al-Muhtadin).

Sheikh Muhyiddin Acheh, Kitab al-Lubab, or Shifa' al-Qulub (affiliated to Kashf
     al-Ghaibiyah) Egypt (n.d.).

Sharh Usul al-Tahqiq, anonymous, al-Mua'arif, Penang, 1356 A.H.

Sharh Matn Jauharat al-Tauhid, anonymous (a translation by one of the Malay
     religious scholars in 1292 A.H.), Surabaya (n.d.).

'Uthman b. Shihab al-Din al-Funtiani (Pontianak), Tanwir al-Qulub, Egypt, 1346
     A.H.

_____. (Pontianak), Taj al-'Arus, Penang (n.d.).

_____. (Pontianak), Fath al-Mutafakkirin, Egypt, 1324 A.H.

'Uqad al-Lajjayn, anonymous (affiliated to al-Yawaqit wa al-Jawahir).

Wan Hassan b. Ishak al-Fatani, Hidayat al-Mukhtar (affiliated to Kitab Bad' Khalq
     al-Samawat wa al-Ard).

Zain al-'Abidin b. Muhammad al-Fatani, Kasf al-Litham, Cairo, 1308 A.H.

_____. 'Aqidat al-Najin, Singapore (n.d.).

_____. Kashf al-Ghaibiyah, Egypt, 1301 A.H.

_____. Irshad al-'Ibad, Singapore (n.d.).

Zainuddin b. Muhammad al-Badawi al-Sambawi, Minhaj al-Salam, Singapore, Surabaya
     (n.d.).

Other Books

Abdullah Yusuf Ali, The Holy Qur'an. Translation and Commentary, Libya (n.d.).

Al-Arqam, No. 9, year I, Kuala Lumpur, 1398 A.H.

Bukhari, Abi Abdullah Muhammad b. Ismail, al-Jami'al-Sahih, Book 1, Paris 1928.

Ibn Hajar al-'Asqalanl, Fath al-Barl, Cairo, 1319 A.H.

Ibn Manzur, Lisan al-'Arab, Beirut, 1955.

HAMKA, Pengantar al-Qur'an al-Karim Bacaan Mulla H.B. Jassln, Jakarta, 1977.

Jeffrey, A., Islam, Muhammad and His Religion, New York, 1958.

Khairuddin Zarkall, al-'A'lam, Beirut, 1959.

Mia Brandel-Syrler, The Religious Duties of Islam as taught and explained by Abu
     Bakr Effendl, Leiden, 1960.

Muslim Ibn Hajjaj, Sahlh Muslim, Cairo, 1955.

Ryan, N.J., The Cultural Heritage of Malaya, Kuala Lumpur, 1975.

Seyyed Hossein Nasr, Ideals and Realities of Islam, London, 1975.

Malay Hikayat

Hikayat Abdullah

Hikayat Nur Muhammad

Hikayat Muhammad All Hanaflyah

Hikayat Si Tanggang.

THE TRADITIONAL MALAY SOCIO-POLITICAL WORLD-VIEW

MOHD. TAIB OSMAN

Introduction

The institution of the Yang Di Pertuan Agong, the paramount ruler of Malaysia, is an innovation born out of a political necessity in the years immediately following the end of the Second World War. The British colonial government had mooted the idea of unifying the nine Malay states under its protection together with the Straits Settlements of Malacca and Penang even before the War had come to an end. For whatever objective it was to achieve, it became clear as the Malayan Union scheme was being unfolded that the sovereignty of the Malay rulers over their own states would have been transferred to the British, and that a more liberal form of citizenship would have been granted to all those who had migrated into the country during the colonial period.[1] The Malays had opposed this political arrangement most vigorously and in later years they displayed the same attitude whenever their birth-right as sons of the soil had been challenged. The racial riots of May 1969 was actually only a repetition of what could have happened if the British had not dismantled the Malayan Union in 1948. With independence in 1957, and later the formation of Malaysia in 1963, the institution of the Yang Di Pertuan Agong was established, bringing with it a new element to the age-old Malay institution of the "raja" or ruler.[2] While the idea of constitutional monarchy according to the will of the people through democratic parliamentary system is a novelty, yet the

Malaysian paramount ruler inherits the concepts of Malay kingship which had evolved over the centuries locally and which had formed the central element of the traditional Malay political world-view.

It is important to know of this political world-view in order to understand the present political structure in Malaysia, not only in the symbol that one sees in the Yang Di Pertuan Agong, or in the structure of the Malay states today, but more importantly, in the political behaviour of the Malays in the context of a democratic parliamentary system, where the representatives of the people are elected by constituencies according to majority vote.

What then is the traditional socio-political world-view of the Malays? This forms the objective of this paper. In other words, this paper sets out to explain how traditionally the Malays conceive of the distribution of power and authority in society and how this concept of power is translated into the relationships that man has to enter into in his everyday life. The structure of such relationships was not born overnight, but has evolved through the centuries following certain phases of history. In the process, many of the cultural identities deemed irrelevant have been unloaded, and many added on, especially in the symbolic expressions, but the core ideas underlying those expressions seem to have survived, although with different interpretations. And the relationships are not confined to those between man and man alone, but more significantly between man and the supernatural, as well as between man and his natural surroundings.

In the relationship between man and man, we encounter not only the superordination and subordination form of interaction, but also the alliances such as to be found in kinship and territorial groupings. Thus, not only do we have to deal with

47

social organisations where the line of power or authority is vertical, distributed upwards and downwards, but also with instances where the interaction between man and man is on a horizontal plane. But what is most interesting is the fact that man's relationship with the supernatural or with his natural surroundings is not confined to his intention in keeping such relationship in harmony based on his belief, conception and feelings with regard to the supernatural and natural environment, but also to the fact that he has learnt to legitimize his man-to-man relationship by making references to the supernatural beings and natural surroundings. The maintenance of social order and hierarchically relative positions between men is often legitimized by myths and beliefs invoking on the supernatural and these are often couched in symbolic forms. At the higher level, we find the dynastic myths and enthronement ceremonies expressing in symbolic form the socio-political world-view and ethos of the state, while at the lower level, we find rituals such as bela kampung (purification of the village) and puja pantai (appeasing the spirit of the sea) which, although addressed to the supernatural, are actually a symbolic expression of man's desire to come to terms with his environment as well as with each other in community life.

The Basic Socio-Political Organisations

There are basically two traditional socio-political systems among the Malays of the Peninsula: Adat Temenggong and Adat Perpatih. While the former is more widespread, the latter is confined to the people of Negeri Sembilan. However, it is in the latter that one gets the survival of what could have been the social organisation of the indigenous peoples in the Malay Archipelago before the rise of the states and kingdoms. The advent of influences from India, through the spread of Hinduism and

48

Buddhism which began from the first century A.D., is credited with the introduction and development of states and kingdoms as socio-political organisations par-excellence in Southeast Asia. However, in the Philippines, some scholars believe that the state which had sprung up in the southern islands was the work of the Muslims during the period when Islam was in the ascendancy, around the thirteenth and fourteenth centuries A.D.[3] Long before this, there had already developed in the Malay Peninsula, Sumatra, Borneo and Java, states and kingdoms which have been popularly characterised by the scholars as "Indianised". Although Islam later on supplanted the Hindu and Buddhistic ideology of kingship which had once supported states and empires like Langkasuka on the Peninsula, Sri Wijaya in Sumatra and Majapahit in Java, it cannot be denied that to an extent the socio-political world-view of the Malays had been formed during the early centuries of the Indian influence in the Archipelago.

But the picture will not be complete if we ignore the fact that while numerous empires and kingdoms had risen and fallen over the centuries, there had existed other forms of social organisation which have survived well into the twentieth century. The local communities, usually based on kinship grouping, must have come into existence during the neolithic period when men in Southeast Asia first learnt to found settlements and cultivate the land. However, even up to the twentieth century, the nomadic way of life, and a loose social organisation that goes with it, is still to be found among the Penan of Sarawak and the Hill Muruts of Sabah and among the Orang Asli of the Malay Peninsula. Local communities, like the longhouses of the indigeous peoples of Sarawak and Sabah or the local kampungs (villages) of the Malays, seem to be the type of social organisation which preceded the formation of states or kingdoms. Kroeber's picture of the pre-state social organisation in the Philippines as a "scatter of small kin-based local groupings known as barangay or banua"[4] would probably apply generally to the rest of the Archipelago.

49

While the state as a social organisation had really shaped the traditional Malay socio-political view, it would be useful to know of the organisation at the local level, which is based on territorial as well as kinship affinity.

The World-View at the Village Level

At the local level, the basic organisation of the Peninsular Malays is the village or the kampung. The size of the village varies, but a typical village is a conglomeration of individual houses each housing a family. It is not known whether such an organisation is a later development from a longhouse which is the typical village arrangement among the interior peoples of Borneo and Sumatra, but the tendency has been that those who have been won over to Islam usually have separate units housing either nuclear or compound families. The same can be said for those converted to Christianity: in Sabah it is known that the Kadazans or Dusuns have the tendency to set up separate unit dwellings instead of the traditional longhouse upon conversion to Christianity. But whatever form it takes, the kampung is not only a local territorial community but one based on kinship ties also. In fact, it is interesting to note that among the Jama Mapun of Southern Philippines, kampung is the general term for relative or kindred and that when they "visit their relatives in Borneo or Palawan, they say they go and live with their kampung."[5]

The socio-political organisation of a village is quite simple. One can usually expect a high degree of kinship ties in a Malay village especially through marriage. Since the British intervention into the affairs of the Malay States in the last half of the nineteenth century, there has been no slavery practised, but prior to that, the lowest rung of the social stratification in Malay society was occupied by the slaves and debt-bondsmen.[6] Thus, at the village level, with the exception of the slaves and debt-bondsmen, the villagers were usually of equal status. If there was any distinction, it would have been based on economic, religious and political factors. The first would be in the form of wealth and extent of land ownership, the second would be in the form of religious knowledge and visible expression of religious piety, and the third would be the leadership position that one held. In the last instance, it was usual for the founder of the village to be made the leader (referred to as penghulu or ketua), and it was not unusual for the subsequent leaders to be chosen from the original family.[7] However, it was common for all the three factors to come into play as the original founder would be in a position to accumulate wealth, and with this wealth he could go to Mecca for the pilgrimage, thus assuring for himself a high religious status as a Haji (one who has performed the Hajj in Mecca) among his villagers. And as Gullick has pointed out, the founder was in the position to provide shelter and help for the newcomers to his settlement. Founders of villagers usually assumed such a station in life that even after death, they were revered as their graves became the centre of popular worship, referred to as keramat in the Malay belief system. At a higher level, the position of keramat is usually reserved for those who in their lifetime had achieved high religious piety and usually referred to as wali, but in popular belief anyone or anything thought to have the power of granting miraculous rewards and wishes would be considered a keramat.[8]

Hence, even at the village level the socio-political world-view somewhat reflects the greater cosmos of the state: the underlying principles are to be seen in the relationship among the villagers themselves, which is bound up in a network of kinship, the relationship between the villagers and the headman, and between the villagers and the invisible supernatural beings

51

around them. In the world-view of the people, these relationships are couched not only in terms of titles used but also in the allusions drawn on other things. The qualities to look for in the headman may be the practical ones such as wealth or possession of property, or warlike prowess and ability in military affairs, but it can also depend on non-worldly qualities like religious knowledge, or show of pious observance of religious duties, and birth-rights which conform to the Malay social hierarchy. In the practical qualities, the headman is expected to look after the welfare of his villagers, who are referred to as anakbuah, thus alluding to the fact that the penghulu is like a strong solid tree from whose spreading branches the numerous fruits hang in comparative security and peace. Thus, in the Malay world-view, the village headman carries the father-image while his fellow villagers that of his dependents. The respect due to him is therefore similar to that due to the head of the family. So when he is rich and has much property, he is better able to look after his community, especially if he is generous. Such a world-view is reflected by the title Orang Kaya-kaya or sometimes shortened to Orang Kaya. By doubling the word kaya, which means "rich", the meaning changes and becomes "in the manner of being rich." Therefore, when the title is used for chiefs and other people of means, the reference is not actually to his wealth, but rather to the quality of "being a rich man", and he is expected to behave like one, generous and open-handed. The quality of being a headman is also the same. However, a rich but miserly headman is not well-liked for he does not fit the picture of a spreading shady tree, especially in time of need.

The second quality, that a headman be a man skilled in martial arts, is consistent with the Malay traditional world-view that a leader should be one to lead his group into battle. Both oral tales and the sejarah, which is the state chronicle written for a sultanate, usually extol men of strength and bravery, who

52

also have a deep sense of loyalty to the ruler. Place-names named after historical or legendary figures who were at one time the chief of the area can easily be identified, such as Teluk Panglima Garang (Bay of Fierce General) in Selangor. In the past when security and peace of the community was always threatened by predatory pirates and other interlopers, a strong and reliable headman added to the sense of security of the settlers.

However, the practical and physical qualities are balanced by religious values which will add to the headman's standing in his community. Not only should he be religious but he must appear to be pious, observing all the tenets of Islam overtly. The imam (religious leader) may have to appear knowledgeable in religious matters, and the community may consult him on intricate Islamic problems expecting him to provide the solution. A headman may not be put in such a demanding position, but he must at all times appear to be pious all the same. In the world-view of the Malays, being pious is important as such a person is regarded as god-fearing, and therefore trustworthy. And lastly, people with titles, especially those bearing hereditary titles of aristocracy, like tengku, megat, nik or mior, or those whose titles are somehow connected with religion, like syed, sheikh or imam, will have primacy over the ordinary people with no titles in being recognised as good village headmen. Taking into account the greater polity of the state, of which the village is only a part, the position of the headman accrues greater importance as he is the link with the outside world, being the raja's or ruler's representative in organising a war party or a corvee' or kerah as it is known in Malay.

The allusion to the village being like a family is to be seen in the fictitious kinship which exists among the villagers. Even today, the term orang sekampung or "belonging to the same village" carries with it certain obligations and privileges. One's behaviour, for instance, is inhibited by the sense of shame

53

toward one's fellow-villagers, even if it is not towards outsiders. This is often reflected by the saying that one does not do dishonourable things in one's usual environment. It is really the extension of the proverb which says "<u>potong hidung rosak muka</u>" (cutting one's nose to spite one's face). The Malay sense of honour is closely bound to that of his family: any dishonour that he brings on himself would also bring dishonour to his family. Therefore, if he is going to commit anything dishonourable, it should be outside his community where his family is unknown, ensuring that anonymity is preserved.

Conversely, outside one's immediate kin group, it is to <u>orang sekampung</u> that one turns to for help and expects help from. This is particularly true in the instance of the recent phenomenon of rural to urban drift: village ties are viewed almost like kin group (<u>saudaramara</u>). Newcomers to the urban areas usually stay with or depend on <u>orang sekampung</u> until they can firmly stand on their own feet. Sometimes such feelings are reinforced by the knowledge of having some kinship relationship, consanguine or otherwise, even if it is a remote one. The Malays refer to this unclear and rather dim kinship ties as <u>bau bacang</u>, that is to say, as far as the odour from the ripened <u>bacang</u> fruit can be carried, one is still related to the other. However, the most important factor is the sense of obligation evoked by such a term: help is usually rendered when asked for, because basically in the Malay world-view, social relationship becomes meaningful when one has his kinsfolk to support him. The importance of having a status in society is further realised when one has nothing to show in terms of power and wealth. But when one can show his affinity to a family or clan, then he has some standing in society. In Negeri Sembilan, when one wants to get married, the support of his <u>suku</u>, especially his close kin and uncles, is necessary. But when one does not belong to any <u>suku</u>, one has to adopt one or to be adopted by one. Known as <u>masuk kadim</u>, one's standing in society is then recognised, and therefore one's marriage will have a smooth passage.

With the acceptance of Islam among the Malays, the need to have a leader learned in Islamic knowledge and steeped in religious observances replaces similar needs in the pre-Islamic era. Looking at the number of customs bearing traces of Hindu beliefs and practices which are still observed and carried out by the Malay villagers, it is not difficult to deduce that those in leadership positions in an ancient Indonesian village were, if not Brahmans, at least priests (pedanda or pendita as they are called in Bali) in some Hindu or Buddhist cults. The intensity of Islamic teaching has not been able to eradicate the Hindu vestiges completely, and neither has it been able to erase older survivals of the old Indonesian beliefs and practices as represented by the institution of the pawang and bomoh. In Malay communities today, the office of the Brahman priest has merged with that of the pawang or bomoh who represents the older cultural stratum that the Malays had gone through.[9] In the incantations of the pawang and bomoh, and in the ceremonies that they perform, vestiges of the Hindu period are still evident. The magical and sacred properties inherent in the mantera, as the incantations are known in Malay from its Sanskrit form, help to boost the prestige of the pawang and bomoh. Indirectly, this factor helps in turn to boost the status of the pawang and bomoh as a community, albeit unofficial, leader.

Pawang is a term given to experts in many areas of skills connected with village life: thus, pawang ikan is the specialist in fishing activities who guides the boat crew to the schools of fishes; pawang lebah is the expert in gathering honey from hives high up in the trees; and pawang bijih is the expert in tin-mining operations who, it is reputed, is able to detect the rich tin veins in the ground using non-scientific methods. While expertise and skills are the qualities of the pawang, the world-view with regard to the institution emphasises not on the practical or technical skills but more on the mystical ability, because in the traditional world-view, all man's activities have to deal with the supernatural world. In fact, the concept of the natural surroundings in the pre-Islamic days which have survived to this day was such that every mountain, hill or river had its guardian spirit, and man, in founding a village or cultivating the crops on land, had to come to terms with his surroundings, which in effect meant maintaining a balanced and harmonious relationship with his spirit neighbours. Even today, in remote villages like Ulu Tembeling in Pahang, the office of pawang padi is still extant even though rice cultivation is no longer the most important economic activity for the villagers.[10] An important ritual which used to be held, and has been passed down till today is the propitiation of the spirits of the sea or river when the fishermen feel that their catches are not as successful as previous catches. Another is the ceremony called bela kampung, cleansing the village of evil influences.

The propitiation of the spirits of the sea takes many forms, although in the past, the sacrificial animal was the white buffalo. Many descriptions have been made of the ritual, and they are not far different from the ritual of protecting the village from evils, or bela kampung. In Malacca, the sacrifice was not a buffalo but a goat, and the arrack was used as part of the offering. A simple ceremony and without the sacrificial buffalo was witnessed once by the writer on the shores of Kelantan.[11] It was a ceremony which took a few days to prepare, and involved a "performance" by a medium, to the accompaniment of wayang kulit music. The paraphernalia included a sacrificial table made of bamboo in the shape of multi-tiered trays. It was beautifully built and decorated. When the time came to hold the ritual, which was in the small hours of the morning before sunrise, small figures of animals made of dough were placed in the multi-tiered altar. The figures, I was told, represented the animals to be given to the spirits. Also in the vicinity were the items which in the past would decorate the boundary of the village. There was also a trayful of offerings hanging in the hut where the orchestra was playing. The ritual consisted of the medium who went into trance and entered into conversation with the pawang who officiated at the ceremony. The medium represented the spirits who, from the conversation, could be understood as bargaining for the sacrifice. The most dramatic part of the performance was the medium prancing about before the altar and taking a close look at the offerings before accepting them. At sunrise, the balai was taken to the sea in a procession and set afloat towards the deep sea.

Sacrifices or offerings in the form of a junk or ancak (basket) in the bela kampung ceremony are also put afloat in the river, and it will drift towards the open sea. Basically, in the case of puja pantai or bela kampung, the idea is to appease the spirits guarding the sea or the guardians of a village. Therefore, the offering is central to the ceremony, and the way it is accepted is often through a medium who goes into a trance, as if he was possessed by the spirits. In the description of bela kampung as studied by a student of mine in Pahang, the notion of coming to terms with the spirits or invisible people (makhluk halus), who are believed to live in another dimension around us, prevailed.[12] In such a ceremony, the pawang tanah is important for through him the ceremony to harmonise the relationship between the people who live there and the spirits living on the same spot is carried out. Much symbolism is used in the ceremony, but it is clear that objects used are related to man's concept of the earth, the water and the air, the three essential natural elements around him. So the person best able to control these natural elements, which fill the space people live in, is looked up to and revered. Although Islam frowns upon such a world-view and prohibits the practice, the practitioner or the pawang not only maintains his unofficial leadership position, but attempts to graft Islamic elements, such as verses from the Qur'an, heroes from Islamic history, or elements of popular Islam, to his primitive beliefs and practices. He thus strengthens his position in the community.

57

Similarly, the <u>bomoh</u>, the expert in curative techniques, has to rely not only on his knowledge of potent herbs but also on his ability to deal with the supernatural.[13] While the <u>pawang</u> and <u>bomoh</u> may not command a strong leadership value in today's village society, he may wield some power, and sometimes in a dysfunctional way, when he dabbles in <u>sihir</u> or black magic. But the traditional Malay socio-political world-view at the village level is a reflection of the more sophisticated order at the upper level of the society, where the social organisation is often referred to as the state or kingdom. It is known that the <u>pawang</u> or <u>bomoh</u> in the past used to possess regalia of office.[14] This strengthens the belief that the <u>shaman</u>, who is the predecessor of the <u>pawang</u> or <u>bomoh</u>, is in fact the forerunner of the king in the Malay socio-political system. One of the proofs of legitimacy to succession in the Malay state is the possession of state regalia consisting of objects of government (<u>alat-alat kebesaran negeri</u>). This tradition has been perpetuated with the Yang Di Pertuan Agong, where the regalia are out for display and form part of the installation ceremony.

The <u>pawang</u> or <u>bomoh</u> today does not occupy the main leadership position in a village community unlike his predecessor, the <u>shaman</u>, who in the pre-state social organisation must have been the headman of his community. The shift in emphasis on the qualities for the leadership position is to be expected because of the socio-cultural changes that have taken place. Mystical charisma and abilities have given way to religious piety in Islam, which also means a strict observance of the ethical conduct, for Islam requires not only submission to <u>Allah</u> as the true path of the believer but also proper conduct towards one's fellow-men. The expressions which project such a world-view are to be found not only in the teachings of religion, but also in examples relating to the life of the Prophet Muhammad and God's other messengers. There are various occasions on which such expressions are expounded: in the formal ritual such as the

Friday congregational prayer in which the faithful are often reminded of their duties as good Muslims by the imam through the khutbah (sermon), which is obligatory before the performance of the prayer itself. In fact, the imam is the repository of knowledge pertaining to Islam at the village level. Typical of a Muslim community, the object is to meet God's approbation as much as possible, and therefore, besides praying five times a day, the following are observed -- fasting during the month of Ramadan, observing the usual ceremonies such as the maulud (birthday of the Holy Prophet) or the israk and mikraj (the Prophet's journey and ascension to heaven), and the activities believed to be approved by Islam which centre around the zikir or ratib (incantation and recitation in praise of Allah and His Prophet). Usually at that level, any doubt or question one has regarding an injunction of Islam is referred to the imam for his opinion, and his advice is often followed.

Although the imam is symbolic of the Islamic status of a village, he is also regarded as a village elder. It is not unusual for an imam to be regarded as an exponent of the bomoh's or pawang's art. At least in curing simple illnesses, he may act as a bomoh, chanting away in Arabic, the Qur'anic verses instead of the jampi and serapah (usually in Malay with a smattering of nonsensical Sanskrit words) of the bomoh. While it is possible to combine the two areas which in theory are opposed to one another because Islam is intolerable of spirit beliefs unless approved by it (for example, syaitan or iblis), it is also possible to draw the line between the two. Wrong interpretation of Islam also accounts for an action to be taken: it may be approved at the village level but disapproved by the learned tradition of the ulama (scholars) at a higher level.

The political leadership is invested in the post of the penghulu, or in the case of small villages, the ketua kampung. In the past, where the central hold was strong, the penghulu was

59

appointed by the Sultan. In the nineteenth century A.D., letters of appointments as penghulu were given so as to provide the legitimacy to rule a district, a river system or a village. As the penghulu, he had the power to decide on the fate of his anak buah. If he was like a spreading tree -- big, strong and benevolent -- then he would have a lot of anak buah. If he was not strong but weak and unjust, he would find many of his anak buah running away from him, and seeking patronage elsewhere. Although the word patronage is used here, it is not implied that the relationship between the penghulu and his anak buah is like that of patron and his client, for in the Malay traditional world-view, kinship and loyalty are very strong. Only in extreme cases where the penghulu is cruel to his anak buah, will the latter desert him but before that they would have to consider kinship ties and other primeval loyalty. The penghulu is often assisted by his ketua adat, tok sidang or tok empat in administering his village. Today, the penghulu (or penggawa in Kelantan) in many Malay states are government servants, looking after a mukim or sub-district, and responsible to the District Officer. The ketua kampung (or penghulu in Kelantan) looks after the village and is therefore closer to the anak buah than the penghulu. Whatever may be the relationship today, the penghulu or the ketua kampung is still looked up to by the ordinary villagers, especially in time of need.

The World-View Regarding the State of Kingdom

Although the village was central to the life of the ordinary people, the palace was still the focus that governed Malay life generally. It might be said that the palace was a pivot in the Malay world, and aptly described by the concept of Paku Alam of the Javanese royalty, where the Kraton is the centre around which the world revolved, including the villages. It might be a palace in the hinterland surrounded by the ricefields as in the case of Java, or it might be the trading ports surrounded on the inland side by villages as in the case of the Malay sultanates. It was the palace that held sway over the realm that it governed. The Malay world, in spite of its variety in speeches and its customs, had the basic structure in that it was the ruler that ruled the centre, and his nobility that governed the outlying districts. Until the nineteenth century, before the advent of British rule in the Peninsula, it was the practice of the Sultans to issue letters of authority to the penghulu to govern and thus collect taxes on the rivers that they governed. Even to this day, in the traditional Malay way, district and palace officials are appointed by the Sultan, and they still bear the ancient titles that in the days of yore also held the power that went with them. In the present time when the administration at the district level is carried out by the District Officer and the political influence is exerted by the Member of Parliament or the State Assemblyman representing the area, the traditional chief has a limited function to play. But when it comes to the adat (customs), and the disputes which should be solved according to the adat law, the adat chief is the person to be consulted. His post carries a small fee and sometimes he is given an office in the District Office. The Orang Besar Jajahan Perak Tengah, for instance, is the traditional district chief of Central Perak and he is given an office in the Parit District Office.[15] This is to show that the Sultan today still appoints his traditional chiefs and they still play a role in the modern administration of the state. We can say that the appointment of the traditional district chief is parallel to the modern administration and at the same time adjunct to it.

Traditionally, the Sultan is the chief and "godhead" in his state. It is believed that the idea of Malay kingship evolved during the Hindu era, and with it the concept of the state (negeri). The extent to which this new institution can be traced

61

to Hindu influence is to be seen in the Hindu titles that these kings bore with them. In fact, before the advent of Islam beginning around the twelveth century A.D., the kings in the Malay Archipelago bore Hindu names. Even the concept of kingship was borrowed from Hindu teachings. The most prominent was the concept of devaraja, in which the king was believed to be the reincarnation of the deva or Hindu deities. Thus, Hayam Wuruk of the Javanese dynasty was not only revered as a king but also as an incarnate of a deva.[16] The concept of Mount Mahameru is still seen in the coronation of Malay kings; in fact, so are many parts of the ceremonies attending a Malay king. For that matter, even the Yang di Pertuan Agong of Malaysia still bears traces of the Hindu idea of kingship. The Mahameru is supposed to be the abode of devas, and it is symbolized in the five-tiered dais known as pancapersada erected for royal ceremonies in the compound of the palace. On this pancapersada, the new king and queen will sit, and undergo a lustration ceremony, again reminescent of the Hindu belief that the king would be cleansed of evil influences. Although the royal ceremony today is very much imbued with Islamic elements, the Hindu origin of the concept of kingship is still to be seen in the symbolism used. The installation of the Perak ruler, for instance, not only carries with it traces of Hindu influences, but the name of the founder of the dynasty who descended on Mount Si Guntang Maha Meru is whispered into the ears of the new ruler so that he would know his pedigree. According to the legend, the forefathers of the Sultans of Perak were the children of Raja Suran who had married in an undersea kingdom. When they descended on Mount Mahameru, the mountain turned golden because the padi there turned into gold, and its stalks into silver. This story has become part of the mythology of the origin of Malay kingship which can be traced to the heyday of Malacca. Those who descended on Mount Si Guntang Mahameru were extraordinary people able to convert everything on the hill into gold and silver. Additionally, they had an impeccable pedigree as they were descended from Alexander the Great of Macedonia (Iskandar Dzulkarnain), Kida Hindi of India, and Nurshirwan the Just of Persia. With such ancestorship, the princes who later became the fountainhead of Malay kings in the Archipelago, showed the extraordinary power they had. This power, called daulat, which comes with kingship, became the cornerstone of the Malay idea of kingship.

The principal prince who descended on Mount Si Guntang Mahameru was known as Sang Sapurba in Malay legends. He showed his daulat in an extraordinary way: the 33 women who slept with him were all afflicted with a skin disease called kedal. It was the daughter of the local chief, Demang Lebar Daun, who finally became his spouse. In fact, the prince entered into a social contract with Demang Lebar Daun, and this guided the future conduct of Malay kings towards their subjects and vice versa.[17] According to this agreement between the prince and the local chief, the subjects of the Malay rulers were not to rebel against them on any account except when the rulers held their subjects in ridicule or contempt. As long as the contract was observed, the harmonious relationship between the ruler and the ruled could be preserved. Thus, the concept of daulat came into being: as long as the Malay ruler observed the contract, he would have the daulat or sovereignty about him. His person was sacred, and to touch any part of his body would be like touching a thing with an excessive amount of mana, and by the same token, his presence would bring about many blessings. There are other beliefs which account for his superior being: for instance, his blood was supposed to be white (not blue as in the case of the Europeans) and not red like that of ordinary mortals. He bore a special title of raja together with his name, and later on in Malay history, the title raja was joined by that of tengku. Whether he was a raja or a tengku, he had the daulat about him and that gave him the legitimation to rule over others, to order them about and the right to be paid obeisance to. Special terms of reference and special words were reserved for his class of people in conversations and correspondence.[18]

Daulat had an accompanying concept called ketulahan. It was ketulahan to challenge the power of daulat: therefore, the concept of ketulahan is not only complementary but also opposite to that of daulat. Simply put, it is forbidden to rebel against those who are powerful and those whose station in life is above oneself. Although this concept had its beginnings in the relationship between the ruler and the ruled, and had given birth to the age-old Malay adage, "panting anak Melayu derhaka pada rajanya" (it is forbidden for a Malay to rebel against his ruler) it had expanded to cover all situations in which one is tempted to go beyond one's station in life. Thus, it is "ketulahan" for an ordinary man to marry a "syarifah" (female form of syed, supposed to be a descendant of the Holy Prophet), or to display the attributes which properly belong to those above him. In the past, there was a class system in Malay society, this usually being represented by an imaginary triangle which reflects this division. At the apex of the triangle stood the ruling monarch, followed by those belonging to the royal class with the titles of raja or tengku. There were lesser members of the class called by titles such as ungku or ku, but whatever the title was, it was ascribed by birth. Below the royal class was the nobility or the titled gentry. Although there was a tendency for scions of this class to follow the footsteps of their fathers, thus maintaining the class, it was not hereditary and the position was usually achieved socially rather than ascribed by birth. Below the nobility was the category of ordinary people who at one time were referred to as the "free man" (orang merdeheka). Right at the bottom of the social scale were the "debt-bondsmen" and the slaves. As a class of people, they became defunct after the advent of European rule in the nineteenth century A.D. when slavery in the Malay Archipelago ended. Even while the class existed, people could still redeem themselves and become "free men" if they could pay their debtors and buy themselves out. If there were really slaves, they were either prisoners taken during a war or the people belonging to the pagan tribes in the interior. The titles prefixed to a person's given name therefore assumes an important place in Malay society because they are indicators of rank of the person. Apart from the raja and the titles of the nobility, there are other titles stemming from religious piety, such as sheikh, imam, maulana, and so forth, or from military prowess, such as panglima or pendekar. Thus, in the world-view of social interaction, titles are the guideposts to proper conduct.

DIAGRAM I

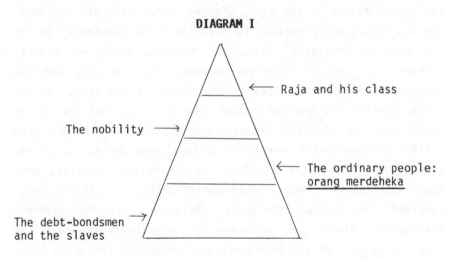

NOTE: The diagram graphically represents the structure of classical Malay society. The line of power is vertical, from top to bottom. Although it is divided into parts, social mobility upwards is possible, but limited, and the upward swing to the raja class is possible through the marriage of a raja to a female commoner or nobility. Such a social structure is buttressed in a world-view which is enunciated by myths, legends, folktales, customs, beliefs, titles, forms of address, dressing and speech.

It was the concept of kingship that held the fabric of Malay society together in the past. An elaborate system was worked out so that the state, symbolized by the king in the centre, would be a viable social organisation. Although the exact boundaries were unknown, and names of rivers or mountains were cited as the boundaries, the territorial concept was purposely kept vague. The phrase often used to describe the extent of authority of the king was <u>segala ceruk rantau pemerintahannya</u> (all the nooks and corners under his rule). The real extent of a king's rule or at least his political influence was usually unknown, and the exact territory controlled by him was questionable. It was in the traditional Malay world-view that the territory extended as far as the influence of the king was felt. In such circumstances, the sacred figure of the king, who was vested with all the power and authority, was important to hold the state together. During the days of Srivijaya, Majapahit, Malacca, Acheh and Brunei, perhaps the idea of far-flung empires was feasible, and the control of the centre rested in the figure of the king, and the actual control was exerted by the army or navy. But the system could also be possible because the empire was divided into smaller enclaves which were ruled by loyal dependents. Later on, these grew into little kingdoms and in later centuries, many began to sprout into little principalities. In southern Thailand, in northen Peninsular Malaysia, and in southern Philippines, there grew a number of principalities under the <u>rajas</u> or <u>datus</u>. By the eighteenth and nineteenth centuries A.D., each small territory had an independent king or chief. In southern Thailand for instance, there were Reman, Yala, Yering, Setun, with Patani, the dominant kingdom. And in what is now the state of Kelantan which was united by Long Yunus in the nineteenth century A.D., there were small states known as Seberang Tok Deh, Kedai Lalat, Jembal, Kubang Pasu, Mahligai, and many others. Vestiges of these principalities are still to be seen in the earthworks which at one time were meant as fortification for them. What was important, therefore, was the world-view that managed to hold each enclave together as a state with the ruler at the head. A glimpse of this attachment to the ruler is best seen in Abdullah's account of the civil war in Kelantan when the protracted battles between the nobility could only bring hardship to the followers, yet they held on steadfastly loyal.[19] Perhaps the Malay ruler had the _daulat_ or sovereignty, and he and his family had around them an aura which would make them respected and obeyed by ordinary Malays. Besides the imposing titles that they bore, which smacked of Hinduism, there was an elaborate system which preserved for the royalty their elevated status. The myth that buttressed the royal house could be seen in the genealogies drawn out for them and the wondrous deeds supposed to have been done by their ancestors.

During the Hindu period, the myth must have been imbued with Hindu mythology to support such a concept as _devaraja_. But with the coming of Islam such a myth was supplanted by another that traces the ancestry of the Malay kings to Alexander the Great, Raja Kida Hindi and Nushirwan the Just. Most of the kings in the Malay Archipelago had their dynastic myths traced to Alexander the Great or to some illustrious figures in the past. There were also other dynastic myths which had strong local flavour in them. Instead of tracing their ancestry to important figures in the past, the sultanates traced their origin to extraordinary circumstances which were often found in Indian literature or in the local folk-lore.[20] The legend of the king being picked up by an elephant is perhaps a well-known motif from Indian literature (the motif of a sagacious elephant), but the motif of the king coming out of the foam of the sea is also a well-known story in the local folk-lore. Whatever the myth adopted by a royal house, it was slavishly copied by the writers of their genealogies or histories and became perpetuated as a well-known belief.

The myth was further supported by the ceremonials and objects signifying those powers. The regalia also provided the

67

legitimacy to rule. In the past, even the bomoh had regalia, showing a close relationship between the power to rule and the power of magic. No ruler of the state of Perak was deemed legal if he had no regalia with him, which usually consisted of keris, swords, tufted spears and decorated umbrellas. The Yang Di Pertuan Agong also has regalia which symbolize his right to rule. It includes cogan alam, cogan agama, a small Qur'an, a keris representing the metals from the different member states, and so on. The trappings that attend the Yang Di Pertuan Agong as a consitutional monarch follow closely the regalia that a Malay sultan has to possess in order to show his power and authority.

The sovereignty of the Malay ruler is also to be seen in the music accompanying him.[21] The nobat is a special ensemble or orchestra which plays at royal ceremonies whenever a ruler holds royal audience or whenever there is a royal function in the palace. Malays believe that the instruments which make up the nobat are inhabited by spirits and they have magical powers. In Perak, only a group of people called orang kaloi could handle the instruments of the nobat. The nobat formed a part of the regalia of the Malay rulers and as such it used to accompany the ruler wherever he went. In the past a nobat could represent the king himself; to hear the sound of nobat playing was enough to make ordinary men stand still as if in the presence of the ruler himself. Today it remains an essential ensemble for the Malay rulers, including the Yang Di Pertuan Agong. However, the sanctity of royalty is maintained by everything that is connected with the nobat, its music, instruments as well as the players.

If the Qur'an features prominently in the installation of the Yang Di Pertuan Agong, thus symbolizing him as the protector of the Islamic faith, the official religion of the country, the right of the Malay rulers to rule was at one time also derived from the power of the supernatural. Apart from the concept of the devaraja during the Hindu period, and the concept of god's

shadow on earth as was propounded during the Islamic period, it
was believed by Malays that each royal house had its guardian
genie (jin kerajaan). When a Perak ruler fell sick and it was
found that he was sinking fast, a trance involving the guardian
spirit of state (Jin Kerajaan) was held.[22] This might not even
be traced to the Hindu concept, or an Islamic concept, for Islam
was opposed to such a belief, but it might have originated in the
primeval Malay belief in penunggu or guardian spirit. The nobat
or the state regalia are believed to be inhabited by the state's
guardian spirits. Thus, the relationship of the state to the
supernatural world had always been maintained throughout history,
except that the forms of that relationship changed from time to
time. It is that relationship, however, which is part of the
Malay world-view regarding his state.

In the days before the advent of the Western powers, a Malay
ruler would appoint his chiefs and penghulus to govern the remote
areas on his behalf. As the rivers formed the main arteries of
communication, especially to the interior, it was customary to
appoint chiefs and penghulus to the river systems that they had
to govern. Besides the rivers, the ports and the sea-emporiums
were important to the coastal states described as the pesisir
type. For the purpose of trading and for the handling of foreign
ships, these principalities had written laws to regulate the
interaction. In fact, the codes of law did not only regulate
commercial and business ventures but also buttressed the class
distinction already in the society. Undang-undang Laut Melaka,
for instance, likened the trading boat to a kingdom where the
rights and privileges of the officials on the boat were similar
to those of the nobility on land. And Hukum Kanun Melaka
safeguarded the position of the rulers further by making it
illegal for any commoner to carry golden-hilted keris or wear
expensive clothes and to go abroad with an umbrella over his
head. All these were taboo as they were reserved for the royalty
and the nobility. The wearing of the golden-hilted keris or

69

expensive clothes and having an umbrella above one's head were only allowed to the commoner on his wedding day, for on that day he was called raja sehari or king for the day. It was like a safety-valve to the society, for on that particular occasion a commoner could pretend that he was a ruler, even for a day.

Literature as an expression and also the vehicle for a particular world-view is undisputed. Writings on the rights and duties of kings are abundant in Malay literature. Most of the works belong to the Muslim period of history, although from the description of the royal ceremonies one can infer the Hindu origin of the institution. The Hindu concept of dharma in which one is paid according to one's deeds on earth is very much bound with the concept of devaraja. When Islam came, the analogy used was that a ruler was like the shepherd who had to look after his flock, for he was God's shadow on earth. Treatises on kingship were written to provide guidelines for the ruler as to his princely duties and what was expected of him. Exemplary stories of just and generous caliphs and kings also abound in Malay literature. At the time of the advent of the Europeans, stories of the injustices and the ungenerous acts perpetrated by members of the Malay royal houses abound. Abdullah bin Abdul Kadir Munshi, who witnessed the transition experienced by Malay society from their feudal structure to one dominated by the Europeans, held a dim view of the cruel deeds of the Malay royalty, although he was full of praise for the just ones.[23] He saw that the leadership would pass on to other groups if the Malay royalty did not change their ways, especially in their attitudes towards knowledge. Abdullah believed that Malay royalty would have disappeared had they not been shored up by the British, and the glamour of some of the members would have dimmed if not for the good education they received. Today, a new èlite has emerged and not less among them are the members of Malay royalty. The reports of cruelty and anarchy that came from the Malay states in the nineteenth century, especially as written by European officials, should not be taken as the norm because such actions were grossly at odds with the ideals set out in the books on kingship or with the moral injunction of the Qur'an. Social justice and generosity were emphasised as the qualities of the rulers in these books, and these formed the guiding principles of Malay kingship as influenced by the Islamic world-view. It is correct to say that the ruler was the hub of that fabric called Malay society up to the nineteenth century A.D., although by that time Malay society, and in fact the whole world, was confronted with a new order brought about by agrarian, industrial and ideological revolutions.

Conclusion

The above is an attempt to present the traditional socio-political world-view of the Malays at two operational levels: the village or kampung, and the state (negeri). To understand the socio-political behaviour of the Malays today, it is essential that we understand the underpinnings of Malay society in the past. Since the end of the nineteenth century, as the result of not only Western influence but also exposition to the new values brought about by industrial, agrarian and ideological revolutions, Malay society has undergone some changes. Some of these have affected the structure of the society tremendously, but because the Malays have retained their basic socio-political structure they have been able to stabilise themselves in facing the change.

The Malays still retain their kampung, and if they are resettled in government-sponsored schemes, the kampung structure is left unchanged. Even if they are resettled in urban areas, the basic structure is adhered to. As long as they live as a homogeneous community, the usual kampung organisation is

71

maintained. What is important is the fact that the world-view which they had held for ages with regard to their social structure organised into kampung, has not changed. Only when urbanisation leads to the break-up of the homogeneity of the Malay community is the established world-view disturbed, because such structural changes also mean the intrusion of a new set of values. Similarly, the traditional set-up of a Malay state is not replaced in its entirety by the modern administration. In fact, it runs parallel to the new bureaucracy set up by the British. The Sultans still retain chieftainships, or Datuks as the titled gentry is known, and in some states, the district chiefs appointed (Orang Besar Jajahan) are given offices from where they can co-operate with the modern administration. The Malays in the rural area still have a great respect for these chiefs appointed by the Sultan, as they act as the intermediary with modern bureaucracy.

Thus, the basic Malay socio-political structure has not changed much over the years. It is difficult to say whether or not the situation was actually influenced by the world-view that prevailed, but certainly, whatever changes had been effected in history, they had managed to conform to the existing world-view with regard to social order. While the structure had undergone some changes during British rule, and had suffered further after independence because of the development projects, the world-view of an average Malay has changed little because he still has the kampung as well as the state structure to stabilise him. The changing structure should not therefore be looked upon as a stumbling block, but rather it should strengthen Malay society in facing the future as their world-view regarding social order is being retained.

NOTES

1. See Mohammed Noordin Soplee, <u>From Malayan Union to Singapore Separation:</u> <u>Political Unification in the Malaysian Region 1945-65</u> (Kuala Lumpur, 1976), p. 24 ff.

2. In his discussion of the Malaysian Constitution in <u>The Constitution of</u> <u>Malaysia</u> (Singapore, 1964), Harry E. Groves had the following to say: "An important feature of the Malaysian Constitution and a unique one in modern government, is that of a monarch elected for a term of years...while the constitution of Malaysia is a modern instrument, drafted in the first instance by foreigners, and necessarily drawing upon the constitutional experiences of Western democracies, it is, nevertheless, in many of its fundamental concepts, consistent with Malay institutions, customs, and practices reaching at least to the 16th century..." (pp. 33 and 35). See also F. A. Trindade, "The Constitutional Position of the Yang Di Pertuan Agong", in <u>The Constitution of Malaysia: Its Development 1957-1977,</u> edited by Suffian, Lee and Trindade (Kuala Lumpur, 1978).

3. See Cesar Adib Majul, <u>Muslims in the Philippines,</u> (Quezon City, 1973). For a discussion on how Islam spread to the Philippines, see his section on "Islam Comes to the Philippines", pp. 51 ff.

4. Quoted by Eric Casino in his <u>The Jama Mapun: A Changing Society in the</u> <u>Southern Philippines</u> (Quezon City, 1976), p. 25; from Alfred Kroeber, <u>Peoples of the Philippines,</u> Handbook Series No. 8 (New York: American Museum of National History, 1943).

5. See Eric Casino's, <u>The Jama Mapun,</u> p. 33. The word <u>kampung</u> in Malay has come to mean the village, a place where a group of people cluster and live together. It is interesting to note that among the Jama Mapun of Southern Philippines, it means "relatives". It must have been an earlier, if not the original usage, of the word, for the village in the Malay sense also carries with it the connotation of people being related to one another. The only exception is perhaps when a village is newly founded or in times of flux as found in the late nineteenth century A.D. in the Western Malay Peninsula.

6. For a discussion of debt-bondsmen and slaves as distinctive categories and classes in Malay social structure, see J.M. Gullick, <u>Indigenous Political</u> <u>Systems of Western Malaya</u> (London, 1965), pp. 98-105.

7. Ibid., p. 35.

8. For a discussion on the different types of <u>keramat,</u> see T.O. Winstedt, "Keramat: Sacred Places and Persons in Malaya", <u>Journal of the Malayan</u> <u>Branch of the Royal Asiatic Society (JMBRAS)</u> 11, no. 3 (1924): 264-79. See also Mohd. Zain Mohmood, "A Study of Keramat Worship (with special Reference to Singapore)" (Ph.D. dissertation, University of Malaya, 1959).

9. Such a view is seen in Sir Richard Winstedt's book <u>The Malay Magician:</u> <u>Being Shaman, Saiva and Sufi</u> (London: Routledge & Kegan Paul, 1961).

10. My field-notes on Ulu Tembeling, Pahang, 21 April - 10 May 1976. Although the _pawang_ doubles as a minor religious official in a village in Ulu Tembeling, nevertheless he is called upon to bless any new venture in planting dry or hill paddy. He officiates at such a function by performing certain rituals, and crowning it all with a prayer. Such an admixture may be frowned upon by the religious authorities, but to simple _kampung_ folk, the two aspects of belief are not incongruous. See also Stewart Wavell, "The Miracle at Beranang", Straits Times Annual (Kuala Lumpur, 1957), p. 21 - 33.

11. My field-notes on Kelantan dated May 1979. The ritual was held on a stretch of beach called Pantai Dasar near Kota Bahru, Kelantan. Although the ceremony started on the previous night, it was not held in earnest until dawn. The main part of the ceremony was held at dawn, culminating with the offering being taken in procession to the sea. Because the ceremony coincides with the morning prayers, _Subuh_, it is a reason why it is frowned upon by the _ulamas_ (religious experts) as a _syirik_ (belief in duplicity of Allah).

12. Abu Dahari bin Osman, "Peranan seorang pawang di sebuah kampung" [the role of a _pawang_ in a village], an academic exercise submitted to the Department of Malay Studies, University of Malaya, 1971. The ceremony was termed locally as Upacara jamuan tanah air (Ritual of the feast to earth and water).

13. See my article, "Patterns of supernatural premises underlying the institution of the Malay Bomoh", Bijdragen tot de Taal-, Land- en Volkenkunde, Deel 128 (1972): 219-34.

14. C.O. Blagden, "Notes on the Folk-lore and Popular Religion of the Malays" JMBRAS XXIX (1986): 6.

15. Field-notes from Perak dated January-February 1980. The Orang Besar Jajahan Perak Tengah is appointed by the Sultan of Perak as one of his traditional chiefs, looking after the central Perak district. Although he is not part of the modern bureaucracy under the District Office, he plays an important role, bridging the usual gap between the local Malay population and the bureaucracy. His selection to the post is based on the fact that he is a traditional local chief and therefore his knowledge of the local population and also of the local adat (customary law) is not to be questioned.

16. Also known as Ayam Wuruk, he was a ruler of Majapahit, an empire which had its centre in Central Jawa and with territories spread over the Nusantara. See Bernard H.M. Vlekke, Nusantara: A History of Indonesia (The Hague 1965), p. 75.

17. Sejarah Melayu (Kuala Lumpur, 1967), pp 24-26.

18. In terms of address, the king is referred to as _tuanku_ while those of royal birth are referred to as tengku or _engku_ for short. The subject addresses himself as _patek_ or _hamba tuanku_. The special words used for the king include _santap_ (to eat), _gering_ (to fall ill), _beradu_ (to sleep), _berangkat_

74

(to leave), <u>bercemar dull</u> (to come) or <u>ulu</u> (head). The common words are <u>makan</u> <u>sakit,</u> <u>tidur,</u> <u>pergi,</u> <u>datang</u> and <u>kepala.</u> The Javanese are more developed in this sense: their language has at least three levels, each used for a different class of people.

19. Abdullah bin Abdul Kadir Munshi, <u>Kisah Pelayaran Abdullah.</u>

20. For example, tales of the origin of kings coming from a clump of bamboos are found in Indian literature. There are also tales of the kings springing from the froth in the sea, which probably is more local in character. For the discussion on the mythic origin of kings, see my article, "Mythic Elements in Malay Historiography", <u>Tenggara,</u> No. 1 (1968): 80-89.

21. See my article, "Some observations on the socio-cultural context of traditional Malay Music", <u>Tenggara,</u> No. 5 (1969): 121-28.

22. Frank A. Swettenham, <u>Malay Sketches</u> (London, 1913), p. 158. For a list of Perak guardian spirits, see "A History of Perak", <u>JMBRAS,</u> Reprint No. 3, (1974): 166-71.

23. Abdullah bin Abdul Kadir Munshi, <u>Hikayat Abdullah,</u> translated by A.H. Hill, Vol. 28, Pt. 3. No. 171.

THE TRADITIONAL WORLD-VIEWS OF THE
INDIGENOUS PEOPLES OF SABAH

YAP BENG LIANG

Introduction

My study on the world-view of the indigenous peoples of Sabah
will focus on the Dusuns/Kadazans and Bajaus (the two major
indigenous groups in Sabah) with occasional references to the
Muruts (the third major group found chiefly in the Interior
Residency). The reason for limiting the scope of the study to
these groups is not only due to a scarcity of published materials
pertaining to the other indigenous groups but also due to the
difficulty which will no doubt be encountered in an attempt to
study so wide a variety of world-views in existence among the
numerous groups of indigenous peoples in Sabah. The 1970
population census,[1] for instance, distinguishes not less than 20
indigenous groups in Sabah, each group having its own distinct
culture and, naturally, a different world-view, too, compared to
the others. Besides that, each ethnic group may consist of
several sub-groups which are culturally different from one
another. The Dusun group, for instance, according to Rutter,[2]
can be sub-divided into two main categories:

(a) The Inland Dusuns, consisting of the Tambunan Dusuns,
the Tegas, the Ranau Dusuns, the Kiau Dusuns, the
Segama Dusuns, and the Tambunwas.

(b) The Coast Dusuns, consisting of the Bundu Dusuns, the

Membakut Dusuns, the Papar Dusuns, the Putatan Dusuns, the Tuaran Dusuns, the Tenggilan Dusuns, the Tempasuk or Kedamaian Dusuns, the Marudu Dusuns and the Rungus. Rutter (1929, pp. 20-21) is of the opinion that the Dusuns and Muruts were the first people to settle in Sabah since before their arrival there were no other people to be found there. They were said to have come from mainland Asia and had initially settled along the coastal areas of Sabah but were later forced to move inland to escape the aggressions of the Bajaus and other newcomers such as the Sulus and Illanuns.

On the whole, the Dusuns are found chiefly along the west coast of Sabah and predominate in places such as Kudat, Tuaran, Ranau, Kota Belud (Tempasuk), Penampang and Keningau with an average population of between 15,000 and 27,000 people in each place. The Dusuns are mainly agriculturists, especially padi cultivators, and perhaps for this reason the term Orang Dusun (meaning men of the orchards or gardens) has been applied to them by the Malays. Most Dusuns, however, prefer to be known as Kadazans.

The Bajau groups, likewise, can be sub-divided into a number of categories. For instance, we can distinguish between the land Bajaus of Kota Belud, the Bajaus and Bajau Laut (Sea Bajaus) of Semporna, the Simunul Bajaus of Sandakan, and so forth. The largest concentration of Bajaus is in the Semporna and Kota Belud districts where they number more than 15,000 people in each place. The Bajaus, especially those of the East Coast, in contrast to the Dusuns, are mostly fishermen and according to some informants the term "Bajau", which has been applied to them by outsiders, is derived from the Malay word berjauh (which means "to be far away") because the Bajaus who were at one time mostly boat-dwellers were always at sea, that is, away from the land.

77

On the whole, very little has been written about Sabah and its peoples and even the few works that have been written scarcely touch on the subject of world-view. Only a handful of writers like Ivor Evans, Thomas Rhys Williams, Owen Rutter and Cyril Alliston have contributed significantly towards the study of world-view. Their works, along with a few other published materials, will form the basic groundwork for my study of the Dusun world-view. However, as these works were written such a long time ago, my study will only deal with the traditional aspects of the Dusun world-view. As the concept of world-view is something that is constantly being formed, changes are expected to occur from time to time in the Dusun world-view but to pinpoint these changes is a somewhat difficult task. According to Arena Wati,[3] many of the ancient beliefs and customs are still very much in evidence among the Dusuns, particularly among those who have not embraced the Christian or Islamic faith and live in the interior regions which are less accessible to external influences. Even among Dusuns who have recently embraced the Christian or Islamic faith, traces of these traditional beliefs and customs can still be found, though to a lesser extent.

My study of the Bajau world-view, on the other hand, will be mainly based on the field-work which I had the opportunity to undertake in 1975 among the Bajaus of Omadal Island, an island off the southeast coast of Sabah in the district of Semporna. This group of Bajaus can be said to be representative of a great number of Bajau communities in Semporna (with the exception of the Bajau Laut) with which it shares a common cultural heritage, belonging as it does to the same cultural stock.

The Dusuns and Bajaus are very different culturally and as such hold very different world-views though it is still possible to trace some common traits between them.

The Dusun World-View

MAN AND GOD

The Dusuns are, to some extent, monotheists and believe in the existence of an omnipotent deity, commonly known as Kinaringan (or Kinorohingan) who, together with his wife, Munsumundok (or Suminunduk), is credited with the creation of the world and everything in it and that includes man, animals, and all features of the physical landscape.

According to some Dusun legends, compounded from several sources,[4] Kinaringan and Munsumundok made man from earth, a portion of which was obtained from Bisagit (the Spirit of Smallpox), and people are descended from him. Men and women of different physiques and complexions were created and that accounts for the different physiques and colours of men on this earth. Kinaringan gave the learned people written guidelines to follow for their future; he taught the illiterate prayers which priests today still use to celebrate festive occasions and to cure sickness.

After Kinaringan had made the Dusuns, he placed them in a basket and washed them in the river. One man, however, fell out and, floating downsteam, stopped near the coast. This man was the father of the Bajaus, people who still live near the sea and are adept at constructing and manipulating boats. After washing the Dusuns in the river, Kinaringan performed a religious ceremony over them in his house but, before he had done so, one man left for the jungle and on his return found that he could not enter the house again for he had become a monkey. This man was the father of all the monkeys.

To provide food for their people, Kinaringan and Munsumundok

79

decided to cut up their daughter, Ponompuuan (also known as Togoriong or Pomonsoi, and from the different parts of her body came all kinds of food: her blood gave form to rice, her head to a coconut (and till this day we can trace her eyes and nose on the coconut), her fingers to bananas, her ears to the sirih-vine, her feet to Indian corn, her throat to sugar-cane, her knees to yam, and so forth. Besides these, all the animals are believed to originate from pieces of her torso.

But Kinaringan and Munsumundok are thought to be all-powerful and beneficent but being too far away they do not directly intercede or take much interest in human affairs unless specifically requested by ritual specialists in the event of community crises, such as famine, flood, drought and disease. For this reason, the propitiation of the Creator beings does not really form an important part in the Dusuns' rituals.

The male deity now lives in the seventh heaven (for there are seven heavens), a place which is infinitely better than the human world, where food is more abundant, where there are no diseases, accidents or loss of property and where there are no arguments, fights or wars. There he has a village populated by his descendants, also known as Kinaringan. It is they who are often called upon to be familiar spirits for the priestesses and who come to them in their seances.

Kinaringan has two sons on earth. One of them, Puruan Tanak, lives under the earth and rules over all the spirits there and also those on the surface of the earth. Most of his subjects on the earth are ill-disposed towards mankind and when they set about harming people or making them ill, appeals will be made to them and to Puruan Tanak by way of a sacrifice.

The other son, Towardakan, who is on earth, is also unfriendly and envious of the Dusuns. According to the Tempasuk

Dusuns, Kinaringan made all men equal, but Towardakan who was envious of men's happiness interfered with this state of affairs and brought it about that some should be rich and others poor. He, too, does not like a good harvest for then all men will be equally well off.

The legends of creation related above are, however, not held in common by all the Dusun groups for great variations of the story can be detected among certain groups.

Among the Tobaron Dusuns, for instance, there is a different legend regarding the origin of the Dusuns and their relation with the Bajaus and the white man. According to this version, Tuminaru (the Creator) and Suminunduh appeared from a hen's egg. Suminunduh soon gave birth to three sons and when they grew up, one became a white man and the other two, a Dusun and a Bajau respectively. The Bajau and Dusun who were always quarrelling were driven across the river by the white man. The white man, possessing the kolian tree planted by the Creator, was destined to be great in the world for this tree bore all kinds of things such as writing materials, cloth, and brass-ware. The Dusun and Bajau, however, continued to quarrel beyond the river and the Bajau made the Dusun swear an oath that if he should build a house seawards of the Bajau, he would die. The Dusun retaliated, claiming that if the Bajau built a house upstream of the Dusun he (the Bajau) would die. That is why till today the Dusuns commonly live upstream of the Bajaus (Evans 1953, pp. 364-85).

Another variation to the story of creation can be found among the Dusuns of Sensuron.[5] According to these Dusuns, the Creator beings, Menemanen and Suminendu, created two special, sacred and wise beings -- a brother, Kaki Kaki, and a sister, Kedukedu. They married and had a son, Kudinkin, and a daughter, Tinaleg. Next came another son, Kempetas, and another daughter, Saneran. All the Dusun people of today are the descendants of

81

Kudinkin and Tinaleg while all the spirits and disease-givers who pose a perpetual threat to the well-being of mankind resulted from the union between Kempetas and Saneran. The difference between men and the spirit beings lies in the way they were created. All men are the children of Kudinkin and Tinaleg whose marriage was good because they had paid the proper ritual fine (sagit) to cut their relationship and to stop offending their Creator. Kempetas and Saneran, on the other hand, did not do so and so theirs was considered an incestuous marriage, and as a punishment their offspring live in an evil world, producing children without character or reason, destined to be forever evil and filthy. The unfavourable state they are in makes them very envious of men and so they contrive to bring harm to men by making them sick, prone to accidents, misfortune, and so on.

At least twenty offspring of Kempetas and Saneran are named by the Dusuns as responsible for much human ill-fortune. These beings are generally termed tamboree (disease-givers). These "disease-givers", mostly human in appearance, are believed to have existed from the beginning of creation and are thus "owners" and "guardians" of animals in the jungle, water, air, trees, plants and fruits of the forest, soil of the fields, and rocks of the mountains. They have one aim in common and that is to stir up mischief among human beings.

Dusuns believe that because man was created especially by the Creator beings, he has a privileged position and is essentially of a different nature, not only from the spirit beings, but also from animals which are primarily created for human food. However, to some Dusuns, the line between man and animals is sometimes ambiguous and in a number of folk stories collected by Evans (1935, pp. 371-491), animals are frequently described in human terms: they are set according to the norms and regulations of kinship, compete in games and help or trick each other, and so forth. In some tales, man and animals are

82

depicted as engaging in all manner of social interaction: they converse with each other, work and assist each other, and they even marry and beget offspring. There are stories of certain women giving birth to animals, for example, a dog, crocodile, or snake, and also stories of animals giving birth to human beings. In some cases, too, animals are depicted as being able to assume human form and vice-versa.

The nearest approach to totemism of which there is evidence are some beliefs of the Dusuns that certain of their ancestors were or became animals. Such ancestor-animals are regarded as sacred and are therefore not eaten. Among the Kedamaian Dusuns, for instance, the python is not eaten because a woman of that village is said to have given birth to such a snake a long time ago. There is also a legend which tells of how a man, Aki Gabuk, of Tengkurus, became transformed into a crocodile and henceforth became the ancestor of all the crocodiles.

Animals who are thought to have been guardians of mankind at one time in the past are also regarded as sacred. The Kedamaian Dusuns, for instance, will not eat the flesh of the hammer-headed shark because a fish of this species, according to local belief, once helped a man of that village to escape from a desert island. Likewise, at Kahung Saraiyoh, the python is regarded as sacred and is not eaten because it is said that such a snake once protected members of a house from headhunters (Evans 1923, pp. 76-78; and 1953, pp. 160-61).

Animals can influence human behaviour in still other ways. For instance, the sight and sound of certain animals are often regarded as omens associated with man's work or health. Some animals when seen or heard or even dreamt of denote impending bad luck, for example, sickness or death, loss of property, failure in warfare, trade, harvest, and house-building. On the other hand, some "omen-animals" are both lucky and unlucky and this depends on how they are encountered. The general idea is that if an "omen-animal" crosses a person's path, thus blocking the way, or goes in a contrary direction, it portends bad luck and it will thus be unwise for the person to proceed on a journey, business transaction, or work in the fields, but if it goes in the same direction, the circumstances are favourable. Among the most commonly mentioned "omen-animals" are the deer, civets, snakes, rats, kingfisher, certain species of the woodpecker, millepedes, centipedes and monitor lizard.

Like animals, most plants, too, are said to be specially created for man's use and are, therefore, not eaten by animals. However, there are certain plants which are undoubtedly created to ensure the survival of animals. Besides providing food, plants are also invaluable to man in other ways. There is a variety of plant substances which can be used to treat illnesses and to provide immunity to certain diseases. The Sensuron Dusuns mention at least 80 types of plants used as treatments for sickness. Plant juices are often drunk as medicines while plant fibres are applied as palliatives to wounds, burns, fractures and sprains (William 1965, p. 36).

Apart from medicinal properties, some plants such as the lempada tree and the komburongoh plant are said to be sacred or imbued with magical properties. The lempada tree is much venerated and feared by the Tempasuk Dusuns because it is believed that Kinaringan had put a curse upon anyone who should violate such a tree, the punishment being that the offender shall suffer and die of incurable ulcers. The komburongoh plant is sacred because it is said to possess certain spirits which can be called upon to be the familiar spirits of priestesses in religious ceremonies. Such spirits are ambassadors to, and negotiators with, the spirits with whom the priestesses deal. Both the lampada tree and komburongoh plant can also be used to treat certain illnesses.[6]

84

MAN AND THE SPIRITUAL BEINGS

The Dusuns, like the Muruts and all the other indigenous
non-Muslim peoples of Sabah, believe that all objects, animate or
inanimate, have or may have a spirit dwelling in them. Spirits
can be found in a great number of places, for example, in the
jungle, in the sea or river, in the hills and mountains, and in
any curiously-shaped objects. In other words, they are all
around man ruling over almost every department of life. These
spirits are of various types and natures. The Dusuns of Bundu
Tuhan[7] mention three principal types: the kodoudouh or spirit
within the body, the tembioruoh or ghost of the dead, and the
rogon or evil in the jungle. The rogon, which is held
responsible for a number of different evils which visit the
people, consists of at least four different types, namely: (i)
rogon mantad id kayu, the rogon from the great trees; (ii)
rogon mantad id watu, the rogon from the great rocks; (iii)
rogon mantad id ba'ang, the rogon from the stream; and (iv)
rogon mantad id gauton, the rogon from the jungle.

Most of the spirits are hostile to human beings and thus
have to be propitiated or warded off by means of offerings.
Those which are implacably hostile must be expelled by means of
magic for, in this case, bribery by means of an offering or
sacrifice will be of no avail. The less malevolent spirits,
however, can be driven from the haunts of mankind by a mixture of
magic and bribery or cajolery.

Among the most hostile spirits may be mentioned the spirits
of diseases or death, such as the duarang, kumohoding,
pamaiyak-baiyak, rogon gaiyoh, ginsahau, and bisagit. These
disease-givers either invisible or in the form of certain insects
or animals, for example, centipedes, scorpions and snakes, will
often attack people whose "soul-substance" is weak and who,
therefore, have little resistance to their attacks. A person's

"soul-substance" can be weakened in many ways, for instance, by acts of malice or if the person suffers from kopohunan (kempunan in Malay), which means "an unsatisfied craving for any food or drink".

In the past, one of the most feared diseases was smallpox which periodically scourged the native population. However, with the coming of the British at the end of the nineteenth century and after many years of medical attention, the disease has ceased to be a threat to the country, the last outbreak being reported in 1914.

Smallpox is believed to be the work of Bisagit, the spirit of smallpox, which figures prominently in some Dusun legends. According to one legend (Evans 1923, pp. 47-49), the disease came about as a result of a pact between Kinaringan and Bisagit. When Kinaringan asked Bisagit for some earth to make his men, Bisagit agreed on the understanding that Kinaringan would share his men with him. After a time lapse, Bisagit claimed his share of Kinaringan's men, stating that this would continue once every 40 years. Thus, every time Bisagit called, all the people would fall ill and half of them would die. Those who died followed Bisagit while those who survived followed Kinaringan. Kinaringan had also pleaded with Bisagit not to kill all the people for then there would be no more people left. To help his people gain relief from the disease, Kinaringan taught them religious chants.

Besides Bisagit, other spirits of smallpox often mentioned were Bulontoi and Goron, described as tall and broad with big eyes and teeth. People were also reported to have seen, in their dreams, spirits of smallpox banging their torches against their left wrists and thus sending out showers of sparks over their sleeping bodies, these sparks being the seeds of the disease.

When an attack of smallpox seemed imminent, the Dusuns often resorted to magic, cajolery or trickery, in order to keep the much dreaded disease at bay. Guardian stones or wooden models of spears and men were often made and set up on the side of the village facing the source of infection. The idea was that protective spirits invoked into the models through a religious ceremony could fight the spirits of smallpox and turn them away from the village. Sometimes, to gain the favour of these spirits, things like fowls, rice, eggs and buffaloes were offered to them by the villagers.

Some Dusuns, however, did not perform any religious ceremony to counter the attack of smallpox as they deemed it a futile attempt since there had been an irreversible pact between the Creator and Bisagit that smallpox would, without fail, kill off one half of Kinaringan's men once every 40 years.

Certain taboos had to be observed as preventive measures when there was smallpox in the vicinity in order to ward off an attack. Some Dusuns, for instance, would avoid eating Indian corn as its grains resemble the pustules of the disease, believing that to eat it would only invite an attack. Caladium roots and some fishes which have red flesh were also taboo as food, the reason being that the former was thought to cause skin irritation while the latter, because of its colour, was thought to cause the rash of the sickness to appear. During an epidemic, too, dogs must not be beaten, and buffalo or cattle meat were forbidden in the house, as they were red, like the eruption of the disease.

According to Evans (1953, p. 194), many years ago during a very serious outbreak of the disease, many fish were caught at Kedamaian and it was thought that there was some connection between the disease and the presence of the fish in such numbers. In 1946, too, it was said at Kedamaian that an outbreak of the disease was expected because of a very heavy fruit crop upcountry, chiefly of langsat with its clusters of small roundish fruits resembling pustules of the disease.

As a protection against disease-carriers in general, a number of magical practices are carried out by the Dusuns, the majority of which serve more to align man with the supernatural forces rather than provide mastery of control for them, in such situations of fear and uncertainty. Among such practices may be mentioned:

(a) the setting up of wooden models of spears and groups of "standing" stones, especially in times of epidemics, directly in front or within the radius of houses to prevent the entry of disease-carriers;

(b) the wearing of amulets or charms to frighten away evil spirits or to procure invulnerability against their attacks. Articles used as amulets are of many kinds, especially those which are rare or unusual, for example, little bundles of some kind of wood or plants with a strong or pungent odour, rhinoceros' teeth, curiously shaped stones and roots, and magical substances made potent through special rituals;

(c) the offering of sacrifices to appease evil spirits on certain occasions, for instance, before or after a journey, before working on a new plot of land, before building a new house or settling in a new place, and during an epidemic. Sometimes a raft or small boat is made to bear away all the troublesome spirits which are felt to be harbouring in the village and causing harm to the people. On the raft is placed food and other offerings to lure the spirits to it. Should the raft run aground near the village, after being set adrift, it is set adrift again immediately, lest the spirits should get ashore again.

If these preventive or protective measures prove to be unsuccessful and an attack of illness or disease results, there are still various means to deal with the situation. Relief can be attempted by using a variety of herbs as medicine combined with a variety of rituals to drive away the influence of evil spirits. Such rituals and in fact all rituals involving the supernatural world are conducted by ritual specialists.

In many places, it is the female specialists who play the most important role, the men's role being confined to the beating of drums and gongs. Female specialists with the ability to conduct seances are believed to possess familiar spirits which can be as many as seven. Many of the familiar spirits are believed to come from Kinaringan's heaven but others are from the lower heavens or even from the underworld kingdom of Puruan Tasak. Familiar spirits are often handed down from mother to daughter, though some are acquired during practice seances. These familiar spirits come to the priestesses when invoked through the use of certain objects, for instance, the komburongoh plant, and assist them during the seances. They act as ambassadors to, and negotiators with, the spirits with whom the priestesses deal and they can even forcefully remove stolen souls from the evil spirits who have taken them.

In a few places, for instance in Sensuron (Williams 1965, pp. 36-37), it is the male specialists who play a major role in rituals, their concern being chiefly epidemics or disasters which affect a great number of people. The male specialists are believed to be in direct communication with the Creator and can do without the assistance of familiar spirits, unlike the female specialists. Contact with the Creator is made through the use of spirit objects in the form of stone or wood figures or in the use of plant parts such as the "heart" of the young banana plant. The banana "heart" is regarded as a symbol of the earth's heart and is thus considered most suitable in effecting a contact with

89

the Creator. Because of their supposed ability to communicate directly with the Creator and their concern with major disasters, the male specialists have a superior social status compared to that of the female specialists. Female specialists are considered best able to deal with aspects of the supernatural affecting daily events, such as birth, illness, death, and so forth.

Though spirits are generally feared, not all of them are malevolent. A number of spirits are believed to be positively benevolent assisting human beings in many ways, such as helping them to recover from illnesses and protecting or rescuing their souls from evil spirits. Among such spirits may be mentioned the dahau, gumponot, gurun, kinorohingan, tumanak, potubogun, sambawon, rumunduk, tampagar and urai/surai. Then there are some spirits, for instance those of rivers, which will remain neutral if they are propitiated while there are a few which will be rather friendly if well-treated, such as the spirits of the sacred jars (gusi) and the spirits of the rice (bambaraiyon), but they, too, will become bad-tempered when neglected.

According to Evans (1923, p. 6), the cult of venerating ancient Chinese jars, which goes back many centuries, is popular among certain groups of Dusun, for example, those of Tuaran and Papar, but among some other groups this practice has been practically abandoned. It is to a kind called gusi, in particular, that sacrifice and prayers are made. The spirits of the gusi are thought to be those of ancestors and they are evilly disposed unless kept in a good temper by sacrifices, when they may be actually beneficent. Rites are performed annually at a festival called mengahau but in times of sickness extra ceremonies may be held. Such annual rites are held with the object of placating the gusi-spirits and of procuring good luck generally. The chief gusi rites usually, but not necessarily, are held soon after the rice planting to ensure a good harvest.

90

The Dusuns believe that if the spirits are forgotten or neglected during the rice season, the rice crop may not thrive. Similar rites can also be performed during pregnancy and for other important human affairs. It would seem, therefore, that the gusi are regarded as a form of intermediator between man and the spirit world.

Though the gusi spirits can to some extent help to ensure a good rice crop, it is really the spirits of the rice or "rice-soul" (represented by a small bundle of rice-stalks) -- something that carries on the life of the crops from year to year -- that plays a more important and direct role in this matter. Without the "rice-soul" man's life would fail.

According to some Dusuns (Evans 1953, pp. 216-18) there are seven (and in some cases, eleven) categories of "rice-souls" and in addition, a class of chiefs, each category having its own qualities or duties. The eight main categories are:

Ohinopot: the chiefs which will give an "inexhaustible" crop to those they favour;

Ohinomod: spirits connected with generosity which will give or look after coconut toddy;

Sambilod: those who look after broken rice and see to it that there is not too great a proportion of it;

Gontolobon: those who give rice in huge quantities;

Momiaud: those who ensure an endless rice crop;

Momiudan: the same as the Momiaud;

Sompidot: those who give full grain in the ear;

91

Kambang: those who make the rice grains swell and become
                large in the cooking pot.

There is also a belief, in some places, that a rich man possesses all the eight categories of "rice-soul" while a poor man, poor in rice for that reason, may have only one or two, and even these souls may desert him to go to a rich man's house where there is plenty of paddy, and will only return when the poor man has a little paddy in store. The bundle of "rice-souls" are hung up in the rice-store and, in certain places, outsiders are prohibited from entering a rice-store for fear that the "rice-souls" will follow them.

As rice cultivation plays such an important part in the lives of the Dusuns, many elaborate ceremonies connected with it have evolved. These ceremonies, performed at every stage of the rice year, are designed to restrain malevolent spirits from damaging or stealing the rice crop, to protect the crop against pests and disease, and to encourage, pacify and protect the "rice-souls".

Among the Ranau Dusuns,[8] there is also a quadrennial rite, known as ambil patod which consists of paying "homage" to a sacred clump of bamboo (patod) thereby ensuring the fertility of crops, domestic animals as well as human beings. This ceremony, performed only by female specialists, is normally conducted before the planting of paddy. The state of the bamboo clump is said to reflect a good or bad season. If many bamboos fall or turn rotten or are eaten by insects, it reflects a bad harvest. In a good year, the bamboo will all be upright and none will fall or be attacked by insects.

All these measures alone are not sufficient to ensure a good harvest for other precautions have still to be taken. Among some Dusuns, there is a string of taboos which regulate their work in the rice fields. For instance, work, as well as all the religious and agricultural rites, must not be performed on certain days of the month which are regarded as rest days. This is to avoid causing injury to the tulandaat, spiritual beings which assist the Dusuns in their work. If injured, they will avenge themselves and the offenders will then face various problems, such as the attack of pests, diseases in the rice crop and domestic animals and, in general, a bad harvest. On a rest day, too, unhusked rice should not be removed from the storage bins, otherwise the tulandaat will attack its contents and the rice will soon be exhausted. Besides this, work in the rice fields should not be done if a person is leaving his village permanently or for a considerable period of time. If work is done, there will be a poor rice crop. Omens should also be heeded; for instance, if a person sees or hears a flying swarm of bees, he must not work in his rice fields on that day or the harvest will not be good.

One of the most important precautions to be taken with regards to ensuring a good crop, is to guard against the occurrence of incest, a crime deemed to be the worst that can be committed by man because it affects the whole community. Incest is believed to damage rice crops. This is because incest and the children resulting from it, being "hot", scorch the crops of the Ompuan (or Tompuan) (a deity who cultivates rice in one of the lower heavens) causing a dreaded red disease to their rice crop. The Ompuan having control of the "rain" river in the sky would punish the whole Dusun community either by creating a severe drought or flood to damage their crops and cause famine. If this happens, two pigs, representing the offenders would be sacrificed on a hill as the blood of the pigs is thought to be capable of curing the Ompuan's crops of the disease.

Among the Muruts, too, incest is regarded with the utmost horror as all kinds of hazards, such as plague, flood, drought,

93

or famine, are ascribed to the act of incest. In the past, the punishment meted out to the offenders was very harsh. Sometimes they were beheaded and their bodies flung into the rivers; sometimes they were buried alive in the same grave and sometimes they were killed in the river up-stream so that their blood might flow past their village and thus wash away the effects of the crime.

THE BELIEF IN THE AFTERLIFE

Belief in the afterlife is a normal feature of animism. At death, the soul leaves the body and continues its existence in another world, under different conditions but not so greatly different from those of the world it has left. The afterworld has been described in various ways by the Dusuns; for example, it is believed to be a broad level plain and all the houses there are new, animals are well-fed and food is always in abundance. Sickness and conflicts are non-existent and everyone is happy and contented, being perpetually young and beautiful and surrounded by their families as in former times. The Dusuns, however, believe that the soul of the dead do not go directly to the afterworld but may linger about its former place for seven days before embarking on its last journey, revisiting its old haunts, doing familiar things and lamenting its last life. In this state, it would create mischief and harm among the living. Thus, when death has occurred, old women would cry aloud, reminding the spirit of the deceased that it must not sojourn in the village but must hurry on to the afterworld. To further prevent the soul's return, the bamboo bier on which the dead has been carried would often be hacked to pieces at the graveside. In some villages, the mourners, after burying the dead, would wash themselves in the river to discourage the soul of the dead from following them home. In addition, the mourners on returning from a funeral would slash with their chopping knives, the steps of the house and the door of the room where death has occurred. Furthermore, all doors and windows of that house would be flung open to let out any harmful spirits. Members of a burial party, too, were often paid sagit consisting of chickens, rice and salt, to distinguish them from the dead after the burial, otherwise it is believed that the deceased, being very grateful for the kindness shown by the burial party would want them as companions in the afterworld.

To get the departed soul properly started on its last journey, a number of objects, such as a water container, rice wine, and models of chopping knives, cocks, hens, and buffaloes, are placed at the graveside as offerings for the benefit of the soul. The Dusuns believe that if models or representative samples of objects, animals or plants are placed by the grave, the souls of these could accompany, and be of use to the soul of the dead in the afterworld. Small pieces of different parts of the buffalo's body are also put in a container and placed at the grave so that the soul of the dead would be able to ride on a buffalo to the afterworld.

Besides fearing the soul of the dead, the Dusuns also fear a great number of evil spirits believed to hover around the house where death has occurred, with the object of stealing the corpse or causing harm in some way. Among the Kedamaian Dusuns, three spirits seem to be feared as body snatchers: the komakadong which is in the form of a flying head with long hair and a trailing stomach; the balan-balan which looks like a human being; and the tandahau which has a bird-like body. The tandahau descends from the clouds and when it seizes a body carries it off into the centre of the sea, and there cuts it up into little pieces to be dispersed in the water. These tranform into fish which the tandahau feeds on (Evans 1923, p 14).

To protect a dead body from such spirits, sharp instruments,

95

like knives, would be placed under the mat on which it lies with their points projecting downwards through the floor of the house, while a spear would be placed upright near the body. A fire would also be lighted near the corpse and as night approaches another fire would be lighted near the house into which bits of rubbish would be dropped from time to time. The foul smell caused by this would help to keep the evil spirits at bay.

The soul of the dead is regarded as "hot" and capable of harming the living. For this reason, sagit (cooling compensation) in the form of a packet of broken rice mixed with rock salt or chopped lemon-grass is often given to those who attend the funeral. Certain taboos have also to be observed to keep away ill-luck. For instance, on the day of the funeral, no one in the village should work in the fields; no boxes, especially those containing goods which are usually kept shut, should be opened; rice should not be taken from the storage bins which are normally kept covered; and no wild buffaloes or cattle must be caught. If these taboos were violated, the "goods" concerned would become unlucky or accursed.

Apart from the soul of the dead, the widow or widower is also considered to be very "hot" or "poisonous" for some time after the death of her/his partner. In some places, they have to observe a taboo period of 33 days during which time she/he is forbidden to speak to or mix with anyone in the village. It is believed that anyone addressed by a widow or widower under taboo will become stupid and confused. But this prohibition does not apply to Dusun strangers or to the Bajaus, Illanuns, and other foreigners.

It is generally believed that the spirits of the dead must make their way to the top of Mount Kinabalu (Nabalu), their final abode. On their way, they will cross and rest at a small stream known as Karaput or Uraput. Another stop is also made at a large

96

rock called Pomintalan where the souls leave signs of their passing: the men, a wrapping leaf of a native cigarette; the women, some thread; and the children, some dirty shreds of their loin-cloths. The souls of the dead will also come across the residence of a deity, Oduk Mongantot (or Minantob), a daughter of Kinaringan, on their way to Kinabalu. She controls the gate to Nabalu, opening it only for those whose time to die has really come. Those who "die" before their time will not be let past the gate but will be sent back to the world of the living where they subsequently revive.

Though Kinabalu is the final abode for the departed souls, their life will not continue there forever. After a certain period, they merge with the mist or get absorbed into the plants and mosses growing in the crevices of rocks which they had once fed themselves. Their places will be taken by new spirits from the world below.

As Kinabalu is regarded as the home of the dead, the Dusuns, in former times, would avoid climbing it since it is regarded as sacred territory. If an ascent had to be made, the dead ancestors must be duly notified by means of a religious ceremony with offering of food such as eggs and fowls. If this ceremony were omitted, those who ventured up the mountain would be taking a big risk as they would lose their way and be unable to return home again. During the climb, too, certain taboos must be observed; for instance, the name of the sacred mountain as well as the names of streams and other related places must not be mentioned.

Like the Dusuns, the Muruts, according to Rutter (1929, pp. 220-23), also believe in some form of human soul which leaves the body at death and has a life thereafter. The spirits of the dead also make their way to the highest mountains in the neighbourhood namely, Mulundayoh and Antulai (Mount Aru). But these places, however, are only the stepping-stones to the afterworld, which is the sky. Life in these places is not so difficult for there are easier conditions of life and plenty of food. The proof that the Muruts go to these mountains at death can be seen in the number of staffs (belonging to the dead) stuck at the foot of the mountains.

There are different kinds of life hereafter for those who have encountered an unnatural death. For instance, those who died by eating the poisonous limuan live in a world thickly planted with limuan bushes which they will cultivate. Those who have been murdered live on a river where there is continual war and everyone is armed. The souls of the dead on the sacred mountains are not entirely cut off from the human world for they can still be contacted by the living. The contact can be effected through a certain practice known as semunggup, once popular among certain groups of Dusuns and Muruts but has long ceased to be practised having been abolished by the British during the period of colonization. This practice consisted of tying up a slave, or imprisoning him in a bamboo cage, after which the whole community would sing and dance around him, prodding him to death with spears and knives. With each prod, they would remind the slave to deliver their messages to a deceased friend or relative.

Apart from these beliefs, some Dusun and Murut sub-tribes also believe in the transmigration of souls. Among the Dusuns, it is believed that at death, some of the seven souls of a person become transformed into swallows, butterflies, beetles or moths. The Muruts, on the other hand, believe that the souls of the dead can sometimes enter the bodies of animals, particularly that of the deer. Men or women who die of sickness or old age, but not those who die of wounds, will be transformed into sambhur deer if in life they were very dirty and infested with lice. This can be "proven" by the fact that the deer is full of lice similar to those which infest human beings. However, a stillborn child or a child who dies at birth, will be transformed into a porcupine. For these reasons some Muruts will not eat deer or porcupine flesh at all while those who do may discontinue this habit should they suspect the deer to be the transformed being of a man. This fact is borne out by the strange or unpleasant taste the meat has.

Among both the Dusuns and the Muruts, the belief in the concept of the soul and the afterlife has contributed greatly to the practice of head-hunting once quite popular, especially among the Muruts, but which has since been abolished by the British. In primitive belief, the soul or the "soul matter" on which life depends rests in the head. A person who has got a head (usually that of an enemy or a stranger) has gained a portion of that "soul matter" which can be of great benefit to himself and the group. Souls of those whose heads he had taken would form a body of followers and supporters in the afterlife. Besides this, the taking of his first head marked a youth's entry into manhood. He could then be considered a warrior and this would enable him to win the favour of the woman he fancied.

In addition to the advantages accruing to the individual from the possession of a head, there were also definite advantages accruing to the community. The possession of heads would help the community to avert sickness and famine and to promote fertility both among the human population and the crops. However, to obtain these advantages, skulls taken in head-hunting had to be propitiated and sacrificed to at regular intervals; otherwise, instead of luck, ill-luck would prevail. Among the Muruts, the skulls would often be decorated with tufts of dried silad grass which was thought to be a sort of medicine for the skulls. Without such treatment, the spirits of the skulls would become offended and bring harm to the community.

A woman's head was normally considered of equal value to a man's and this could perhaps be attributed to some reasons as suggested by J.H. Hulton (in Rutter 1929, p. 186): that a woman's head was more difficult to obtain, as a community in time of trouble sent the men to work where there was danger while the women worked close to the village; that the desire was to cause a permanent reduction of the enemy population and the death of a woman would certainly have more effect on the birth-rate than that of a man; that a female head might increase the fertility of the successful village; and that there was also the possibility that a woman's hair was desired for ornaments.

As in other areas of life, many taboos and omens were observed in connection with a head-hunting raid. Evans (1922, p. 103) mentioned a number of taboos which had to be observed by the women folk when the men were engaged in a head-hunting raid.

a) The women must not weave cloth, or their husbands would be unable to escape from the enemy as he would become uncertain in which direction to run. In the weaving of cloth, the backward and forward movements of the shuttle represent the uncertain or confused movements of a man trying to escape from the enemy.

b) Women must not eat rice from the winnowing tray for the edges of it represent mountains over which their men would be unable to climb.

c) Women must not sit sprawled, or with their legs crossed, else their husbands would not have strength for anything. On the other hand, it would be lucky for the women to keep walking about, for then the men would have strength to walk far.

Rutter (1929, pp. 190-91) also mentions a few taboos observed by the Murut women:

a) The women must not sleep during the day, but only at night, otherwise the men would be heavy, would trip, and fail to see obstacles.

b) They must not eat bananas or limes, lest the men's bones become soft and their muscles slack.

c) Each woman must light a piece of resin-gum (damar) every night and place it on a large stone to enable the men to see clearly.

Sometimes before a raiding-party set out, divination was resorted to in order to find out whether the warriors would be successful or not. Among certain groups of Muruts, it was customary to examine the liver of a pig to foretell the future. If the liver was marked with deep lines, it foretold of misfortune; if it contained hollows, some of the warriors would be killed; if diseased, the warriors would be wounded; and if flabby, the warriors would be inert in action. But, if the liver was firm, red and healthy-looking it portended success. If the liver looked unhealthy, the raid would be abandoned.

Often associated with the practice of head-hunting was the custom of tattooing. Among some groups of Dusuns and Muruts, the tattoo was formerly a sign that a man was a warrior. He was not eligible for tattooing if he had not been on a raid. As for a woman, she was not eligible for tattooing if she was not deemed an expert at women's crafts, for example, basket-work and weaving. Tattoos had other uses besides this.

According to Rutter (1929, pp. 117-19), among the Muruts, it was said that the straight tattoo lines on a woman's forearm, from the wrist up towards the elbow, represented torches, since a woman was regarded to be so foolish that when travelling to the afterworld, she might lose her way if she was not equipped with a

101

torch. Furthermore, tattoos could help the spirit of the dead win the favour of the ferryman who would then ferry him across a great river and provide directions for the remainder of his journey to the afterworld. A man who was not tattooed would have to paddle or pole himself on a log across the river.

Among the Muruts of Kuala Kaputu,[9] there is a legend accounting for the origin of tattoos which were said to provide safety from crocodiles. According to the legend, a crocodile once procured the help of a midwife of the Murut village to assist its mate which was having difficulty in laying eggs. When she had helped the crocodiles successfully, they promised her that if the people of her village wore a tattoo on each shoulder or two tattoos around their legs, all crocodiles recognizing these would never harm them. There is also a belief among the Muruts of the Pangaran and Salang villages that when a tattooed man dies, God would be able to see his tattoos glowing on his body like the sun and allow his soul into heaven.

The Bajau World-View

THEORIES OF ORIGIN

The origin of the Bajaus is not very clear though there are some legends pertaining to it. Among such legends are those related by the Bajaus of Omadal (Semporna), Cyril Alliston and Najeeb Saleeby.

According to the Bajaus of Omadal, once there was a ruler in Johore by the name of Sultan Iskandar Alam. The Sultan had a daughter, Sitti Zairan Kabaran, whose beauty won the admiration of two brothers, Selangaya Bongsu and Haklom Nuzum, who sought

102

her hand in marriage. As the choice was difficult to make, the Sultan suggested that the brothers should compete in a boat race and whoever won the race would marry the princess. Due to some misadventure, Selangaya Bongsu lost the race to his younger brother and, being very upset, refused to return to Johore but continued sailing aimlessly until he eventually reached the Philippines. In the Philippines, Selangaya Bongsu decided to settle in the Sulu Archipelago. From there a number of his descendants, the Bajaus, made their way to Sabah.[10]

The version as recorded by Cyril Alliston was as follows: Long ago in Johore, there was a Sultan who had a daughter, Dayang Ayesha, whose remarkable beauty won the love of both the Sultan of Brunei and the Sultan of Sulu. The Sultan of Johore, thinking that the Sultan of Sulu was a better match for his daughter, accepted his proposal and with that the princess was sent off to Sulu, escorted by several warships. On their way to Sulu, the Sultan of Brunei managed to kidnap the princess. As a result of that, the followers of Princess Ayesha, fearing the wrath of the Sultan of Johore, dared not return home. Instead, they became sea-gypsies, depending on the sea for their livelihood, sometimes engaging in piracy. Later, some of them settled on isolated islands and along the northwest and northeast coast of Borneo while the others preferred to stay in boats as sea-gypsies till this day.[11]

The version as given by Najeeb M. Saleeby was that the Bajaus (Samals) were carried by strong winds from Johore to the Sulu Archipelago somewhere around the fourteenth century. The number of Bajaus arriving in the Sulu Archipelago was very large and almost the whole archipelago was peopled by them. However, though they were numerically greater than the Sulus who were the original inhabitants of the archipelago, the Sulus were able to subjugate them. The relationship between them and the Sulus were like that of a slave and his master or a subject and his ruler.[12]

The legends related above maintain that the ancestors of the Bajaus now found in the Borneo-Philippines region were originally the inhabitants of Johore, a state in the Malay Peninsula, but moved to the new region due to certain circumstances. However, due to a lack of written materials, it is difficult to ascertain how far the above account is true. Sopher[13] is of the opinion that the ancestors of these Bajaus were originally from the Riau-Lingga Islands and that before coming to the Borneo-Philippines region they were already boat-dwellers. Sopher based his theory on the fact there are cultural, linguistic and physical similarities to be found among the inhabitants of the Riau-Lingga Islands and the Bajaus of the Borneo-Philippines region. Sopher believes that the migration of the Bajaus from the Riau-Lingga region which took place somewhere in the fourteenth century was, in some ways, prompted by the trade which was then flourishing in Brunei and Jolo between the Chinese and the local people. The Chinese were greatly interested in the marine products which could be obtained from the innumerable island environments off the North Borneo coast and especially in the Sulu Archipelago. Those products could easily be gathered by the Bajaus who were expert swimmers and divers.

Apart from trade, there were other factors which could have prompted the migration of the Bajaus from their original homeland, such as the pressure of over-population which prevented them from getting an adequate supply of marine products; conflicts with the other local people; their inherent love of adventure; and the uncontrollable wind and sea currents which brought them to new places.

In the past, the Bajaus were mostly boat-dwellers and this could be attributed to a number of reasons. Some say that the Bajaus loved a sea-roving life and thus had no wish to bind themselves to any particular place. Others claim that they had a cowardly disposition and when hurt or threatened would simply move off to another place rather than confront their aggressors. Some Bajaus even explained that they felt safer in their boats and would fall ill if they were to live on land.[14]

Nowadays, however, a large number of Bajaus have become house-dwellers though a few, especially the Bajau Laut, still prefer to be boat-dwellers and lead a nomadic type of life. Most of the Bajaus who have settled on land are strand-dwellers, perhaps because of their fishing activities which no doubt require an easy access to the sea.

MAN AND SOCIETY

Leadership

According to the Bajaus of Omadal, the first group of Bajaus to come to Sabah was sent by a certain ruler of Sulu who was said to have suzerainty rights over the state of Sabah. It was said that before colonizing Sabah, the British had earlier sought the permission of the Sultan of Sulu. The permission was granted by the Sultan on the understanding that some of his Bajau subjects would be allowed to settle in Sabah. This was taken as a precautionary measure to prevent Sabah from falling completely into the hands of the British. The group of Bajaus sent to Sabah was also directed to return to Sulu once a year to pay homage and tribute to the Sultan.

The first place to be settled by these Bajaus on coming to Sabah was Omadal Island. It is not clear why the island was chosen as their place of settlement. According to some Bajaus, the choice was made by the Sultan of Sulu himself as Omadal was deemed to have a strategic position. Others are of the opinion that the settlement on Omadal was purely accidental; the Bajaus having travelled a long way from Sulu finally decided that it was time to make a stop and Omadal appeared to be the most suitable place then. Later, however, because of the problem of over-population, some Bajaus migrated to other islands in the vicinity of Omadal, such as Bum-Bum, Danawan, Si Amil and Menampilik, though they still maintained a close relationship with their kinsmen on Omadal.

In those days, most Bajaus preferred to make their homes on isolated islands rather than on the mainland of Sabah and for a large number of Bajaus this pattern of settlement has persisted to the present day. This form of settlement gave them a feeling of security as there were no strangers with whom they need to contend. Moreover, in those days, as the Bajaus of Omadal explained, they were afraid to live on the mainland of Sabah for fear of a certain tribe, the Sagai, who practised head-hunting. The existence and activity of this tribe were also mentioned by J. Valera[15] as follows:

> It was many years ago, that is, before the colonization
> of Borneo, that not only Dayaks attack people to take
> heads, but also Sagai-i, a kind of tribe who is said to
> be in Ulu Sirodong, Tawau district. It was the custom
> of this tribe that when any of the royal family is
> dead, the rayat were sent out to attack other tribes
> and bring home heads.

When the Bajaus first came to Sabah they had five leaders, appointed by the Sultan of Sulu, to lead them. These leaders -- Panglima Abdul Haman, Panglima Lauhari, Orang Kaya Angalon, Orang Kaya Apang and Melanti -- who were said to be the descendants of Selangaya Bongsu first gathered at Omadal Island but were later assigned to separate regions. Panglima Abdul Haman was assigned to Omadal Island; Panglima Lauhari to Galam-Galam; Orang Kaya Angalon to Golom-Golom; Orang Kaya Apang to Kubang; and Melanti to Silawa; all in the district of Semporna. These leaders who were designated as the headmen of their own regions were also requested by the Sultan of Sulu to select a number of officials to assist them in their administrative duties. As a result of this, there arose a number of other officials bearing the title of Maharajah, Pahlawan, Pengharapan, Munari, Imam, Khatib, Bilal, Nakib, Ulangkaya, etc., each with a different duty and status. The Maharajah, Pahlawan, Pengharapan, Ulangkaya and Nakib were responsible for the peace and safety of the village; the Imam, Khatib, and Bilal were responsible for spreading the Islamic faith among the Bajaus; while the Munari was responsible for keeping the villagers informed of important news and ceremonies as well as collecting alms for the poor and tribute for the Sultan of Sulu. These officials after being selected by the headmen were sent to the palace of the Sultan of Sulu where they were given proper training for their posts. According to Bajau custom, these posts or titles were hereditary and on the death of the officials, the posts would be inherited by their brothers or sons. If there were no brothers or sons, the posts would be given to their nearest kin, such as cousins or nephews, preferably descendants of previous office-bearers. These new sets of officials were not required to undergo training at the palace of the Sultan of Sulu and as such their ties with the government of Sulu gradually weakened and eventually came to an end.

Nowadays, a number of these traditional posts, such as Pengharapan, Pahlawan, Ulangkaya and Munari, have lost their importance and serve no function though the titles are still maintained by the Bajaus. The Panglima and Maharajah (usually held by village headmen) as well as Imam, Khatib and Bilal, on the other hand, are still highly regarded and continue to function as before. These leaders, however, do not have much authority or power over the other villagers as they are looked upon mainly as advisers though they no doubt play an important role in the society.

Right from the start, all these important posts were held only by men. Though there are now female _Imam_, _Khatib_ and _Bilal_, they play only a secondary role and serve mainly as assistants to their male counterparts.

Kinship

To the Bajaus, the circle of relatives acquired through birth, marriage or adoption, are regarded with much respect for they play an important part in their lives. Separate terms are used to refer to the different sets of relatives. Relatives acquired through birth are known as _maglung_ while those acquired through marriage and adoption are known as _pamilatan_ and _danakan ni-ipat_ respectively. Within the category of _maglung_, relatives are further distinguished as _danakan sekot_ (close relatives) and _danakan tah_ (distant relatives). A person's _danakan sekot_ include all members of his nuclear family -- grandparents, grandchildren, great-grandparents, great-grandchildren, siblings' children, siblings of parents and their children. This set of relatives having the closest ties of kinship occupy the most important place in a Bajau's life and it is to them that he normally shows his greatest concern and obligations. The _danakan tah_ consisting of all other relatives outside the circle of _danakan sekot_ are by comparison less important.

A person's behaviour, responsibility or obligation towards his circle of relatives is not only determined by the closeness of kinship ties but also by other factors such as age, generation, and sex. Among the Bajaus, the young are expected to treat their elders with respect and to look after them when they are old. The older folks should not be addressed by their names but by certain terms, such as _ema'_ for father, _enggo'_ for mother, _siaka_ or _kakak_ for older relatives of the same generation, _babo'_ for aunts and _bapa'_ for uncles. It is permissible for the older relatives, on the other hand, to address the younger relatives by their names though this seldom happens. Most Bajaus in addressing their younger relatives prefer using affectionate terms such as siali or oto' for males, and arung, inda', siali for females. The terms oto' and inda' can also be used for older relatives of the same generation.

In the Bajau society, it is the male relatives who are expected to be the breadwinners for the family and are responsible for the welfare of their female relatives. The women being considered the weaker sex are regarded as most suitable to be housewives though they can often help their male folks at home, for example, to dry fish and mend nets. As such, among the Bajaus of Omadal, no woman is to be found earning her own living. Should a woman be separated or divorced from her husband, she can always turn to her brothers, uncles, or other male relatives for assistance.

Relatives, though generally known as danakan or kaum pamili, are sometimes referred to as saga sehe or sehe-sehe which means "friends". The use of the term saga sehe or sehe-sehe reflects the intimate relationship between an individual and his relatives who are looked upon as his companions, advisers, and helpers in times of need. As the Bajaus do not mix freely with other people, it is not surprising, then, that for most of them relatives are their only friends or companions. Most Bajaus feel secure in the company of relatives and thus it is a common practice for relatives to live in close proximity to one another. As relatives are greatly trusted, they do not feel the need to fence their houses or to partition their houses into rooms though there may be several families living together.

Marriage between relatives is also very common as they are considered the most suitable partners. Thus, among the Bajaus of Omadal, marriages between first and second cousins appear to be most common. This form of marriage is also preferred as it can help to strengthen the kinship ties of the families concerned though it does not guarantee a permanent union as divorce is fairly common, too. Not all categories of relatives, however, can be chosen as marriage partners. Relatives who are too closely related are forbidden to marry as this union which is regarded as incestuous is considered "hot" and liable to bring harm not only to the couple involved but also to their descendants. For instance, they may be cursed with diseases, insanity, infertility, accidents, or ill-luck generally. However, if a union between two fairly close relatives should take place, a special ceremony called <u>animan sial</u> or <u>animan pasuk</u> can be performed to "cool" off the offence and ward off any ill-luck. In this ceremony, some gold, usually a ring, is thrown into the sea as a form of offering to appease the spirits of the sea. Apart from this, some blood is extracted from the couple with a special golden needle called <u>pengugit</u>. Sometimes a white cock will also be killed and its blood sprinkled over the couple. This cock will not be eaten but thrown away after the ceremony. Such a ceremony is either performed on the third day of the wedding or when the couple suffers from misfortune.

On the whole, the kinship system of the Bajaus is of the bilateral or cognatic type where relatives of the mother and father are regarded with equal importance and thus similar terms of address are applied to them. The inclusion of the two sets of relatives in the same terminological category also means that there is some significant similarity in the customary behaviour due to both of them. Male and female relatives, too, are regarded to be of equal importance and this is reflected in the use of similar terms of reference for most of them, such as <u>embo'</u> for grandparents, <u>moyang</u> for great-grandparents, <u>kaki</u> for cousins, <u>empu</u> for grandchildren and <u>kemenakan</u> for nieces and nephews. However, to differentiate between the sexes, the terms <u>lelah</u> (male) and <u>danda</u> (female) may be used, for instance, <u>empu lelah</u> (grandson) and <u>embo' danda</u> (grandmother).

MAN AND THE SUPERNATURAL BEINGS

The Bajaus of Omadal and Semporna in general (with the exception of a group of Bajau Laut) are Muslims and have been so for quite some time now though the exact date of their conversion to Islam is difficult to determine. Some Bajaus explained that they had been Muslims even before they came to Sabah. According to Tregonning,[16] Islam was brought to Borneo by Indian and Arab traders and merchants along the sea-routes probably in the fifteenth or sixteenth century. The Bajaus being seafarers and coastal dwellers probably had some contact with these Muslim traders and could have been influenced into embracing Islam then.

Being Muslims, the Bajaus do not share many of the Dusuns and Muruts' traditional beliefs, such as those pertaining to the creation of the world, the gusi cult, the practice of somunggup, head-hunting and tattooing. However, they do share certain beliefs with these groups, one obvious example being the belief in a great number of supernatural beings which are believed to have a great influence over man's fate and fortune. The adoption of Islam, in their case, did not result in the suppression of animistic beliefs and practices which are still very much in evidence among them.

Among the host of supernatural beings in the Bajaus' belief system may be mentioned three main categories: the jinn, bantu syaitan (ghosts and devils), and souls of the dead.

Jinn

The jinn whose origin is obscure are powerful supernatural beings with very special attributes believed to influence man's life greatly. There are various types of jinn and each Bajau clan is believed to possess its own jinn which differ from the jinn of other clans. The jinn are generally benevolent and can assist man in the form of familiar spirits. A familiar spirit is usually in the charge of a special member of the clan, chosen personally by the jinn to be its mediator with the human world. The person in charge of the jinn, whether male or female, is known as orang yang berjin or just kelamat (medicine-man). With the aid of the jinn, the orang yang berjin acquires special abilities and can cure other members of the clan of all sorts of sickness, especially those caused by tulah (supernatural curse). Besides this he also has the ability to perform miracles, such as the ability to stop a storm, to change wind directions, to mend broken objects without using anything, and to dim the eyesight of enemies. The possession of a jinn within a certain clan is hereditary and at the death of an orang yang berjin, the jinn is passed on to one of his kinsmen who is deemed most suitable.

Some orang yang berjin are more fortunate than others and can be assisted by more than one jinn which naturally enhances their power and influence. In Kampong Galam-Galam (a Bajau village on Bum-Bum Island, Semporna), for instance, there was once an old woman, Dumiha, who was said to possess two different kinds of jinn, Jin Duata and Jin Tuan-aulia, and as a result of that acquired extraordinary power. Jin Duata was said to manifest itself only during the day while Jin Tuan-aulia would manifest itself only on Friday nights. Of the two, Jin Tuan-aulia, who was believed to originate from the Tawi-Tawi Island in the Philippines, was more well known. According to a legend, Jin Tuan-aulia was once a human being, too, but because of his extremely pious nature, was transformed into a jinn with very social attributes. It was said that he could even assume the form of various animals and insects, such as the snake, centipede and fire-fly. The origin of Jin Duata, on the other hand, is obscure. Nevertheless, like Jin Tuan-aulia, Jin Duata, too was believed to be positively benevolent and would assist man through the medium of an orang yang berjin.

112

The orang yang berjin is regarded as very special and to some extent sacred and hence should always be treated with reverence. A person who is disrespectful or violates certain taboos with regard to an orang yang berjin risks supernatural punishment in the form of tulah. A person under the influence of tulah will suffer any kind of mishap, such as illness, accident, and loss of property or luck. Animals, too, are not safe from such tulah should they violate certain prohibitions. For instance, it was said that even birds flying over the sacred residence of Dumiha would be accursed and fall dead.

In the Bajau society, an orang yang berjin has certain privileges over other members of the society. One obvious example is the privilege to use beds and sometimes umbrellas, too. Ordinary men who attempt to sleep on beds without the prior permission of the jinn face the risk of tulah and may fall ill. As a result of this prohibition, the use of beds is infrequent in most Bajau communities. Though it is still possible for ordinary men to use beds by seeking the permission of the jinn, most Bajaus would rather do without beds believing that even with the permission of the jinn, the safety of those involved is not fully guaranteed. Moreover, it is rather expensive to own a bed for there are certain obligations to be met. A person desiring to use a bed must provide the orang yang berjin with certain gifts, such as clothes, pillow-cases, or money (usually amounting to half the price of the bed). Besides this, if he were to furnish his bed with anything at all, such as pillows, mosquito-net or mattress, he is required to give the same things, in similar amounts, to the orang yang berjin not only at the initial period but throughout the whole period the bed is used. Failure to do so would only court an attack of tulah.

The Bajaus believe that an orang yang berjin is not only powerful and influential in his lifetime but continues to be so even after his death. At death he is looked upon as a saint who

113

can still assist man in many ways. Thus, his tomb, which is usually made more special than those of ordinary people, is often frequented by people seeking supernatural help to relieve them of all kinds of predicaments. A request for help is often accompanied by a vow to offer the saint certain gifts, like umbrellas, flags, perfume, or money, should the request be answered. If such a vow is not fulfilled, the penalty can be very heavy and the person concerned may fall ill or even die. Sometimes, however, he will be given prior warning in a dream; if he dreams of being bitten or about to be bitten by a snake, that means he will be in danger unless the vow is fulfilled. If the vow is fulfilled in time, he will be forgiven and no harm will come to him.

Belief in Tulah

The belief in tulah is an important aspect of the Bajau world-view. Apart from the reasons mentioned earlier, tulah can also befall a person for a number of reasons, for instance, showing disrespect towards one's elders by criticizing, cursing, scolding, abusing or opposing them. Forgetting one's responsibility towards one's parents, relations and ancestors, for example, by leaving the village permanently without ever returning to see to their welfare or needs, can also bring about tulah. This belief still predominates the lives of the Bajaus of Omadal, preventing many of them from leaving their island home though the living conditions there are far from satisfactory. A number of Bajaus who have migrated still return occasionally to the island to avoid getting tulah. Quite often those Bajaus who fall ill suddenly on leaving the island would associate the illness with tulah and in order to cast off the effects of tulah would return to stay for a considerable period on the island. It is also believed that being stingy with one's parents, grandparents or other elderly relatives, for instance, by withholding something that is readily available and very much desired by them, is yet another reason for tulah.

114

There is also hereditary tulah, such as tulah embo' and tulah matalau. The Bajaus attribute the existence of these two tulah to certain events that happened in the past. According to one legend, tulah embo' came about when some ancestors of the Bajaus today brought home a curious vessel (later named embo' which means "grandfather" or "grandmother") which they found near the sea. After the vessel was brought home, everyone in the house fell seriously ill for three consecutive days, developing sores on their bodies which they found difficult to cure. Then, one night, in a dream, a Bajau was told that they could only be cured if they performed a magembo' ceremony using the same kinds of objects they found in the vessel. These objects, contained in a similar vessel, should be set adrift on the sea after the ceremony. Among the things required for the ceremony that persists till today are some padi, a coconut, turmeric, jalawastu (an aromatic herb), a wooden vessel, some black cloth and a semi-completed pandanus mat. Till this day, the descendants of all those Bajaus involved in the incident are susceptible to tulah embo'; and when an attack of the tulah is suspected, the magembo' ceremony will be performed.

Tulah matalau, on the other hand, came into existence with the birth of a certain child. According to a legend, the child was once born with sores all over his body and his condition became normal only after a magmatalau ceremony, dictated in the midwife's dream, had been performed. The objects required for the magmatalau ceremony are quite similar to those required for the magembo' ceremony, including things like rice, an old coconut, turmeric, jalawastu, a brass vessel, three cigarettes made from tobacco and nipah leaves, and a semi-completed pandanus mat. As in the case of tulah embo', the descendants of the affected person are highly susceptible to tulah matalau.

A hereditary tulah is considered extremely dangerous, even more dangerous than the attack of evil spirits. However, as described above, there are ways and means to cast off the effects of such a tulah. The same is true for other kinds of tulah, too. The person deemed best able to effect a cure from the attacks of tulah is once again the orang yang berjin and the methods employed will depend, of course, on the type of tulah encountered and the type of jinn he possesses. While under treatment, the patient and all members of his household are often required to observe certain taboos. For instance, they should refrain from bathing, eating any spicy or oily food, or certain kinds of fish, and sleeping on a mattress. Failure to comply with these taboos would only cause a prolongation of the ailment.

Hantu Syaitan

While the jinn are generally benevolent, the hantu syaitan are mostly malevolent and they are found both on land and sea. One of the most frequently mentioned ghosts is the hantu bangkit or pangguah believed to make their haunt on Omadal Island. This is hardly surprising as Omadal has been a popular burial ground of the Bajaus since ancient times, and as such, is directly linked with the existence of the hantu bangkit which is said to originate from burial grounds. In the past, it was a common practice for the Bajaus of Semporna to bury their dead on Omadal Island even if it meant having to travel a very long way. This was so because Omadal, supposedly the first place settled by those Bajaus on coming to Sabah, was regarded as their homeland and, consequently, an appropriate burial ground for their dead. Even now some Bajaus who have settled elsewhere prefer to bury their dead on Omadal Island for, according to traditional custom, it is necessary to bury the dead alongside their ancestors, otherwise they, the living relatives, will be punished with tulah. However, most Bajaus who have settled on distant lands and have been partially exposed to foreign influences, are no longer ruled by such a traditional custom, preferring to bury their dead near their new homes.

The Bajaus believe that some of the dead, especially those who have sinned in their lifetime and those who were buried without due respect to traditional customs, will transform into hantu bangkit and work mischief among the living. This ghost which can appear at any time of the day is described as a skeleton having a long chin, reaching up to the chest, and enveloped in a sheet of white cloth. It has an extremely foul smell and is thus frequently surrounded by flies. The ghost can be frightened away by whipping it with a broom of lidi or a stick used for roasting fish or even by reciting some verses from the holy Qur'an.

Apart from the hantu bangkit, there are other types of evil spirits such as the selok, balbalan, kokok, gelap and menanggalam. The selok which usually flies at night is described as having the form of a human head with an exposed trailing stomach, similar to the appearance of the komakadong in the beliefs of the Dusuns. It is extremely dangerous for anyone attacked by it will suffer a shortness of breath, chest pains, frequent vomitting, and may even die if not given prompt treatment.

The balbalan looks like a human being but differs in that when it sits, its knees are higher than its shoulders. Like the selok, the balbalan also flies at night but attacks its victim slowly, unlike the swift action of the selok. The victim will experience much pain, his body will turn yellowish, and he will feel weak, lethargic and sleepy. If a person has been attacked by the balbalan, others around him have to observe certain taboos so as not to aggravate his illness; for instance, they should not bring into his house red fish, bamboos or long sticks. The victims of the balbalan and selok can only be cured by drinking the juice of the patau leaf and blessed water in which turmeric has been soaked.

117

The kokok which always appear as a group are not as harmful as the selok and balbalan as their main intention is to make a friend or companion out of their victim. These ghosts are usually found during the rainy season and in places where there are mangrove trees. People who encounter them will be hypnotized into following them into the jungle. Under their influence, the victim will gradually lose his memory and if not rescued will live with them as a hantu kokok, too. To look for the victim, it is necessary to play the tagungguh (traditional musical instruments of the Bajaus) as the kokok which are very fond of them will manifest themselves at the sound of the music. When found, the victim is usually in an abnormal state: his hands are stiff and his body slippery. He is also terribly shy of man and will refuse to eat. However, he will soon recover when given a bath. One way to keep the kokok at a distance is to be nude as the ghosts dislike and are afraid of seeing people in the nude.

The gelap is an evil spirit that dwells in the sea and is often seen as a bright light though it can assume the form of a human being. It is fond of sinking boats and drowning its victims. To keep the gelap away, some Bajaus when going out to sea will bring with them some limes and tuba (a substance used to poison fish) as these are greatly feared by the spirit.

Like the gelap, the menanggalam also appears in the form of a bright light. People who encounter them will be so petrified that they lose their speech. Sometimes they will even die as a result of the extreme fear.

Apart from those already mentioned, there are other kinds of evil spirits which are not known by any specific names but known generally as hantu syaitan or iblis, which threaten the well-being of man. Some of these evil spirits, for instance, are fond of attacking women who are pregnant or in labour. For that reason, pregnant women are often advised to let down their hair

118

when travelling at night so that evil spirits would not be able to see them clearly. Besides that, it is also advisable for them to carry sharp objects for these are feared by the evil spirits. While in labour, too, they should be protected by placing around them certain objects, such as knives, thorns, tongkai leaves and gajah lemon peel. These objects which are either sharp or have a pungent smell will keep away evil spirits.

MEDICINE-MEN

As in Dusun society, there are certain persons in the Bajau community who are deemed capable of dealing with evil spirits and these include the orang yang berjin and other medicine-men generally known as kelamat. The ordinary kelamat, like the orang yang berjin, often work with the aid of familiar spirits (not jinn in their case) and thus possess miraculous strength and ability. They are especially noted for their ability to cure people of a great number of diseases, particularly those believed to be caused by evil spirits, such as malaria, chicken-pox, insanity and paralysis. Such skills can be acquired through many ways, such as through the will of god, the assistance of familiar spirits, inheritance, revelations in dreams, and, most commonly, through training under a veteran kelamat.

People who are possessed or attacked by evil spirits can be recognized through their abnormal characteristics: they will be pale, stiff, unable to talk, and afraid to be with people. To ascertain whether a person is really the victim of evil spirits or not, the kelamat can either go into a trance or rub a piece of ginger over the patient's body. If the patient is really possessed by evil spirits, he will scream and cry when the ginger is administered to his body. After diagnosing the nature of the patient's illness, the kelamat will then proceed with the treatment. The type of treatment will of course depend on how

119

severe the case is. In less severe cases, the patient is merely given some ginger to eat and also a bath accompanied by prayers.

In more severe cases, for example, in the case of paralysis or chicken-pox, the treatment will take on a different form and will be held for a period of three consecutive nights. If the evil spirits are felt to be particularly obstinate, a small boat or pitulak will be built and loaded with various kinds of food as well as models of men, representative of the patient and members of his household, to lure the spirits away from there. To set the boat on its proper course, it is also equipped with wooden models of the captain, steersman, and guard armed with certain weapons. It is believed that the evil spirits lured and trapped in the boat will be carried away by the boat once it is put to sea and the patient will then be able to recover. In view of this, great care has to be taken when putting the pitulak to sea to make sure it does not drift back to shore. If it should do so, the evil spirits will have a chance to land and work mischief on people once more. Should the pitulak land near another village, that village will also be attacked by the dreaded disease and another pitulak will have to be built to set the evil spirits adrift again.

Apart from their ability in the art of medicine, most kelamat are believed to be experts in the art of magic and witchcraft and thus are much feared by other members of the society. Magic and witchcraft are methods aimed at influencing or controlling events of the social and physical world with the aid of supernatural power. The two differ in that magic may be either malevolent or beneficent while witchcraft is invariably evil.

In the category of magic may be mentioned the ilmu pugai, a love charm aimed at inducing or fostering love between people of the opposite sex; ilmu hopai, aimed at weakening enemies to render them lethargic and thus easily defeated; ilmu panglias, aimed at making a person invincible and impenetrable to any weapon; and ilmu doa kosog aimed at endowing a person with enormous physical strength to enable him to defeat his enemies easily or lift very heavy objects. A number of these arts, such as the ilmu hopai, ilmu panglias and ilmu doa kosog are said to have been frequently practised in the past when the Bajaus were constantly harassed by pirates and other foreign intruders. Nowadays, however, such magical arts are rarely resorted to because of the relatively peaceful environment around them.

In the field of witchcraft, there are two notable practices, namely ilmu bungkang and ilmu selimbil, both of which are aimed at causing injury or death to the victim. Ilmu bungkang is performed with the use of turmeric, chalk, needle, and a half-coconut shell. These objects, arranged in a particular manner, will be planted at a place frequented by the victim and while doing this, the kelamat will call on the evil spirits to work harm on the victim. The victim of bungkang will have these symptoms: severe headache, high temperature, swollen legs and fainting fits. However, he can be cured with the help of another kelamat.

Ilmu selimbil, on the other hand, is performed with the sole intention of killing the victim. In this case, two knives tied together in the form of a cross, will be directed by the kelamat to seek and kill the victim. Should the knives return with blood stains, it is taken as a sign that the victim has been killed.

The Bajaus are aware that the practice of magic and witchcraft, along with a number of their traditional observances, are not in line with the teachings of Islam. However, they believe that God (Allah) has a forgiving nature and will accept or forgive all men, including those who have sinned. Thus, even though they have been Muslims for a long time now, such

121

traditional practices are still adhered to, and even regarded as being essential in their lives. Magic and witchcraft, for instance, give them a sense of security in the face of enemies who may not be easily repelled by ordinary means.

SOULS OF THE DEAD

Like the Dusuns and Muruts, the Bajaus also believe that life does not end with the death of the physical body. They hold that the soul will continue to live in another world which is different from the one it is accustomed to on earth. At death, the soul departs from the body to make its way either to heaven or to hell, the destination being determined by two major factors:

a) Man's conduct while on earth: Most Bajaus believe that people who behave well and are always performing good deeds for the community will be assured of a place in heaven. Likewise, women who die of childbirth and boys who die of circumcision will also be given a place in heaven as their deaths are regarded as kematian sabil (deaths in the course of duty). On the other hand, those who are evil will probably end up in hell. However, there are some Bajaus who believe that since God has a forgiving nature, all men, whether good or bad, will be given equal treatment in the afterworld.

b) Proper burial: To be assured of a good life in the afterworld, the dead has to be buried with due respect to customs and religion and this responsibility lies with his immediate family and relatives. Failure to fulfil this obligation will only bring about tulah in the form of sickness, accident, or other forms of ill-luck, for those concerned. It is believed that

122

whatever is done by the living for the dead will have definite effect on his life in the afterworld. Thus, in the Bajau society, apart from the elaborate burial rites, prayers and feasts, there are other practices which aim at helping the soul of the dead to find salvation and comfort in the afterworld. One such practice is the giving of alms in the form of money, food, clothes, or other possessions of the dead to ensure that the dead will not lack anything or suffer poverty as these things donated to others will be indirectly received by him in the afterworld. Sometimes, to be doubly sure that the dead will be comfortable in the afterworld, some of his treasured possessions will be interred along with him so that they can continue to be of use to him. It is also felt that the dead will miss his children or grandchildren, especially the little ones, and will want them as companions in the afterworld. Thus, to prevent the dead from stealing the souls of those he left behind, some areca-nuts, serving as their representatives, will be buried with him.

The occurrence of death is much feared by the Bajaus for it is believed that when there is death in the village, evil will prevail and people who are not cautious will fall victim to it. They not only fear the appearance of the hantu bangkit but also ill-luck generally. To avert ill-luck, certain taboos have to be observed by the whole village for a period of seven days after death has occurred. The following are some of these taboos:

a) No one should break anything or sneeze in the house of the deceased, otherwise death will also occur in the house of the person concerned.

b) No one should burn any food, remove lice from the hair,

123

> or perform any work, such as weaving, sewing, or
> carpentry.

c) The house of the deceased should not be washed.

The Bajaus believe that the souls of the dead are always
keeping a watch over the activities of the living and can also
assist them in times of trouble. However, such assistance cannot
be taken for granted for whether or not it will be given depends
on how well the souls of the dead have been treated. People who
treat them well, for instance, by keeping the compounds of their
graves clean and by holding periodical feasts in memory of them
can hope for their help while those who neglect them will be
punished with <u>tulah</u>.

Conclusion

An important element in the traditional world-views of the Dusuns
and Bajaus is the belief in a host of supernatural beings. In
their view, the world is populated not only by man and animals
but also by all kinds of spiritual beings which live in close
proximity to man and can be found dwelling in various features of
the natural landscape, such as the sea, rivers, mountains, trees
and plants. These spirits, most of which are malignant, are
believed to have a strong influence over man's fate and fortune.
It is felt that there is a direct link between these supernatural
beings and many events in man's life, such as the personal crises
of birth, sickness and death, individual fortune, success in
hunting, yield of crops, and so forth. Man's well-being, then,
will depend largely on how well he can accommodate himself to
their whims and fancies. However, man is not completely helpless
in the face of these supernatural beings as there are ways and
means to deal with them. For instance, spirits which are

malignant can be expelled by means of magic, bribery or trickery while those which are beneficent can be invoked or even adopted as familiar spirits to assist man in various ways. Thus, the nature of man's relation and attitude towards these supernatural beings are in many ways determined by the spirits' disposition and attitude towards man.

Apart from the attention given to supernatural beings, the Dusuns and Bajaus also pay much attention to omens and taboos which regulate their conduct in many aspects. There are birth taboos, marriage taboos, death taboos, taboo days when no work must be done, etc.

Such primitive world-views are also heavily influenced by the past. People act and judge others in accordance with the norms and values laid down by their ancestors. In other words, events in the past are looked upon as a general guide for present and future behaviour in ceremonial practices, economic activities, child-training and other departments of life.

These traditional world-views have survived for innumerable years now and are still tenaciously held by the respective groups. However, like most other world-views, they are not static and changes have occurred from time to time albeit at a very slow pace. Some changes have resulted in the obliteration of certain traditional beliefs and practices, such as those pertaining to jar-worshipping and tattooing among certain groups of Dusuns and Muruts, while others have added new dimensions to their worldviews, such as the adoption of Christianity and Islam among certain groups of Dusuns, Muruts and Bajaus. In most cases, the advent of these universal religions has not succeeded in obliterating the major part of their traditional world-views which have persisted to the present day. However, further changes in their world-views can be expected in the near future as the peoples of Sabah become increasingly drawn into the

125

process of modernization which began after the Second World War and has gradually become intensified after Sabah became a state of Malaysia in 1963. Among other things, the process of modernization brought about the introduction of Western medicine, secular education and modern systems of communications. These social amenities will undoubtedly bring or add new dimensions to the natives' world-views as they bring them into closer contact with the world at large.

NOTES

1. Banci Penduduk dan Perumahan, Colongan Masyarakat (Kuala Lumpur: Jabatan Perangkaan Malaysia, 1970), pp. 87-96.

2. Owen Rutter, The Pagans of North Borneo (Hutchinson & Co. Ltd., 1929), pp. 37-40.

3. Dusun (Kota Kinabalu, Malaysia, 1978), p. 8.

4. Ivor H. N. Evans, Religion, Folklore & Custom in North Borneo and the Malay Peninsula (Cambridge, 1923), pp. 45-49; idem, The Religion of the Tempasuk Dusuns of North Borneo (Cambridge, 1953), pp. 16-18; and Fred Sinidol & Martin Benggon, "The Creation - A Folk-Story from Penampang", Journal of the Sabah Society 1, No. 1 (1961): 43-48.

5. Thomas Rhye Williams, The Dusuns (A North Borneo Society) (Holt, Rinehart & Winston, 1965), pp. 11-18.

6. Ivor H. N. Evans, Among Primitive Peoples in Borneo (Seeley, Service & Co. Ltd., 1922), p. 165; and The Religion of the Tempasuk Dusuns of North Borneo (Cambridge, 1953), pp. 61-62.

7. Harold Allen Bair, "Notes on Kapir, the Kadazan Religion, as practised in Bundu Tuhan", Sabah Society Journal III, No. 1 (April 1966): 45.

8. E. White, "A Dusun Fertility Rite", Sarawak Museum Journal VI (July 1955): 254-56.

9. John H. Alman, "Notes on Tattooing in North Borneo", Journal of the Sabah Society 1, No. 4 (1963): 81-83.

10. Yap Beng Liang, "Orang Bajau Pulau Omadal, Sabah" (Satu Kajian Tenkang Sistem Budaya), (M.A. dissertation, University of Malaya, Kuala Lumpur, 1977), pp. 39-40.

11. Threatened Paradise - North Borneo and Its Peoples (London: Robert Hale, 1966), pp. 23-24.

12. The History of Sulu (Manila: Filipiniana Book Guild, Inc. IV, 1963), pp. 32-40.

13. The Sea Nomads (Syracuse University, Memoirs of the National Museum, No. 5, 1965), pp. 352-53.

14. Sixto Y. Orosa, The Sulu Archipelago and Its People (The Philippines: New Mercury Printing Press, 1970), pp. 62-63.

15. J. Valera, "The Old Forts of Semporna", Journal of the Sabah Society, no. 4 (1962): 40-41.

16. Under Chartered Company Rule, (University of Malaya Press, Singapore, 1958),
    p. 2.

REFERENCES

Abdullah Hassan. "Kepercayaan-Kepercayaan dan Ilmu Dukun di Kelompok Taou Sug
    (Sulock) Daerah Sandakan", B.A. Thesis, 1973/4, University of Malaya, Kuala
    Lumpur.

Alliston, Cyril, Threatened Paradise - North Borneo and its Peoples, London,
    Robert Hale Ltd., 1966.

_____. In the Shadow of Kinabalu, London, Robert Hale, Ltd., 1961.

Alman, John H. "Death of a Dusun", Journal of the Sabah Society, Vol. 1, No. 4
    (1963): 39-49.

_____. "Notes on Tattooing in North Borneo", Journal of the Sabah Society,
    Vol. 1, No. 4 (1963): 78-88.

Appells, G.N. "Social Groupings Among the Rungus, a Cognatic Society of Northern
    Borneo", Journal of the Malayan Branch of the Royal Asiatic Society
    (JMBRAS), Vol. 41, Pt. 2 (1968): 193-202.

Arena Wati. Dusun, Kota Kinabalu, Malaysia, 1978.

Bair, Harold Allen. "Notes on Kapir, the Kadazan Religion as practised in Bundu
    Tuhan", Sabah Society Journal, Vol. III, No. 1 (April 1966): 45-51.

Burrough, P.A. "Stick Signs in the Sook Plain", Sabah Society Journal, Vol. V,
    No. 2 (Dec 1970): 83-97.

Dundes, Alan. "Folk Ideas as Units of World-View", Journal of American Folklore,
    84 (1971): 93-103.

Dundes, Alan, ed. Every Man His Way, Prentice-Hall, 1968 .

Enriquez, C.M. Kinabalu, The Haunted Mountain of Borneo, London, 1927.

Erchak, G.M. Dusun Social & Symbolic Orders, Sarawak Museum Journal, Vol. XX, No.
    40-41 (Jan, Dec, 1972), (New Series): 301-13.

Evans, Ivor H.N. Among Primitive Peoples in Borneo, London, 1922.

_____. Religion, Folklore and Custom in North Borneo and the Malay Peninsula,
    Cambridge, 1923.

_____. "Some Dusun Fables", Sarawak Museum Journal, Vol. VI (July 1955):
    245-47.

_____. The Religion of the Tempasuk Dusuns of North Borneo, Cambridge, 1953.

Geertz, Clifford. "Ethos, World-View & the Analysis of Sacred Symbols", Every Man His Way, edited by Alan Dundes. Prentice-Hall, 1968.

Harrison, Tom, and Barbara. "The Prehistory of Sabah", Sabah Society Journal, Vol. IV (1969-70).

Hatton, Frank. North Borneo, London, 1885.

_____. The New Ceylon, London, Chapman & Hall, Ltd., 1881.

Holly, S. "The Origin of the Idahan People", Sarawak Museum Journal, Vol. VI, (July 1955): 257-62.

Jabatan Perangkaan Malaysia. Banci Penduduk dan Perumahan Malaysia Golongan Masyarakat, Kuala Lumpur, 1970.

Jack Maik bin Huashia. "Spirit Boats", Journal of the Sabah Society, No. 4 (1963): 23-27.

Jones, W.T. "World-Views: Their Nature & their Function", Current Anthropology, Vol. 13 (1972): 79-109.

Keith, Agnes. Land Below the Wind, London, 1939.

Mendelson, E. Michael. "World-View", International Encyclopaedia of the Social Sciences, Vol. 16 (1968): 576-79.

Mokhtar Ali bin Ali. "A Berunsai at Lanas", Sabah Society Journal, Vol. 1, No. 4 (1963): 89-92.

Molokum, Jipanus. "Monogit - A Native Custom", Journal of the Sabah Society, Vol. 1, No. 2 (March 1962): 17-19.

Orosa, S. Y. The Sulu Archipelago and Its Peoples, New Mercury Printing Press, The Philippines, 1970.

Redfield, Robert. Human Nature & The Study of Society, edited by Margaret Park Redfield, The University of Chicago Press, Chicago & London, 1962.

Rutter, Owen. The Pagans of North Borneo, Hutchinson & Co. Ltd., 1929.

Saleeby, N.N. The History of Sulu, Publications of the Filipiniana Book Guild, Inc. IV, Manila, 1963.

Sinidol, Fred & Benggon, Martin. "The Creation - A Folk-Story from Penampang", Journal of the Sabah Society 1, No. 1 (1961): 43-48.

Sopher, David E. The Sea Nomads, Syracuse University, Memoirs of the National Museum, No. 5, 1965.

Tregonning, K.G. Under Chartered Company Rule, University of Malaya Press, Singapore, 1958.

Valera, J. "The Old Forts of Semporna", Journal of the Sabah Society, No. 4 (1962): 23-27.

White, E. "A Dusun Fertility Rite", Sarawak Museum Journal VI (July 1955): 254-56.

Williams, Thomas Rhys. The Dusun (A North Borneo Society), Holt, Rinehart and Winston, 1965.

Yap Beng Liang. "Orang Bajau Pulau Omadal, Sabah", M.A. Dissertation, University of Malaya, 1977.

Zaini bin Mohd. Isa, Kebudayaan dan Adat Resam Kadazan dan Murut, Pustaka Aman Press, Kelantan, 1969.

WORLD-VIEW OF SOCIAL BELONGING AMONG THE CHINESE IN MALAYSIA AND SINGAPORE: THE CASE OF SECRET SOCIETIES, CLANS AND DIALECT-GROUP ASSOCIATIONS

LEE POH PING

It cannot be said that the Chinese in nineteenth century Singapore and Malaya had a political view of themselves after the fashion of modern nationalists. They did not conceive of themselves as a nation in the modern sense. This is due not only to the fact that they were migrants and did not have a state they could identify with but also because nationalism in the modern sense did not affect them until the very late nineteenth century. After all, even in China then, Sun Yat-Sen, desperate to create nationalistic feeling among the Chinese, compared them to a heap of sand. The political view they had of themselves was that they were part of the middle kingdom. This was more in the nature of being part of a civilization and of being subjects of an emperor. Even then the Chinese migrants to Malaya and Singapore were deemed to have fallen foul of the emperor who was a Manchu who did not take kindly to the Chinese leaving the middle kingdom.

This did not mean, however, that the Chinese migrants had no concept of themselves as a collectivity or as people who could group together along certain lines. Such groupings that they had were social in nature but these, especially the secret societies, bordered on the political even if this political aspect was vague and not so explicitly and systematically laid out, as is the case with many modern revolutionary and nationalistic movements. It is proposed here to discuss the socio-political identity of the Chinese, specifically the kind of identity that had as its basis

131

what I will call natural and voluntaristic attributes.[1] There is
no intention here to strain the meaning of words from what were
originally meant, still less to resort to any jargon. Natural
attributes here is taken to mean those attributes that pertain to
blood or common ancestry and those that pertain to common speech
or dialect and territory; in other words, those attributes found
in traditional societies everywhere that is normally conducive to
affinity among people. By voluntaristic attributes, I mean
basically those attributes that are not normally natural, and
that solidarity among such people involves an act or action that
transcends adherence to natural attributes. Observe that such
voluntaristic organizations are not necessarily the same as
voluntary organizations. Voluntary organizations are normally
formed with no coercion involved, whereas the voluntaristic
organizations here discussed, the secret societies, suggest no
such absence of coercion. In fact, secret societies are formed
on the basis of coercion, whether it is in a physical or a
ceremonial form.

The motives of the majority of the Chinese who migrated to
Malaya and Singapore were naturally mixed. Some came because
they wanted to escape from China and others because they were
kidnapped or forced involuntarily to come. But in the main, the
motive had been to make a living and then a fortune which would
stand them in good stead when they subsequently retired, as was
their intention, back to China. Thus, to this business of living
and prospering, they had of course to think on collective lines
not only because no man was an island unto himself but also
because the alien environment they found themselves in compelled
them first to organize among their own kind, and the circumstances of the nineteenth century forced them to think on
voluntaristic lines. The circumstances were the unsettled nature
of the Chinese together with the absence of recognition of those
who had natural attributes. This was where the concept of the
secret societies became useful. Their doctrine of brotherhood

that could embrace the Chinese without natural attributes was adopted and this concept of brotherhood took on multifarious political, social-welfare and criminal terms. To be sure, the secret societies did not explicitly claim to be solely any one of these three. Rather their concept or "ideology"[2] was such that it could cover all three. Where the circumstance suited, one of these three would be given emphasis. But before this can be discussed, it is first necessary to consider the manner in which solidarity or brotherhood is arrived at, for the methods employed reveal a world-view that gave much scope to physical and spiritual violence.

The physical threats could range from beatings to actual killing. Munshi Abdullah, the noted Malay scholar, wrote of the readiness of the secret societies in early nineteenth century Singapore to use force when they executed one who refused to join. He also noted the presence of arms in a secret society hidout he was led to where he saw "ten large shields, 3 muskets leaning against the wall".[3] Many other observers also testify to this possession of arms by the secret societies together with their usage.

Added to this was the sense of awe and fear that was created by the initiation and oath-taking ceremonies the secret societies imposed on their members. These included forcing a new member to drink the blood of some older members to symbolize their new-found brotherhood. Spiritual threats were also used. Some flavour of this can be gleaned from a look at the first article of the two rival societies then in existence in Singapore, the Triad Society and the Ghee Hok. The first article of the Triad states:[4]

From the moment that you have entered the Hung League you must quietly fulfil your duties, and keep to your own business. It has always been said that filial love

133

is the first of all virtues; therefore, you must respect and obey both your parents, and obey and venerate your superiors. Do not resist your father and mother and, so violate the laws of the Hung League. He who does not keep this command, most surely, will not be suffered by Heaven and Earth, but he shall be crushed by fire thunderbolts! Each of you ought to obey this.

That of the Ghee Hok states:[5]

After entering the Hong Gate (the Ghee Hok), a member of the Hong family must above all things obey and honour his parents, he must also abstain from injuring the parents of a brother Hong. If he breaks this oath may he within 100 days die by being cut to pieces or in the five seas, his flesh floating on the surface, and his bones sinking to the bottom.

If the concept of solidarity was not a gentle one, it nevertheless formed the backdrop of the political, social and criminal manifestations of the secret societies. The ideological basis of their political view essentially arose from the nature of their origins. All secret societies in China are presumed to have originated from what is called the Peach Garden trio. The legend is that in the second century A.D., a legitimate dynasty in China was threatened, and three strangers, Liu Pei, Kuan Yu and Chang Fei met in a peach garden and bound themselves under an oath of brotherhood to be loyal to each other until death, to save the threatened state and to serve the people. Thus, in the oath-taking of members, some of the verses refer to the Peach Garden trio. For example:

This night new incense is blended with the old incense;

In a peach garden Liu, Kuan and Chang pledged fraternity. The brethren have faithful hearts and loyal spirits; since the ancient times their names are perpetuated and renowned in the world.[6]

The secret societies, in this case, the Triad Society or the Hung League and the dominant group of secret societies among the Chinese migrants, did not become a regular political body until the Manchu conquest of China though the Triad Society constantly alludes to the Peach Garden trio. With the Manchu conquest, many who resisted it became part of the Triad, vowing to restore the old Ming Dynasty. The Triad themselves appeared as a regular political body from the time of the Manchu period in China.[7]

It cannot be said that the secret societies among the Chinese migrants in Malaya and Singapore, whether they were brought directly from China or were first formed by Chinese migrants in Malaya and Singapore, were consciously political. Many of the leaders of these secret societies disavowed any conscious political basis when the British authorities were thinking of proscribing them. They declared their intention to be that of the maintenance of law and order, and referred to the fact that they did not urge the Chinese to cut off their queues, such cutting being a conscious anti-Manchu act and hence consonant with the political aims of the Triad in China.

Nevertheless, they had sounded and acted political at certain times, particularly when anti-foreign feelings in China spilled over to Malaya and Singapore. Then the secret societies became to some extent involved in fanning such feelings. This was even more so when the Chinese or those in the secret societies felt threatened by the British in Singapore and Malaya, irrespective of whether that threat was economic or otherwise; then the secret societies played on anti-British feelings. Thus, during the many riots in Singapore in the nineteenth century, there were many instances of secret societies playing on Chinese or racial feelings, condemning those who sided with the British as being traitors or not pure Chinese. In the 1876 Post Office Riot, in Singapore, a certain pro-British Chinese leader was condemned as not being of the Chinese race "but is the offspring of a mixture of Barbarian and Chinese blood so he can deceive and change and raise trouble."[8]

The concept of brotherhood also involved mutual help. It was as if they were all part of one family, the members enjoined to consider the secret societies as they would their parents. Thus, Article 5 of the 36 articles of the oath states that:[9]

> After having entered the Hung League, you ought to be faithful and loyal. You must consider the father of a brother as your own father; his mother as your mother; his sister as your sister; and his wife as your sister-in-law.

And members of this family were expected to protect their own kind, help each other in times of difficulties and so on. In fact, the 36 articles of the oath are replete with instructions concerning helping one another.[10]

Sometimes the philosophy of mutual help extended even to justice in work arrangements. This was observed by an English official who wrote in 1849 that secret societies in the gambier and pepper plantations in Singapore organized the workers to accept lower wages in difficult times so as to prevent unemployment.[11]

The secret societies turned criminal when they could not perform the two social and political roles. Because their ideology was not explicitly social and political, the methods they employed to enhance solidarity were also conducive to criminality. And this was often the case as the political aspect manifested itself only to perceived external threats which were not often, while the social aspect could be used as a rationale for criminal actions. Thus, the nineteenth century is replete with incidents of secret societies being involved in basically criminal activities such as kidnapping, street fighting over territory, and so on.

But as the twentieth century came, the secret societies were proscribed by the colonial government. At the same time, the Chinese in Malaya and Singapore were exposed to modern political influences from China. In addition, Chinese society became more settled and there was increasing recognition that there were more and more Chinese with natural attributes. The voluntaristic aspect became less important compared to ties based on blood and common dialect and territory. Such natural ties came to pervade Chinese group identity.

The first of these is that people of common blood, that is, people descended from a common ancestor, whether real or fictive, can be considered as part of a family or a clan. Specifically, it was presumed that people with the same surname had such an attribute. Hence, they should group together not only because of such common sentiments but also for what other mutual activities they could engage in. Thus, many such clans existed in traditional Chinese society. For the purpose of this paper, it suffices only to document one. In the Foon Yang clan association, it is stated that any "lawful citizen residing in Malaysia and bearing the surname Kok" was eligible for membership.[12]

Similarly, those who spoke the same dialect could also group together. However, such a view of social identity had complicated manifestations not only because of the variety of dialects spoken but because a common dialect was often identified with a common territory. For example, there are five major dialects spoken by the Chinese. They are Hokkien, Teochew, Cantonese, Hakka and Hainanese. In most cases, people speaking the same dialect came from the same territory. In some cases, however, the same territory may be the homeland of two different dialect groups, such as the southern part of the province of Kwang Tung (廣東) which is inhabited by the Hakkas and the Teochews. At the same time, a wider territory such as a province may have different dialect groups originating from it, for instance, Kwang Tung province which has Cantonese, Hakka and Teochew speakers. Thus, an explicitly state dialect-group association such as a Hakka association will have only Hakka-speaking members, whereas a territorial association such as the Kwang Tung Association will have Teochew, Cantonese and Hakka speakers. It is not the purpose here to go into further detail over such complications except to say that the basis for affinity was often both dialect and territory. For documentary examples of this, the Yungting (永定) Association of Perak states that all Chinese from the district of Yungting in the province of Fukien (福建) were eligible for membership.[13] Though the dialect is not mentioned here, the Chinese referred to are Hakkas. A second document, The Rules of Perak Eng Choon Kong Hoey, also states that any Chinese from Perak who hailed from the district of Eng Choon (永春) in China could be members.[14] Such members are Hokkiens.

Unlike the secret societies, however, the methods employed by such groups to enhance solidarity did not involve physical coercion while the ceremonial aspect was not spiritually intimidating. This ceremonial method was that of ancestor worship. The belief was that while ancestor worship had an irreducible value of its own in cultural terms, it could also reinforce mutual sentiments through ceremonial reverence for elders who had departed. This practice is almost always found among the clan associations and frequently so with the dialect-group associations. Thus, the rules of the Kwangtung Association, a dialect-group association in Perak, states as one of its major activities that the association should "hold regular worshipping ceremonies to pacify the spirits of the departed elders. Spring worshipping shall be held on the day before Cheng Meng (a day set aside by the Chinese for the worship of their ancestors) and autumn worshipping shall be held on the thirteenth of the seventh moon each year."[15] But in the case of the clans whose very raison d'etre is common ancestry, it should be expected that even greater emphasis would be placed on this practice. Some examples can be given to show the care and importance normally given to this. The Tzeng Clan Association states as one of the objectives of the association that it "shall be to honour and make sacrifices to our ancestors, to exhibit and make known the virtues of our ancestors, (and) to obey and carry out the teachings of our ancestors".[16] That of the Foon Yang Association (clan association) encourages all members "to worship ancestors".[17] The care shown is indicated by this statement of the Tzeng Association under the heading "Anniversary and Sacrifices to the Dead":

> In order to be careful with the observance of rites at funerals and in making sacrifices to the dead, the association shall observe the Spring and Autumn Festivals when sacrifices will be made to our departed ancestors, and also observe the day of establishment of the Association as an anniversary, when celebration and re-union dinners will be held. How and when such celebration and re-union dinner will be held shall be decided by the Standing Committee and the Standing Committee shall inform all the members in writing seven days beforehand in order to enable the members to be ready to take part.[18]

Unlike the secret societies, such groupings did not normally become political or criminal. They, however, had a mutual-help philosophy. Thus, some of the functions of the Perak Kwang Tung Association were to "deal in matters concerning the welfare of persons of Kwang Tung origin and philanthropic works" and to "work for the welfare of the members",[19] while that of the Foon Yang Association (clan association) were to "render mutual aid among the clansmen" and to "look after the welfare of the clansmen".[20]

But the most important ramification of these groupings based on natural attributes is in the business of making a living. For the purposes of giving credit, of trusting members not to cheat, of depending on the reliability of members in matters pertaining to work and so on, such can be achieved only through mutual trust of a very high degree. The way to demonstrate this ramification is to show the identification of dialect group with occupations, and three examples need only be given. In a survey undertaken,[21] the names of important members of three dialect-group associa- tions, namely, the Hakkas, the Cantonese, and the Hokkiens, in Ipoh were given together with their occupations. Here, only the surnames are given to conceal the identity. The following is the list for the Hakka Association:[22]

Surname	Occupation
Hu	businessman
Liao	miner
Yeh	miner
Hsia	businessman
T'ang	printing agency owner
Yao	businessman
Kuan	clerk
Ch'm	teacher
Hsia	bank employee

Surname	Occupation
Chang	miner Hsieh businessman
Hu	teacher
Pan	miner
Hu	bank employee
Lan	businessman
Ch'en	miner
Tseng	businessman
Lan	sawmill owner
Hsin	Chinese medical practitioner
Lau	sawmill owner
Lee	miner
Lau	miner
Tseng	miner
Hu	miner
Chung	teacher
Li	miner
Ch'in	miner
Liang	miner
Wu	miner
Liang	miner
Liang	miner
Hu	miner

Below is the list for the Cantonese Association:

Surname	Occupation
Yeh	retired government officer
Chou	businessman
Hu	retired businessman
Ch'en	contractor
Lo	businessman
Hsieh	miner

Surname	Occupation
T'u	miner
Ch'en	contractor
Ho	goldsmith shopowner
Liang	fishmonger
Li	businessman
M'eng	goldsmith
Li	businessman
Lui	reporter
T'ang	printing agency operator
Hsieh	businessman
Huang	reporter
Huang	goldsmith
Chou	hawker
Li	contractor
T'u	florist
Kuan	clerk
Kuan	waitress
Ts'ui	housewife
Chang	clerk
Kuan	clerk
Lin	coffin-maker
Ho	housewife
Chuan	businessman
Yu	businessman
Liang	oilmill owner
Kuan	interpreter
Tu	salesman
Ts'ui	goldsmith
Lo	businessman
Li	contractor
Ch'u	businessman
Lui	foundry owner
Tu	teacher

Surname	Occupation
Lo	salesman
Huang	businessman
Li	businessman
Ch'en	contractor
Ts'ui	housewife
Lui	coffin-maker
Hsieh	businessman
Ch'en	contractor
Li	businessman
Lo	businessman

Below is the list for the Hokkiens:

Surname	Occupation
Ch'en	spare part agent and housing developer
Ch'en	housing developer
Huang	rubber estate owner
Yao	oil-palm estate owner and housing developer
Lin	businessman
Ou	furniture wholesaler
Huang	workshop owner
Ou	businessman
Huang	workshop owner
Huang	spare parts agent and shopkeeper
T'u	rubber estate owner
Li	businessman
T'u	retired teacher
Lin	spare parts agent and shopkeeper
Lui	spare parts agent and shopkeeper
Huang	spare parts agent and shopkeeper

Surname	Occupation
Huang	spare parts agent and shopkeeper
Lin	retired teacher
Yeh	businessman

This survey shows that miners (tin-miners) are mainly Hakkas, that artisans and other urban service workers are generally Cantonese, and that trade and business is mainly the province of the Hokkiens. Dialect-group solidarity is thus reinforced by economic activity.

To conclude, this essay does not suggest that the Chinese in Malaya and Singapore did not group together on other lines during the colonial period. Some grouped on the basis of their long domicile in Malaya and Singapore, a domicile reinforced by a common non-Chinese language such as English and Malay. An example of this was the Straits Chinese British Association. However, such Chinese constituted only a very small minority and many among them were drawn to the dialect-groups. For the majority, their socio-political identity was found in the groupings discussed.

NOTES

1. I am indebted to Jean Chesneaux for this important distinction. See Jean Chesneaux, ed., Popular Movements and Secret Societies in China 1840-1950 (Stanford, Stanford University Press, 1972), p. 6.

2. I use this word "ideology" advisedly, not simply to mean a systematic set of beliefs but some kind of world-view.

3. Munshi Abdullah, "Concerning Tan Tae Hoey in Singapore", Journal of the Indian Archipelago VI (1852): 547.

4. Gustave Schlegel, Thian Ti Hwui, The Hung League or Heaven-Earth-League (Batavia: Lange & Co., 1866), p. 135.

5. Vaughan, J. D., Manners and Customs of the Chinese in the Straits Settlements (Singapore, Mission Press, 1879), p. 115.

6. Schlegel, op. cit., p. 123.

7. Ibid., p. 3.

8. Singapore Daily Times, 19 December 1877.

9. Schlegel, op. cit., p. 136.

10. Ibid., pp. 135-44.

11. See J. Thompson, "Agricultural Labourers", General Report of the Residency of Singapore drawn up principally with a view to illustrating its agricultural statistics, Journal of the Indian Archipelago III, (1849): 767.

12. Rules and Regulations of Foon Yang Association, Perak 【吡叻汾陽公會】 (Jalan Yang Kalsom, Ipoh), pp. 1-2.

13. Rules of the Perak Yungting Association, Ipoh 【霹靂永定同鄉會】 (Jalan Ali Pitchay, Ipoh p. 2).

14. Rules of the Perak Eng Choon Kong Hoey 【霹靂永春會館章程】 (Russell Street, Ipoh), p. 1.

15. Rules of the Perak Kwang Tung Association 【霹靂廣東會館章程】 (Jalan Ali Pitchay, Ipoh), p. 14.

16. Rules of the Perak Tzeng Clan Association 【霹靂曾氏宗親會章程】(Ipoh), p. 1.

17. Foon Yang Association, op. cit. p. 1.

18. Tzeng Clan Association, op. cit. p. 9.

145

19. Kwang Tung Association, op. cit. p. l.

20. Foon Yang Association, op. cit. p. l.

21. I am indebted to Mr Tham Ah Fun, a former student of mine, for help in this survey.

22. Names taken from the sixteenth committee of the Association (Pi-li-k'e-shu kung-hui). 【吡叻客屬公會第十六屆一九七七／一九七八年度職員表】 (The surnames are romanized according to the Matthews Dictionary).

23. List taken from the 1977 committee of this association (Nan-hai hui-kuan). 【吡叻南海會館公元一九七七年度職員表】.

24. List taken from the 1975 to 1976 committee of the Pi-li Hsing-aun Hui-kuan. 【吡叻興安會館一九七五／六年度職員一覽表】.

WORLD-VIEW OF THE INDIANS WITH REGARD TO THEIR SOCIAL IDENTITY AND BELONGING IN MALAYA, c.1900 - 57

R. RAJOO

Broadly defined, the world-view of a people is their character-istic outlook of the universe. It is concerned with the inside view of a man in a particular society, that is, the way he typically sees himself in relation to his world. Thus, the self is the axis in the study of any world-view.[1]

The concept of world-view implies that man in the course of life constantly comes into contact or confrontation with certain things which profoundly influence his outlook and behaviour in relation to all else. According to Redfield, man by nature everywhere comes into confrontation with three major phenomena, that is, nature, God or the supernatural, and man himself.[2] Thus, briefly the concept of world-view includes the individual's perceptions of the world, the influence of God or the supernatural, nature and man's relations to it; man's relations with man and such aspects as the structure of and basic conflicts in society.[3] However, since all world-views are related to human experience, it is possible to have variations in people's outlook. A people desperately in need of food would view the world differently from those among whom the need for food may not be so insistent. Yet, despite such variations, there is always a standard outlook of people in every society.[4]

In the study of any world-view, the emphasis is usually on the cognitive elements. But not all aspects of the world-view are expressed in words. There are aspects which may not be verbalised but are acted out in human behaviour. Thus, it is necessary to look into both the cognitive and cognative aspects of human life to understand the world-view of a particular society. Such an approach would be useful to study a complex society such as the Indians in Malaysia. The Indians here were made up of diverse subgroups and were also literate, semi-literate and non-literate. Then there were Indians who lived in the plantations and others who lived in the urban centres. Both had different experiences and different views or outlook on life.

Bearing such complications in mind, this paper on the world-view of the Indians with regard to their social identity and belonging has taken into consideration the following aspects: verbal expressions or folk-tales, personal histories, ideas about and reactions towards kinship, religion, politics, leadership, tradition and modernity and ethnic relations. The material on which this paper is based was collected through interviews, observation, participation and the investigation of literature available on the Indians in Malaysia. There is a greater emphasis on the South Indian world-view in this paper, attributed to the fact that the writer is more familiar with this group than with the rest, and the non-availability of material on the other Indian ethnic groups during the preparation of this paper. Nevertheless, the study attempts to cover the whole of the Indian community including the Ceylon (Sri Lanka) Tamils. The study is holistic in approach and the method adopted here is both synchronic and diachronic.

On the whole, the Indian world-view with regard to his social identity and belonging in Malaya has been influenced by such factors as socio-cultural background of the Indian immigrant, his original motive for migration, method of migration, the pattern of settlement in Malaya, closeness to

148

India, his achievements or failures in Malaya, the attitude of the British government and the European employers towards him, and finally, the subsequent adjustment made by him in his new environment. A brief account of the history and settlement of the Indians in Malaya will be useful here to understand the above assumptions.

History and Settlement of the Indians

By and large, the Indians who had settled in Malaya before 1957, that is, when the country achieved independence, belonged to those Indians and their descendants who had come directly from India from the last quarter of the nineteenth century. In 1957 there were 820,256 Indians living in Malaya compared to 470,180 in 1921.[5] They belonged to two broad categories, namely, the rural plantation or estate workers and the urban settlers. Between the two, it was the plantation workers who constituted the larger number, that is, between 65 per cent and 70 per cent while the rest were the urban dwellers. Thus, the modern migration of the Indians to Malaya came to be synonymous with labour migration. What were the socio-cultural and economic backgrounds of these Indians?

The plantation workers and those manual groups in the urban centres attached to the railways, public works, etc., were mainly brought as "cheap labour" or coolies under the indenture and kangkani[6] systems of migration, initially to work for a period of 3 - 5 years. The plantation workers were put in the sugar, tea, coffee and coconut estates and later in the rubber and oil-palm estates under strict supervision. In India, though some of them owned small quantities of agricultural land, most of them were landless agricultural labourers who worked for their high caste Indian landlords, usually occupying a position of serfdom or

149

near-serfdom. In many instances they were indeed serfs or slaves as they were also referred to as <u>adimais</u> (slaves).[7] In addition, however, there were sprinklings of weavers who had lost their traditional occupational pursuits to the British manufacturers. These downtrodden Indian masses were induced to emigrate to Malaya like in other colonial territories under the British rule. They were given "free passage" to travel and were promised a "better life" abroad.

But, of course, not all of them came under the "freepassage" contract system for there were also some who came as free labourers paying their own passage, especially after the abolition of the <u>kangkani</u> system of emigration, and perhaps these were generally better-off.

The labour migrants had a certain cultural homogeneity in that about 80 per cent of them were Tamil-speaking South Indian Hindus while the rest were Telugus, Malayalis, Canaris and Oriyas from North India. In the Hindu social hierarchy, they belonged to the non-Brahmin middle-ranking and lower castes (<u>jatis</u>) such as the Goundar (who usually would identify with the high caste Vellalas in South India), Padaiyaci, Kallar, Anampadiyar, Vanniyar and Muttu Raja on the one hand, and the Adi-Dravida "untouchables" such as the Pallar, Paraiyar and Chakkiliyar (cobbler) on the other. Between these two categories there were the washermen and the barbers. Among the (Andhra) Telugus there were the Kamma and Reddi and the "untouchables". The Malayalis generally belonged to the Nayar caste. The urban working class too had the same caste categories except that there were also such non-Brahmin categories as Tevar.

Besides the working class Indians, the urban Indians constituted two major segments, that is, the educated and the commercial classes. These two segments were made up of diverse ethnolinguistic categories. Broadly, they were classified as

150

South Indians, North Indians and Ceylon Tamils (Jaffnas). The South Indians comprised mainly the Malayalis, and high caste and upper or middle class Tamils. The North Indians included the Punjabis, Sindhis, Gujeratis, Bengalis, Marwaris, etc.[8] The three major groups further divided themselves as Hindus, Christians, Muslims and Sikhs each of which had its own sub-sects. These various sub-categories had their own caste divisions such as Brahmins, Vaisyas, Ksatryas or Chettiyars, Vellalas, Kayasths, Jats, Ramgarhias, Raj Puts, Patel, Patidar, Muci, etc.

In terms of economic activities, the North Indians except for the Sikhs engaged in business. The Sikhs usually joined the police force while many also served as watchmen and some became dairy farmers and so forth. The Malayalis and Ceylonese entered white-collar services both in the government and private sectors. Among the South Indian Tamils, the Chettiyars were money-lenders and financiers, the Vellalas were small-scale businessmen while the educated Brahmins and Christians took up white-collar jobs. The Muslims on the whole concentrated in various kinds of business enterprises.

By 1957, some changes had generally taken place in these patterns of economic activities. For instance, many Sikhs made tremendous progress in professional fields and business while some from the working class came to occupy lower grades of clerical and technical services. A considerable number took up the teaching profession especially in the urban areas.

An interesting aspect of the Indian settlements in Malaya was that wherever the Indians went they tended to congregate on the basis of linguistic, territorial or religious groups. Even specific castes were concentrated in certain localities. These patterns of settlements thus not only created "Litte Indias" but also "Little Madras", "Little Delhis", "Little Jaffnas", and so forth.

It is indeed a less complex matter to study the world-view of a folk or simple society than a complex society. The Indians in Malaya not only belonged to a complex society but also had moved from one area to another under different circumstances. Therefore, they were likely to have different images about themselves.

Bharati, in his study of identification among the East African Asians, suggests that "the standards for the study of identification in a specific society is the self-image and the alter-image of its members. The self-image is the sum total of notions of them, the alter-image the sum total of notions about another group, particularly about a group with which there is close interaction".[9]

This is a useful suggestion to understand the convictions of a people with regard to their social identification and belonging. First of all, who did the Indians identify themselves with in Malaya?

In his study Bharati stresses a point when conducting his study in Africa (1964) that, "there was no such a thing as a common self-image of the Asian settlers in East Africa, just as there was no common self-image among the Indians in South Asia".

This statement also holds good for the Indian settlers in Malaya, and of course, it would be the same among the Indian Diaspora everywhere. In one situation they would identify as Indians but in another they would like to be identified as individuals or on the basis of their sub-groups such as Tamils, Malayalis, Telugus, Dravidians, South Indians, North Indians, Punjabis, Sindhis, Gujeratis, Bengalis, Jaffnas, etc.; Hindus, Muslims, Sikhs, and Christians; Brahmins, Chettiyars, Vellalas, and so forth. The same Indians in another situation would identify themselves as Malayan Indians or Malaysian Indians.

When Indians were in the midst of non-Indians, they would refer to themselves as Indians or Malayan/Malaysian Indians but among themselves they would identify with a specific linguistic, territorial, religious or caste category. In the same way, when Indians were confronted by a common problem they would get together as Indians but otherwise their identity was not Indian but pertaining to their specific sub-groups. The Tamils, for instance, in reference to non-Tamils would identify themselves as Tamils (or Dravidians) but among themselves a person from a middle ranking caste would distinguish himself as "Tamil" as against a "low" caste, and in the same way a high caste Hindu, namely, a Brahmin or Chettiyar in reference to other Tamils would distinguish himself by his caste category. On all such occasions an Indian would use the same term "community" (samugam) as in Indian community, Hindu community, Chettiyar community, etc. The same was applicable to the Sikhs, Malayalis, Gujeratis, Jaffnas, Christians, etc. A Sikh would close the doors of his gurdvara to another Sikh just as one Hindu would close his temple to another. Thus, the notion of this "we group" holds different connotations according to different circumstances.[11] The narrower the category the greater was the "we group" emphasis. The term "Indian" was perhaps frequently used by the English-educated but, again, only in specific situations. This was because the notion of an Indian identity is a comparatively new one. This was realized only about a hundred years ago for the Indians in Malaya and only a few hundred years ago in India.

Some Indians now think that the sub-group consciousness among them is more emphasized now than it was in the pre-war period. In actual fact, it was equally pronounced even in that period. In the pre-war era, it was largely confined to the upper classes and castes, whereas in the post-war period it spread to a wider proportion of the Indian community, as a result of greater participation in community and national affairs and politics.

The fact was that the Indians came from different territories, speaking different languages, following different religions and practising different castes. There were very few converging factors or commonalities among them. To a South Indian unlettered worker a North Indian was always a "Bengali" who had come from "some other land" just like him. In India, an Indian's identity was first to his family or household, then to his kindred or extended jati (caste) group, and lastly to his village. No further loyalty or identity was demanded of him in a modern political sense. The Indians also migrated as individuals and individual sub-groups and not with any sense of belonging to a "community" as such. Their aspirational levels were thus individualistic and sub-group oriented. Their subsequent identity as Indian was circumstantial, necessitated by certain political events both in India and Malaya. But the same Indian, usually educated, had a great pride as an Indian belonging to a great country that had a very superior ancient civilisation and that his religion was the oldest religon in the world. This feeling of superiority that the Indian came to conceive is believed to be only about two or three hundred years old, that is, since India came into contact with the West.[12] It is also attributed to the role of the Indian social, cultural and political heroes such as Raja Ram Mohan Roy, Tilak, Rabindra Nath Tagore, Ramakrisna, Vivekananda, Gandhi, Nehru and Subash Chandra Bose (Netaji). But such a notion had little effect in changing the traditional Indian society into a single structural block. Thus, one can see an apparent contradiction in the Indian mind, that while on the one hand he was proud of being an Indian, on the other his pride was in something else, not as an Indian.

When the Indians came to Malaya they transplanted their typical segmented and compartmentalized Indian society in an extended form. There was nothing to prevent them from doing so. On the contrary, they were helped by the British to create their own world so that their stay would be comfortable and "very much at home".

154

Upon arrival the Indians established numerous associations for each individual group through which in-group identity and interest was stressed. This prevented the Indians from forming a single structural block. The absence of an Indian identity in the pre-war era was pointed out by a number of visiting Indian officials or leaders, namely, V.S. Srinivasa Sastri, an Indian agent in Kuala Lumpur, Dr. Lanka Sundram, another Indian official, and Nehru. Writing about Indians in Malaya in 1935, an Indian, M. N. Nair made the following observation:

> Indians are fond of forming numerous associations wherever they go and Malaya is no exception to this general rule. In Malaya, there are various communal and denominational associatic's in addition to various Indian associations, spread all over Malaya. There is no cohesion and unity between these various associations, and there is not one single association competent to speak on behalf of the Indian public.[13]

There were of course some educated Indians who genuinely identified themselves and formed the Indian associations (but these were mere social clubs). They even ventured further to form the Central Indian Association of Malaya (CIAM), the first political body claiming to represent the Indians. However, this was formed only after a long struggle and there is reason to believe that it was formed after Nehru apparently chided the middle class Indians for their indifferent attitude towards the community during his visit to Malaya in 1937. He also called for the unity of the Indians during his visit. In one of his messages to a Tamil weekly, he said:

> Not knowing Tamil, I am unable unfortunately to profit by it but I hope it stands for the freedom of India and for the uplift of her masses. All newspapers which advocate these great causes have my good wishes. I

155

hope also that it will work for unifying the various elements of the Indian population in Malaya...(Letter reproduced in Dravida Kesari, 27 May 1937)

The world-view of the Indians and what they identified with in Malaya provides an interesting study. As the largest number is, in fact, plantation workers, it is apt to begin with them.

The Plantation Worker

The primary identification among the plantation workers was with one's kin, caste-group and ecological unit, that is, the estate. This was also true of the urban Indians except that the ecological identification among them was the village in South Asia. From his verbal expressions relating to his life we learn that, except for some, the plantation workers had little of the ego-identification. Very often we hear him say: "I came to Malaya as a canji-k-kuli (contract labour or coolie). My work is one of serfdom under the white man (vellai-k-karankitta adimai velai). I came to Malaya to make a living (pilaikka vanten). I came here because I was told by the recruiting kangkani (alkattara kangkani) that I can do easy work and earn a big sum of money in the estate (tattattule). I was given a 'free ticket' and money for other expenses".

Jain observes that the plantation was a "closed, protected and sheltered" system.[14] The plantation worker's notion of his ecological boundary in Malaya is clearly depicted in the above statements. He would say (and even sing): "that estate/this estate/but when you have no estate to go, you run". When he learned through his experiences in the estate that life was one of struggle fraught with uncertainties (niccayam illata

156

<u>pilaippu</u>), he would blame the <u>kangkani</u> for bringing him here under false promises. This is evident in many of the estate songs. The following is given as an example:

> Oh, Kangkani, Kangkani,
> One with the black shirt
> Did you not bring me
> With a promise
> To chase the crow away from the sugar
> But, alas (now)
> There are the thorny <u>lalang</u>[15]
> And the shells of the rubber seeds
> Which prick and bring me pain.[16]

> Oh, Kangkani, Kangkani,
> One with the black shirt
> Did you not bring me on <u>janji</u>[17]
> But (now) you are killing (me).

> Oh, lady of the house, Virayi!
> Would you not rise from your sleep
> The Kangkani is here to chase you
> Hurry up for the roll-call
> The <u>dorai</u>[18] too has come
> In his car with its rattling noise
> And the <u>kirani</u>[19] has come, too,
> Speaking his language of '<u>kis-mus</u>'
> (English).

From the above expressions, one would expect an estate worker to react strongly against those forces such as the <u>kangkani</u>. Instead, there was absolute conformity and a sense of resignation. This was an extension of his outlook upon the universe which he acquired in his village life as a helpless agricultural labourer in India. Why did he not go back? Because things were no better there. At least here he was assured of a job, there was a place to stay, and there was a fixed income. He would say he was born a "coolie" because he was destined to be so. It was his talaiviti or karma (fate). He was grateful to the manager for having given him a job and would even pray for his manager's welfare. He avoided any confrontation with the kangkani, kiranis (clerical staff), and the manager (dorai). They were like his guardian deities (kaval teivam) who were very powerful and would not hesitate to inflict punishment if confronted.

Everything in the estate worker was oriented towards a mechanical mode of behaviour. Life was emotionally governed. He took great interest in sensual pleasures, reflected in his over-indulgence in alcoholic drinks and he cared very little about his ego-identity. He had no concern in world affairs. His world revolved round the estate and his immediate concern, in fact, major concern, was to keep harmonious relations with his dorai, kirani, and the kangkani to whom he would even pay homage in the form of special gifts during the festival of his goddess, Mariyamman, just as he would make offerings to the goddess in order to appease her.

There were, of course, exceptions to this general pattern of behaviour. Many middle-ranking non-Brahmin castes such as the Goundar, Kallar, Vanniyar, Reddi, etc. had a better perception of the self and among whom there was also greater ego-identification. Their life was governed by a certain degree of rational action which found expression in higher motivation for saving and cautious spending. There was also a greater perception that they had come to a "foreign" country to earn and return as wealthy people so that they could be better persons in their natal village on their return.

RELIGION

Religion was and is one sphere of life that distinctly characterized social identity and belonging among the Indians, the Hindus in particular. The religion of the estate and of the urban Hindu workers was a combination of peasant Hinduism and folk religion as found in South India. The religious behaviour of these workers was an expression of their anxiety-stricken day-to-day life. It was a religion which has been termed "Little Tradition" about which a great deal has been commented by Srinivas and others.

The religious life of an estate worker was not one of intense devotion and he worried little about other worldly affairs. However, he believed in the existence of some powerful supernatural forces which influenced his life and he also believed that he had to pacify them so that they would not interfere without reason in his life. He believed that there was a Goddess Mariyamman (Mari, in short) capable of curing diseases like smallpox, chickenpox, cholera, etc. and thus he erected temples wherever he went to this goddess (just like in the village communities in India) and propitiated her periodically. No intense devotion was demanded from devotees but periodical ritual offerings and worship. When a person had chickenpox or cholera, a devotee would say "Mother Mari has come". He would immediately make every effort to appease her so that her anger would not be aroused out of negligence. Mariyamman was worshipped by the entire estate community through an annual festival celebrated on a grand scale for about three days. On this occasion, the deity was also "pleaded" to "descend" upon the devotees so that it could be ascertained whether she was happy with them. Once the celebration was over and offerings made, the devotees felt less anxious about the goddess who would be attended to thereafter only when there was a crisis.[20]

In addition, the plantation workers also held a belief that there were certain noxious spirits which would come to endanger their life by attacking them. To keep these away the workers also worshipped certain guardian deities such as Muniyanti, Munisvaran and Maturai Viran, who possessed both malevolent and benevolent qualities. Again in return for their services, these deities were given offerings periodically for, if neglected, they would not hesitate to punish their transgressors, being of the revengeful type.

The workers, of course, knew of the Great Tradition gods and goddesses but they were of little concern to them. Even the god Subrahmanya was usually worshipped in the form of a Little Tradition deity rather than as one of the Great Tradition gods.

However, occasionally a temple of the Little Tradition may come under the influence of the Great Tradition religion, as is common in urban areas, and thus would undergo transformation (Sanskritisation or Akamisation) by adopting attributes of the Great Tradition Hinduism. In such cases, the Little Tradition devotees identified themselves with Great Tradition Hinduism but the majority of the workers knew little about the differences nor were they always prepared to accept such a change.

KINSHIP

The workers' major concern was not with regard to identity with their natural world, nor with the supernatural forces but their relations with their families and other kinsmen. Among them, the morality of social action was usually judged in terms of kinship ties and roles. The pattern of settlements further reinforced kinship identity among the Indians, especially the plantation workers. All relationships between husband and wife, parents and children, brothers and sisters, brothers' and sisters' children

160

were held in ritual connection. There was emphasis on male children, especially the first-born. Male children were preferred for both economic reasons (one would say "one can live like a king if one had three sons") and ritual needs. Upon the death of the father, the eldest son took over the commissions and omissions of the family. Children were expected to be obedient to their parents and contribute towards the family's purse. The family was the most sanctified sphere in the life of the Indians. Among the Hindus this was sanctioned by the emphasis on ancestral worship and the observance of rites de passage. Even after death, the soul of the person continued to have relations with the family. Among the South Indian Tamils, kinship ties were further strengthened through marriage between brothers' and sisters' children. Between two brothers and their children, one will stand for the other (as substitute) on ritual matters. Frictions and separation did develop among them but during a dispute with an outsider (ayalar), they would unite and identify as one (conta-k-karar). Non-conformity to such family norms would result in total exclusion from all kinship ties. One can understand why kinship ties were so strong among the Indians making them continue to identify with their kinsmen in their native village in India. To an Indian mind, however educated he may be, this was a natural thing. The authority of elders was to be respected, and on matters of importance such as marriage, parents alone had the right to make decisions. However, a father's major concern was not in providing education or guaranteeing a better socio-economic future for his children but in getting them married off as soon as they had attained "marriagebale" age (vayacukku vantatum). A good father was one who would not prolong the marriage of his daughter after her first puberty.

The society considered male-female relations as an important matter. Just as age constituted a significant factor in family relations, so too was male superiority over the female. The

English notion of superiority-inferiority in male-female or husband-wife relations could be quite offending to the Indian mind because the Indian society's view of husband-wife relations was sanctimonious, supported by the saintly values of the Indian world-view. The good (ideal) wife (pativrata) regarded the husband as a sort of god. There was always a distinction between a "woman of the family" (kutumpa-pen) and one who was not. Upon attaining her first puberty, a girl (or "woman") should maintain strict reservation in her relations with men and the outside world. She should dress in a particular manner following the Indian tradition (valakkam, paramparai or marapu). She should not smile at a stranger nor should she be seen in the company of men. All these were translated into a kind of ritual behaviour.

Here again, although these were considered as the standard world-view of the Indians on matters of familial and kinship values, there were differences between the various castes, which can be termed as "orthodox" and "non-orthodox". The further one goes down the caste ladder the greater the evidence of fluidity in the adherence to such rules. These are complicated issues in Indian society, but within the society they were understood and adhered to accordingly.

One important point is that these values stressed at the micro-family level were then transferred to the macro-kinship, caste (jati) and community levels giving a characteristic standard outlook of the Indians in terms of social identity and belonging. The family here becomes the model for the macro-level behaviour. It may not be out of place to quote Mandelbaum's views on the subject with regard to Indian society:

Relations within a family are in certain important ways similar to relations within a jati and in a community. We should scarcely expect it to be otherwise;...It is a module, a regular structural segment, of the jati, just

162

as the <u>jati</u> is a module of the community. Every person is born into a family as into a <u>jati</u>, and into one only. He cannot readily opt out of either family or <u>jati</u>.[21]

The Indian world-view on this matter in Malaya was not very far from this observation. There was of course no such rigidity as in India but it was there perhaps in a modified form. The conditions prevalent in Malaya and the large number of people involved, the constant contact with India, continued arrival of Indians until independence, etc., all contributed towards this. The existence and continuity of this world-view of the Indians can be further seen in the section dealing with caste.

The Urban Indians

Among the higher castes and classes of the Indian "community" there was a greater emphasis on ego-identification and also alter-identification about one another. There was always pride in one's success or achievements in life, be it in education, occupation, business or even on matters pertaining to religion, culture and caste. Thus, the pride was always seen in identification with one's kin group, caste, religious or territorial sub-groups. The economically successful Punjabis, Malayalis, Ceylonese, Chettiyars, Vellalas, etc., would always say "We so and so ..." in reference to other sub-groups. There was greater perception of world affairs and motivation to exploit the available opportunities in these groups. Among them there was even greater emphasis on morality of social action in identification with sub-groups. Such an approach towards problems of life resulted in associations being formed and separate temples for each sub-group being built. Each sub-group

163

would also try to assert its importance against another sub-group. Thus, there was greater emphasis on notions of superiority-inferiority statuses. One group would say, "We did not come here as coolies ...", another "We came here as an educated community", and yet another "We came here...but now we occupy such and such a position ..." Such sentiments indeed created situations whereby the various sub-groups began to compete with one another in occupational and educational pursuits. A Malayali informant once told me: "In the pre-war period there were many Ceylonese occupying the position of clerks and conductors in the estates but later the Malayalis slowly monopolised those jobs ...". A prominent Punjabi, a Sikh, in Kuala Lumpur, said: "Most of our people came here as policemen and watchmen. But there were so many who rose to high ranking officials. So many became professionals ... Many became businessmen, even as owners of tin mines." These are indeed statements of facts. But in the manner they were said, there was always an emphasis on sub-group achievements, a pride in identification with a particular sub-group.

RELIGION

As previously stated, the urban Indians constituted Hindus, Christians, Muslims and Sikhs. Greater emphasis will, however, be placed on the Hindus from whom a great deal can be inferred on the subject of the world-view with regard to social identity and belonging. Others will be taken up wherever necessary.

The upper caste Hindus identified themselves with the Great Tradition Hinduism. But this was in no way a uniform structure. It was composed of several strata and each sub-group identified itself with one of these strata. At the same time, at some point they all identified as Hindus, including the Sikhs who would say their religion was a reformed type of Hinduism.

164

When seen in the real situations, the Hindus adhered to the following sects: The South Indian Tamils and the Ceylon Tamils emphasized the Siddihantic tradition based on the Tamil Saivism, the Telugus, the Vasnavite tradition while the North Indians and the South Indian Brahmins, the monastic Vedantic tradition of Senkara. The South Indian Saivites worshipped the Pan Indian Hindu gods such as Siva, Ganesa, Subrahmanya and goddesses such as Amba, Laksmi and Sarasvati. The North Indians worshipped Visnu and his incarnations, such as Rama and Krisna and the above-mentioned goddesses. The Tamils would claim their authority from the Tamil saints and their devotional works, Tevaram and Tiruvacakam, while those adhering to the Vedantic tradition emphasized the Vedas, Upanisads and Bhagavatgita as their authority. The North Indian Hindus also gave importance to the teachings of Arya Samaj, Sanatan Dharm, or the Brahmo Samaj. The South Indian Hindus emphasized the building of temples wherever they went (as was expressed in an ancient Tamil adage: "Do not stay in a place where there is no temple") on the basis of this tradition or sect. The more orthodox Siddhantins usually denounced identity with the Vedantic Sanskritic tradition. The plantation workers usually identified their religion with the Saivite tradition. The orthodox Saivites would not like identification with the Little Tradition religion which they termed the worship of "village deities" (kirama teiva valipatu) or "minor deities" (ciruteiva valipatu). However, when confronted by certain persistent crises, they would also attend to the deities of the Little Tradition but they would try to keep this secret. The high-caste orthodox Hindus as well as the middle-ranking castes practised ritual pollution and besides those vegetarians by birth, others also had great reverence for vegetarianism.

There was yet another group of educated Indians who took their religious model from Ramakrisna, Vivekananda and Aurobindo and later Sivananda and Satya Sai Baba and also founded associations in their names. As regards religious practices, this group emphasized the reading of texts and devotional prayer and there was less concern for ritual Hinduism.

In terms of social identification, the higher caste and upper class Hindus always considered their religion as superior to the religion of the working class Hindus. They also thought that their religion was the oldest religion, the most "tolerant" religion, and so forth. On such occasions, they would try to support their views with quotations from Ramakrisna, Vivekananda, Max Muller or some other Western writer and there was always a pride in belonging to this old and most tolerant religion. One could find such pride not only among the Hindus but also among the Sikhs, Christians, and Muslims. A Sikh devotee said that his religion was good because it forbade even smoking and taking alcoholic beverages. Such statements were usually made between the various religious groups on a particular aspect of the respective religion.

KINSHIP

The Indian values of kinship as seen earlier were even more emphasized among the higher castes and classes, whether one was a Hindu, Christian, Muslim, or Sikh. Respect for elders and male dominance were even more intense compared to their counterparts in India. There was also greater stress on having male children and this was expressed in the following proverbial saying: "Even a king would become a pauper if he had five daughters".

Caste

Some years ago during a verbal war between the Malayan Tamil

Youth Bell Club and the All-Malaya Dravidian Association (Dravidar Kalakam or D.K.), the anti-caste movement, the former attacked the latter for holding on to a "dead snake". The "dead snake" was the caste system in Malaysia. I had the occasion to refer this topic to a former secretary of the D.K. The secretary immediately referred me to a court case of one Kalivarathan and asked me whether the caste system was really dead. The case was about the removal of the dead body of Kalivarathan, a "low" caste, by a few "high" caste Hindus for burial in the graveyard belonging to the high-caste Hindus somewhere in Kedah. In the final verdict, those responsible for removing the dead body of Kalivarathan were found guilty and hence convicted.

All categories of Indians wanted the caste system to be abolished because it was based on superstitious beliefs (muta nampikkai). They believed that the Aryan-Brahmins were solely responsible for introducing this evil institution among the non-Brahmins to suppress them, an ideology they borrowed from the South Indian-based Dravidian Movement or Dravidar Kalakam. No Brahmins ever entered plantation life and there were only a few in the urban areas, especially in Kuala Lumpur. Yet, the caste system was there among all categories of Indians whether Hindus, Christians, Sikhs or Muslims, and the Brahmins were responsible for this. Although among the Muslims, the caste system did not exist in the same manner as among the Hindus, yet there was endogamous marriage akin to the caste system. A group of urban working-class and lower middle-class Indians got together and invited the founder-leader of the D.K., E.V. Ramaswami, from South India to come to Malaya in 1927. Upon arrival E.V. Ramaswami urged the non-Brahmin Indians to form the D.K. in Malaya to abolish the caste system among the Indians in the country. In 1932, the first conference of the All-Malaya Dravidian Association (akila malaya dravida mahajana sangkam) was held in Penang in which some prominent high-caste Hindus including Vellalas, Chettiyars, and Nayar took part.[22]

167

Yet, despite such calls on the abolition of the caste
system, the Indians found it necessary to identify with a
particular caste. A person of a high caste (this term was a
relative one, as one could be "high" and "low" at the same time
in relation to one above and below) was proud of being a member
of a particular high caste and even would affix his caste label
to his name. He would not eat in the home of a "low" caste
person and would resent his daughter marrying a lower caste.
When a "high" caste Hindu came to know that his daughter loved a
"low" caste boy he would feel as if the whole world had come to
an end. There were cases of certain middle-ranking Vellala
castes sending their daughters back to their native villages in
India when the latter fell in love with "low" caste boys. Such
incidents occurred even as late as the 1950s.

In Malaya, it was not the classic verna system, that is,
dividing the Hindu society into Brahmins, Ksatryas, Vaisyas and
Sudras but the sub-caste jati system that was operational. Thus,
the jati division was found not only among the high-caste Hindus
(including Sudras) but also among the "low" caste "untouchables"
who had their own sub-divisions, such as Pallar, Paraiyar, and
Chakkiliyar on a hierarchical basis. A Pallar would not marry
into the family of a Parsiyan and the latter would behave in the
same manner in relation to the last sub-caste. Perceptions of
identification in terms of caste resulted in the formation of
caste associations, especially among the Tamils in view of their
large numbers. The importance given to social identification
with the higher castes prompted many lower caste men to claim
membership to particular higher castes in each locality. This
was usually done in the urban areas since in the plantations
there was face to face contact between members of the different
castes which made this difficult, at least until recent years.
The caste system has since undergone several changes but on
ritual aspects only. On marriage and intra-group identification
it still holds a significant place. Though inter-caste marriages

have been on the increase, the number has always been small, and it is still not welcome between extremes in caste categories.

Politics and Leadership

There was generally an apathetic attitude towards politics among the urban Indians. Until World War II the plantation workers had no notion of the subject and even after that it was a blurred view. Politics as a secular ideology was unknown to most Indians. Even among the educated, politics was thought to be only for those persons interested in it. An old proverbial saying vividly puts the Indian political view thus: "Whether Rama rules or Ravana rules, what does it matter to me?" Thus, community problems were expected to be solved by such persons who were the "leaders".

Before the war, no community level leadership evolved in the plantations. The protected and sheltered plantation system did not permit the evolution of such a leadership. The workers accepted the authoritarian form of leadership provided by the manager and the kangkani. Nevertheless, the kangkani, having come from the same level as the workers did have a considerable influence on the people and the latter also consulted him on all matters of importance.[23] The role of the kangkani declined after the war and with the coming of trade unionism (the National Union of Plantation Workers or NUPW) and later the Malayan Indian Congress (MIC), the plantation workers came to be associated with national movements and politics.

But how did the Indians perceive of political ideology when politics finally came into their community?

We noted earlier how the urban Indians struggled to form the

169

CIAM. It was not a spontaneous response to solve community problems as such. The few Indians who were involved in the CIAM were in fact influenced by the Indian Nationalist Movement in India and also had the support of the Agent of the Indian Government in Malaya. There were a few like Dr. P. K. Menon and Dr. Soosay who made radical statements with regard to British treatment of the Indians in Malaya[24] but all this had little effect on the overall political view of the Indians. Again, many Indians joined the League of Indian Independence and the Indian National Army (INA) of Netaji to free India from British rule. However, these were the educated and business class Indians who seemed to have supported the movement and the Indian National Army (INA) to safeguard their own interest.[25] One must also take cognizance of the charismatic role of Netaji here. No doubt a few hundred thousand estate workers were taken to construct the Siamese "death" railway but these workers did not go on their own "free will". They were forced to go and there are many even today who blame those who were responsible for this.

Among the Malayan Indians, political perceptions were usually coloured by traditional factors. Thus, political participation too was not based on any ideological convictions as such. It was the individual personalities or groups that mattered. This can be understood from the Indian view of leadership.

The Indians by and large held two kinds of leadership in high esteem: the tradition-based and the charismatic. A leader must be one who must be religious, able to speak the community's language, and he must respect the culture of the group. A leader who does not possess these qualities could not be a good leader nor would he be able to genuinely attend to his people's problems. Alternatively, one must be a charismatic leader like Gandhi, Nehru, and Netaji. We can draw a somewhat similar local analogy here: the trade unionist Dr. P.P. Narayanan, the secretary of the NUPW, to some extent was viewed along this line in the 1950s and 1960s. He was viewed as a liberator of the plantation workers from the evil grips of the employers. Thus, he was called "P.P. the Big Brother" (P.P. Anna). In the same way, the South Indian Dravidian Movement Social Reform leaders like E.V. Ramaswami, C.N. Annadurai (the leader of the Dravidian Progressive Movement or Dravida Munnerra Kalakam) and the founder of the Tamil Unity Movement in Malaya in the 1950s, G. Sarangapani, a Singaporean, reflected such qualities for whom the lower and lower-middle class Indians had great veneration.

Such a political world-view created some peculiar problems both in the pre-war and post-war period in Malaya, and later Malaysia, among the Indians.

In the pre-war period one sub-group would oppose the appointment of a member from another sub-group to the Federal or State Council to represent the Indians.[26] In the post-war era, that is, after 1946, when political participation was given to a wider Indian population, the numerically preponderant Tamils rejected the leadership of a non-Tamil in the MIC. Such an opposition came from the newly emergent Tamil educated group in Malaya.

Perceptions of Cultural Identity

There were some who had a somewhat different perception of Indian identity with regard to the Indians in Malaya. While by and large they remained as members of the different sub-groups, they also emphasized an Indian identity and thus tried to represent the Indians and Indian problems. This was a very small group mainly comprising Western educated intellectuals who had been subjected in varying degrees to the influence of the Indian

171

national and cultural heroes in India.[27] It was this group which successfully formed the CIAM in the pre-war period and later identified itself with Netaji's League of Indian Independence and the Indian National Army founded in 1942. The founders of the MIC in August 1946 had also been inspired by the Indian Independence Movement in India. However, the position of this leadership was quite an ambigious one. While on the one hand it took its lessons from the Indian leadership in the subcontinent, it stressed that its role was to identify with the interest of the Indians in Malaya on the other. However, though it wanted to identify the Malayan Indian interest from a Malayan outlook, it was not prepared to lose its cultural identity. It was even critical of those culturally alienated Westernized Indians in the urban areas. It also stressed that Indian interest in Malaya was inextricably interwoven in the preservation of an Indian identity. Arasaratnam's observation may be aptly cited here:

> Culturally, the Indian leadership frowned at any tendency to alienate themselves among any section of the community. They wanted the Indian community to preserve its integrity. This was even encouraged by Government policy, as communalism lay at the very basis of public policy in Malaya. The Indian community was getting its share of recognition because it was a separate and identifiable community, and its continuing advancement lay in such identity.[28]

But to take such a view verbatim, uncritically, would be misleading because, as we have already seen, among the Indians themselves there was no such thing as a homogeneous view of cultural identity and sense of belonging.

Viewed in terms of cultural identity, to all Indians India was culturally and spiritually superior as reflected in its past glory, its archaic religion, mythology, philosophy, huge temples,

172

cultural experts and cultural performances, that is, drama, dance, music, etc., its numerous feasts and festivals, and language, especially Sanskrit and Tamil. But this notion of India's cultural richness did not mean that the loyalty and identity of every Malayan Indian was stretched to India as a nation as such. On the contrary, his main concern was with his own village (ur) or the region from which he came.

When Indian emphasis on cultural identity was seen in real situations it took a complex form. This was observed as Great Tradition and Little Tradition on the one hand and the Dravidian Tradition on the other, in so far as the more orthodox (conservative), ritually inclined Hindus emphasized the Great Tradition religion. Besides them, there were the Western-educated Hindus who adhered to the saint-cults of devotional Hinduism. There were also a similar orientation among the Sikhs. Alcoholic drinks and even smoking were forbidden according to the teaching of Sikhism and, thus, the more orthodox Sikhs would stress religious behaviour on this basis.

Those who emphasized identity with this higher form of religious practice also undertook reform activities to eliminate Little Tradition practices and other such practices which were believed to be degrading to the dignity of the Indian "community" in a multiracial society. As regards the Hindus, such attempts could be viewed as a process of "Sanskritisation" since the more educated Indians usually tended to identify with the Sanskritic Great Tradition. Sanskritisation did not mean the study of Sanskrit or the adoption of vegetarianism and teetotalism. One may or may not become a vegetarian or a teetotaller but may undertake the worship of high caste deities and also attempt to convert Little Tradition temples into Sanskritic or Akamic temples, show a desire to know the Hindu scriptures and may even attempt to learn the Indian classical dance (bharata-natyam) and music (karnataka cankitam) because all these constituted

173

important aspects of the Great Tradition religion-cum-culture. This change usually took place when there was an improvement in the socio-economic and educational position of the lower castes. There were, of course, different degrees of Sanskritisation. While the "lower" castes Sanskritised by taking the model of the non-Brahmin middle-ranking castes, the latter would take the model of the non-Brahmin high castes, and so forth.[29]

As against Sanskritisation, there were the non-Brahmin Tamil-educated lower middle class and working class Indians who viewed their cultural identity in terms of the puritanical non-Sanskritic, pre-Aryan Dravidian culture. They took their ideological model of the Dravidian Movement (D.K.) and the Dravidian Progressive Movement (DMK) from South India. Thus, they rejected Sanskritic Hinduism and condemned the caste system, Hindu mythologies and Hindu Brahminical rituals, denouncing them as based on superstitious beliefs.

But this movement itself was a complex one. For example, while the anti-Hindu groups opposed all identity with Hinduism, there were those orthodox Hindus who stressed an identity with the non-Sanskritic Tamil Siddhantic religion.

In the 1950s, the D.K. and the DMK movement featured a significant aspect of the socio-cultural life of the Tamil majority which also found expression in the emergence of the Tamil Unity Movement through the "Festival of the Tamils". Evidently, the movement also influenced significantly the pattern of Indian politics and leadership in Malaya.

The point is that the Dravidian Movement too wanted to modernize[30] the Tamil society by de-emphasizing the religious elements which were considered superstitious (in South India the Movement has been referred to as the Backward Class Movement). On the other hand, it stressed the use of the pure form of Tamil without Sanskritic influence, the study of Tamil classics such as Tirukkural, and Silappatikaram. In the field of aesthetic art, it de-emphasized dramas and films with Hindu mythological themes and substituted dramas and films with secular (reformist) themes like Or iravu, Para Sakti, Manchara -- all written by the DMK leaders such as C.N. Annadurai and M. Karunanithy (both became Chief Ministers of Tamil Nadu later) in Madras.

At the same time, there were also those in the urban areas who had had a Western education to whom Sanskritisation or Dravidianisation meant nothing at all. They disclaimed any identity with India or the aspirations of the India-born educated Indians. There is reason to believe that this group preferred rapid Westernisation because it wanted to dissociate itself from the rest of the other Indians since the latter was a grim reminder of the indenture system and the "coolie" or estate culture. At the same time, there were those Western-educated Indians who loved Western gadgets but this did not mean that they wanted absolute Westernisation. Some would even object to their daughters taking part in ballroom dancing or even wearing Western dress. The Western-educated urban Hindu youths, on the other hand, thought that ballroom dancing had nothing to do with Hinduism. Thus, the Hindu Youth Movement comprising entirely of English-educated youths even organized ballroom dances as part of its social activities. Both the urban orthodox Hindu parents and the anti-Hindu Tamil-educated youths vehemently criticized the attitude of the English-educated youths. In one of the Hindu youth functions in Kuala Lumpur, an orthodox Hindu parent indeed asked the youths to remove the term "Hindu" and call their movement by some other name. To the orthodox Hindus, the Western ballroom dance was against the Hindu religion. On the other hand, to the anti-Hindu Tamil-educated youths Western dance was against "Indian culture" or "Tamil culture". There were still others to whom all this meant nothing and yet they considered themselves as Indians in some way.

Ethnic Relations

In pre-war Malaya the economic-ecological adaptation of the Indians both in the plantations and urban areas had cast them in comparative isolation from the indigenous Malay society. Moreover, the major concern of the Indians in this period was not centred on relations with the Malays but with the British rulers and European employers.

Nevertheless, the Indians by and large did have some limited social contact with the Malays and this indeed brought about certain perceptions about one another.

The Indian attitude towards relations with the indigenous Malays during this period was one of accommodation and adjustment. Both the estate and urban Indians generally regarded themselves as being able to get along well with the Malays, as compared with the Chinese to whom "money" was the major concern. The Indians, somehow, saw that there were certain common cultural values between them and the Malays.

One would expect that there should have been greater interaction between the Malays and Indians leading to intermarriage. One explanation for the absence of such interaction was religion and the Indian view of kinship. Older Indians always thought that marriages within one's inner or own group (contam) would be more lasting than those involving an outside group. A retired doctor, a Brahmin, said: "I know of at least a dozen of my friends whose family life has been broken because all of them married outside the community. Marrying outside one's own community simply would not work." The point is that when Indian parents got their sons and daughters married they wanted their daughters-in-law, sons-in-law and their children to be able to become part of their families and play their kinship roles.

176

Conclusion

As presented in the foregoing pages, the world-view of the Indians with regard to their social identity and belonging in Malaya both in the pre-war and post-war periods was significantly influenced by their pre-emigration background and the conditions prevalent in Malaya. Back in India, their world was confined to their household, the jati, and the village. No further loyalty was demanded of them. The Indians reconstructed in a modified form such a world over the years in their new environment.

Undoubtedly, Malaya was a haven for many, if not all. Malaya was also considered a foreign country (ayal ur or natu) and the thought of returning to one's native village as a wealthy person was always there. But for many that was only a desire, an ideal view, as can be seen from their original motivation for emigration. As for the plantation workers, except for a few high-caste Hindus, the main concern was a struggle for survival and, to this extent, to maintain harmonious relations with their employers.

The post-war period brought significant changes in the attitude towards going back to India. Some by now had even cut off family ties with their kinsmen in their native village in India. An old retired plantation worker, a woman of about 60 years old, in an estate near Kuala Lumpur said:

> I lost my husband and a son in Siam during the Japanese occupation. But after the war I did not go back. I had no reason to go back because I had my other children here who are now married and have their families here ... But I went to India recently to see my sister and brother ... My children sent me there to see them...

177

There were yet some older Indians who desired to return to India but their local-born children were not willing to go.

There was, however, one other trend that characterized Indian perception of cultural identity. While there were the Western-educated urban Hindu youths who went through the process of Westernization, there were the orthodox Hindus who emphasized aspects of the Great Tradition Hinduism. Such a notion among the latter resulted in the emergence of many religious movements during the post-war period.[31] A few even sent their daughters to South India to study Indian classical music and dance. There was concern among the orthodox Hindu/Indian parents with regard to cultural "drift" among their educated youths. In another direction, on the other hand, the rural Tamil-educated and urban working class youths tended to show greater interest in the Great Tradition religion, perhaps a trend resembling the characteristic of social change in modern Indian society in India, that is, while the high-caste Hindus Westernize their life-style, the lower castes adopt Sanskritisation as a form of modernization.[32] In Malaya this was seen to happen as a continuous process in the larger Malayan Indian community from the beginning of the 1930s. Even many youths who were once staunch supporters of the anti-Hindu Dravidian movement were reported to be turning towards Hinduism. However, there is also reason to believe that this change was due to the stress faced by these Hindus caused by the modern competitive living in a multi-racial society. The reason why many urban middle class Hindus too now turn to the saint cults of Swami Sivananda, Swami Satya Sai Baba, etc., which emphasize devotional Hinduism based on congregational worship can also be attributed to this.

The Indian youths now take an active part in politics and even are articulate on political issues but, unfortunately, their views are coloured by primordial sentiments detrimental to the effective role that they could otherwise play.

Many Indians still regard India as a country superior in spiritual and cultural matters. Holding such a view they naturally continue to receive cultural experts, namely, spiritual leaders, singers -- both classical and modern -- and film stars, especially from South India. But this does not mean that they want to identify themselves with India in any way. Youths who visit India return with a certain amount of dissatisfaction not only because of India's poor economic status but also other matters. The Malayan-born Indian youths usually feel that they are different in many ways in their outlook compared to their counterparts in India. Such a notion evidently has made them identify themselves more with Malaya, and later Malaysia, as Malayan Indians and Malaysian Indians.

NOTES

1. Robert Redfield, Human Nature and The Study of Society, Vol. 1, edited by Margaret Park Redfield (The University of Chicago Press), 1962, p. 270.

2. Ibid.

3. Juha Pentikainan, "Life History and World View" (Paper presented at the Tenth International Congress of Anthropological and Ethnological Sciences, New Delhi Madras Session, 1978).

4. David G. Mandelbaum, The World and the World View of the Kota, Village India, Studies in the Little Community, edited by McKim Marriott (Chicago: The University of Chicago Press, 1955), p. 224.

5. See Kernial Singh Sandhu, Indians in Malaya (London: Cambridge University Press, 1969), p. 182.

6. A Tamil word for a labour-supervisor in the plantation.

7. Dharma Kumar, Land and Caste in South India (London: Cambridge University Press, 1965), pp. 10-48.

8. In 1957, of the total number of Indians, 634,681 were Tamils, 72,971 Malayalis, 27,670 Telugus, and 84,934 North Indians. See Arasaratnam, Indians in Malaysia and Singapore (London: Oxford University Press for the Institute of Race Relations, 1970), p. 48.

9. Agehananda Bharati, "Patterns of Identification among the East African Asians", Sociologus 15 (1965): 129.

10. Ibid., p. 130.

11. R. Rajoo, Communalism and Factionalism Among the Indians in Malaysia, Manusia dan Kasyarakat, (Department of Anthropology and Sociology, University of Malaya, Kuala Lumpur), forthcoming.

12. See Agehanando Bharati, Hinduism and Modernisation, Religion and Change in Contemporary Asia, edited by Robert F Spencer (Minneapolis: University of Minnesota Press, 1971), p. 99.

13. Indians in Malaya (Kuala Lumpur, 1937).

14. See Ravindra K. Jain, South Indians on the Plantation Frontier in Malaya (Kuala Lumpur: University of Malaya Press, 1970).

15. Malay word for a tall and coarse grass.

16. I am grateful to Dr. R. Dhanadayudham, Department of Indian Studies, University of Malaya for allowing me to use the originals of these songs in Tamil.

17. Malay word for "contract" or "promise".

18. Tamil word for "manager".

19. Malay word for "clerk".

20. For more information, see R. Rajoo, "Patterns of Hindu Religious Beliefs and Practices Among the People of Tamil Origin in West Malaysia" (M.A. thesis, University of Malaya, Kuala Lumpur, 1975).

21. David G. Mandelbaum, Family, Jati, Village, Structure and Change in Indian Society, edited by Milton Singer and Bernard S. Cohn (New York: Wenner-Gren Foundation for Anthropological Research, 1968), p. 34.

22. Tamil Nesan, Vol. 8, 10 August 1932.

23. See Ravindra K. Jain, "Leadership and Authority: A Case Study of Indians in Malaya (c.1900-1942)", Leadership and Authority, edited by Jehan Wijeyayewardene, (Singapore: University of Malaya Press, 1968), pp. 163-73.

24. See S. Arasaratnam, Indians in Malaysia and Singapore, pp. 96-102.

25. Ravindra K. Jain, South Indians on the Plantation Frontiers in Malaya, p. 427.

26. Ibid., p. 86.

27. See Edward Shils, The Intellectual Between Tradition and Modernity: The Indian Situation (The Hague: Morten & Co., 1961), pp. 20-21.

28. S. Arasaratnam, op. cit., p. 101.

29. See M. N. Srinivas, Social Change in Modern India (Berkeley: University of California Press, 1968), pp. 1-45.

30. See Milton Singer, When a Great Tradition Modernizes, An Anthropological Approach to the Study of Indian Civilization (London: Pall Mall Press, 1972).

31. See R. Rajoo, "Religious Movements among the Urban Hindus in Malaysia" (Paper presented at the Tenth International Congress of Anthropological and Ethnological Sciences, New Delhi, Madras Session, 1978).

32. See Bernard S. Cohn, The Changing Status of a Depressed Caste, Village India. Studies in the Little Community, edited by McKim Marriott (Chicago: The University of Chicago Press, 1956) pp. 53-77.

REFERENCES

Amarjit, Kaur. "North Indians in Malaya, A Study of their Economic, Social and Political Activities with Special Reference to Selangor 1870s - 1940s". M.A. thesis, Department of History, University of Malaya, 1973.

Ampalavanar, Rajeswary. "Social and Political Developments in Indian Community of Malaya, 1920-1941". M.A. thesis, Department of Indian Studies, Faculty of Arts, University of Malaya, Kuala Lumpur, 1969.

Arasaratnam, S. Indians in Malaysia and Singapore. London: Oxford University Press for the Institute of Race Relations, 1970.

Benedict, Burton. "Factionalism in Mauritian Villages". British Journal of Sociology 8 (1957): 328-42.

Bharati, Agehananda. "Patterns of Identification among the East African Asians". Sociologus (Berlin) 15/2 (1965): 128-42.

_____. The Asians in East Africa. Chicago: Nelson-Hall Company, 1972.

Brown, Norman, W. "The Content of Cultural Continuity in India". Modern India. An Interpretative Anthology, edited by Thomas R. Metcalf. London: Macmillan Company, 1971.

Cohn, Bernard, S. "The Changing Status of a Depressed Caste", Village India. Studies in the Little Community, edited by McKim Marriott. Chicago: The University of Chicago Press, 1956, pp. 53-77.

Dharma Kumar. Land and Caste in South India. London: Cambridge University Press, 1965.

Dotson, Floyd, and Dotson, Lilian. The Indian Minority of Zambia, Rhodesia, and Malawai. New Haven: Yale University Press, 1968.

Firth, Raymond, et al. "Factions in Indian and Overseas Indian Societies". British Journal of Sociology 8 (1957).

Jain, Ravindra, K. "Leadership and Authority in a Plantation: A Case Study of Indians in Malaya" (c.1900-1942), Leadership and Authority. A Symposium, edited by Gehan Wijeyewardene. Singapore: University of Malaya Press, 1968, pp. 163-74.

_____. South Indians on the Plantation Frontier in Malaya. Kuala Lumpur: University of Malaya Press, 1970.

Mahajani, Usha. The Role of Indian Minorities in Burma and Malaya. Bombay: Vora & Co., 1960.

Malhi, Ranjit Singh. "The Punjabi News Papers and Sikh Organisations of Kuala Lumpur". Graduation Exercise, Department of History, University of Malaya, Kuala Lumpur, 1976/77, p. 69.

Mandelbaum, David G. "The World and the World View of the Kota, Village India. Studies in the Little Community", edited by McKim Marriott. Chicago: The University of Chicago Press, 1955.

_____. Family, Jati, Village, Structure and Change in Indian Society, edited by Milton Singer and Bernard S. Cohn. New York: Wenner-Gren Foundation for Anthropological Research, 1968.

Nair, M.N. Indians in Malaya. Kuala Lumpur.

Pentikainen, Juha. "Life History and World View", Paper presented at the Tenth International Congress of Anthropological and Ethnological Sciences, Madras, 1978.

Rajoo, R. "Patterns of Hindu Religious Beliefs and Practices Among the People of Tamil Origin in West Malaysia". M.A. thesis, Department of Indian Studies, University of Malaya, Kuala Lumpur, 1975.

_____. Communalism and Factionalism Among the Indians in Malaysia, Manusia dan Masyarakat. Department of Anthropology and Sociology, University of Malaya, Kuala Lumpur, forthcoming.

Ramachandra, G.P. "The Indian Independence Movement in Malaya 1942-1945". M.A. thesis, Department of Indian Studies, University of Malaya, 1970.

Redfield, Robert. Human Nature and The Study of Society, Vol. 1, edited by Margaret Park Redfield. The University of Chicago Press, 1962.

Sandhu, Kernial Singh. Indians in Malaya, 1786-1952. London: Cambridge University Press, 1969.

Singer, Milton. When a Great Tradition Modernizes. An Anthropological Approach to the Study of Indian Civilization. London: Pall Mall Press, 1972.

Sinha, Surajit. "Tribal Cultures of Peninsular India as a Dimension of Little Tradition in the Study of Indian Civilization". A Preliminary Statement, Traditional India: Structure and Change, edited by Milton Singer. Philadelphia: The American Folklore Society, 1959, pp. 298-312.

Srinivas, M.N. Social Change in Modern India. Berkeley: University of California Press, 1968.

Staal, J.F. "Sanskrit and Sanskritization". Journal of Asian Studies 22/3 (1963): 261-75.

Subramaniam, S. "Politics of the Indians in Malaya, 1945-1955". M.A. thesis, Department of Indian Studies, University of Malaya, Kuala Lumpur, 1974.

Wiebe, Paul, D. and Mariappan, S. Indian Malaysians. The View from the Plantation. Delhi: Manohar, 1978.

LANGUAGE AND THE WORLD-VIEW
OF THE MALAY PEASANTS

ASMAH HAJI OMAR

World-view is defined as the way a certain people perceive life and this perception may be reflected in or influenced by various media, language, culture, religion, and so on. As such, examining people's perception through any of the media mentioned means examining the relationship between this medium and their thought processes.

There are two schools of thought on the subject of language and reality. The first posits that language reflects reality, while according to the second, language creates reality.

It has been a long known and accepted fact that language is an index to culture. This means that language reflects the culture of its speakers -- the way of life they lead as well their physical and social environment. Such a function is borne by the vocabulary of the language concerned.[1] As such, the language of a people engaged in agriculture is expected to be rich in the vocabulary of agriculture. For instance, in this language there will be a range of terms to denote a particular grain based on its shape, colour and taste, as has been attested by the vocabulary of the Malay dialect of Kedah.[2] Such a language may not have the terms for the different types of wind and waves in the sea as do the language of people who are all the time involved with the sea.

In the same way, a language with a complex system of lexis on religion and beliefs does certainly indicate that its speakers are in possession of a religious system and sets of beliefs. The antithesis is a language which may not be as rich in such a vocabulary, as the society which upholds it may not have such a complex system of religion and beliefs.

The view that language reflects reality stems from the premise that language is the product of man's perception of his environment and of his understanding of reality. From perception comes conceptualization, in which Man is able to make use of verbal symbols to record his thoughts and experiences. It is these two processes, perception and conceptualization, that have been responsible for the emergence of a language of one community that is different from that of another. That is to say, a certain people perceive differently from another, and a group of people in a particular environment have their own type of perception, based on the environments around them and their experiences in life. Hence, as mentioned earlier a language with a rich treasury of ri~ rarming terms is certainly to be one that is spoken by people who are in the pursuit of this type of occupation. This shows that the speakers concerned, being involved as they are in rice-farming, are able to differentiate the realities in their rice-farming environment and type of life better than those people whose daily pursuits are more in the line of fishing.

Man's perception and conception of the realities around him include his view of the world, and this is recorded in his language. As such the elements in his language that reflect his world-view are not only confined to the lexical but include the grammatical ones as well. For example, a language which does not have a category of gender, especially in the human nouns, reflects a world-view of its speakers in regard to the treatment of the sexes in his everyday life. It is highly probable that

185

the speech community concerned has a social system which does not discriminate the various sexes in certain aspects of their life. The Malay language is one such language, and we see that in the traditional way of life, especially among the peasants, there is equal responsibility among the men and women in the search for a livelihood for the family. For example, rice-farming has always been the responsibility of men and women. Both the sexes go out to the field to tend the land, plant and harvest rice, although there is a division of labour of some sort, once they are in the field -- the men doing the heavy work such as ploughing the land and threshing harvested rice, and the women the planting and weeding as well as the cutting of rice stalks. With this background, there never arose any view that the tapping of rubber was an industry which belonged only to the male category, when rubber was first introduced to the Malay society at the end of the nineteenth century. With the Malay fishing communities, it is only the men who go out fishing. However, the women, although they stay at home, carry out their share of the responsibility of seeking a livelihood. The concept of the livelihood being the responsibility of the men alone is, then, not an indigenous one.

A different way of treating the sexes, as reflected in the grammatical gender, is seen in languages which have the gender system. Examples are the European and the Semitic languages. Although the European or Western way of life tends to show equal treatment to both sexes, this concept of equal responsibility came into being only recently. Western society sought to place their women in roles separate from the men. The women were to be admired and revered while the job of earning the family's bread was the responsibility of the men.

Whilst the English language indicates the existence of gender only for the pronoun of the third person singular, the Arabic language seems to have masculine versus feminine genders for most pronouns, in the singular, dual and plural numbers. And this system of gender is not limited to the pronouns but it governs the nouns, the verbs and the adjectives as well. This high degree of gender differentiation reflects a similar phenomenon in real life, specifically in the view of the Arabs towards the sexes. It is a well-known fact that the Arabs practise a strict rule of male-female segregation in all aspects of life.

The second school of thought on language and reality claims that people's perceptions are influenced by the patterns in their language. It seems a bit more difficult for people to accept the fact that language creates reality, and hence influence the people's world-view, instead of reflecting it. There have been some extremist interpretations of this. Witbold Doroszewski, quoting Akhmanohova, says this thesis means that a language which has a rich vocabulary on fishing will cause its speakers to have a predilection for the fishing industry and thus pursue this occupation intensively.[3] Although this is not a good illustration it does contain some truth. On the other hand, how does one explain the different world-views of two rice-farming communities if it is not for the differences underlying their speech systems?

The fact about a people's world-view stemming from language can be better explained by citing the way people react to certain words, phrases or sentences. In Malay, the word Barat (the West) evokes various reactions. On the positive side it means progress, modernization, knowledge, science and technology and so on. Conversely, when applied to the moral and social side of life, it means permissiveness and yellow culture. It goes to show that the word Barat can influence various world-views of the people depending on the context in which it is used. Among the Malay speakers one can strive to progress like the orang Barat (the Westerners) but one cannot behave socially like them. Hence, teknologi Barat is good but pergaulan secara Barat is not.

In the same way, a request with the word <u>tolong</u> will conjure up a reaction from the respondent, different from that which is evoked by one without the word concerned. This in itself shows that among the Malays, there is a world-view concerning the nature of interaction in requests, and that this view is much linked to or rather influenced not only by sentence-structure but also by modulation and lexical items.

The correlation between language, thought and culture is not confined to having thought and culture as the contents of language, but it also means that language does to a certain extent influence the thought and behaviour of its speakers. This means that a people speaking a particular language perceives life and acts differently from those speaking another language, and this difference in the perception and behaviour of two linguistically different peoples are related to the differences in their linguistic organization, that is, in the systems and structures of their lexis and grammar. In other words, these two people are expected to have two different world-views as one may speak a language with a system of verbal inflection while the other may not, and so on.

Each language is said to have a <u>weltanschauung</u> which causes its speakers to see the same phenomenon both sensory and non-sensory in a way different from speakers of other languages. The formulation of this conception of language has come to be known as the principle of linguistic relativity, and has been usually associated with Wilhelm von Humboldt. Strictly speaking, Humboldt was not the first to conceive this linguistic relativity hypothesis because mentions of it had already appeared in the writings of his immediate predecessors, Johann Georg Hamann and Johann Gottfried Herder.[4] In the United States this linguistic relativity hypothesis was probably introduced by Franz Boas. However, it was made known by Edward Sapir's formulation and application of it on the languages of the American Indians, and

188

Sapir's conviction and efforts in this field continued in the work of Benjamin Lee Whorf. It is, however, not surprising that in the United States, this hypothesis has come to be known as the Sapir-Whorfian hypothesis on language, thought and reality, as suggested by the title of the book containing selected writings of Benjamin Lee Whorf, Language, Thought and Reality.[5] According to the Sapir-Whorfian hypothesis, "the notion of linguistic relativity could be developed and in a much more telling and effective way by noticing differences not only in 'lexation' but also in grammatical structure".[6]

While it has been an accepted fact that the complexity of vocabulary reflects that of culture, it has by no means been attested that the complexity of morphology and syntax is an index to the complexity of culture. On the other hand, for many natural languages the correlation is to the reverse; that is to say, the more complex a culture is the more simple are the morphology and syntax of its language. Languages which have developed sociologically in terms of their function as languages of wider communication or as media for the accumulation of knowledge as well as media for the latest developments in science and technology, have indicated a development towards a simplification of their linguistic systems. Such languages, as evidenced in their histories of development through the centuries, are English and French.

In this correlation of cultural complexity versus linguistic simplicity, what is true for a certain set of languages may not be true for others. Malay, for instance, has shown a development towards a linguistic complexity in phonology and grammar, along with the complexity of functions that it has to fulfil, in particular the function of a scientific language. The Malay language be it in the nomenclature of Bahasa Malaysia or Bahasa Indonesia has in less than half a century added to its inventory not only items of vocabulary , phonology and grammar from foreign

189

sources, specifically English, but has also adapted systems and structures which were once completely unknown to the society speaking that language. Such borrowings and adaptations have added degrees of complexity to the language in terms of vocabulary and grammar.

There are many studies on thought and perception of a particular community which employ the principle of linguistic relativity as expounded by Humboldt in Europe and perpetuated by Sapir and Whorf in the United States. However, in my opinion the Humboldtian principle of relativity and the Sapir-Whorfian hypothesis are applicable only after a language has been given shape and has grown to the capacity that complements the social development of its supporting community. That is to say, the fact that language influences perception belongs to a level high up in the linguistic and social development of the speech community.

As mentioned earlier, it is rather difficult to believe that the vocabulary and the patterns that are characteristic of the speech system of a particular community exist prior to the physical and cultural milieu of the community concerned. Rather, the vocabulary and the patterns grow within specific physical and cultural contexts and in tempo with them. At the same time, another process to the reverse takes place, whereby the patterns that have been crystallized play their role in influencing the thought and perception of the speakers concerned.

In the light of the above, the study undertaken, that is, the world-view of the Malay peasants in relationship with their language, is given the framework of the two hypotheses which are really interrelated with one another, and that is, that language reflects as well influences people's world-view, as seen in the following diagram:

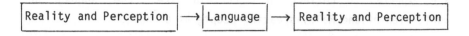

Reality and Perception → Language → Reality and Perception

This study will focus on the Malay language of the Kedah peasants. This is due to the fact that in the Malay-speaking areas of the archipelago Kedah has appeared to be one that has a highly established system of peasantry, practising wet-rice agriculture, which dates back to the very early centuries of the Christian era. Chinese voyagers of the tenth century A.D. did not fail to record the fact that the people of Kedah were already cultivating wet-rice and had their own system of irrigation besides having well-grown fruit gardens.[7]

Although the Kedah dialect is just one of the many dialects of the Malays, the differences between the dialects are not as great as to imply basic differences in their grammatical systems and structures. A wider divergence may be imputed to their lexical items, but even in a single regional dialect, lexical items may differ from one language register to that of another. As an example, a dialect with two different sets of people, one a rice-growing group and the other a fishing group, may reflect two different sets of lexical items in the speeches of these two groups. However, since the verbal systems concerned are in dialectal relationship with one another, the systems and structures are fundamentally the same. As such they may share a common world-view, diverging from one another only at certain points, perhaps in their perception of climatic conditions and such like experiences.

On the basis of what has been said above, this study presupposes that the correlation between languages and the world-view of the Kedah Malay peasants will also reflect that of the other Malay-speaking peasants. As peasants are only part of a large community, the findings on their language and world-view

191

are expected to reflect to a certain extent the language and world-view of the Malay-speaking people as a whole.

The following discussions are presented under these main headings:

1. Grammatical patterns as interpretations of experience.

2. Grammatical categories and semantic components.

3. Concepts of animateness versus inanimateness and human versus non-human.

4. Concept of male versus female.

5. Concepts of shape and size.

6. Colour terms.

7. Terms for tastes.

8. Classification of padi grains.

Grammatical Patterns as Interpretations of Experience

It is not possible to deal exhaustively with the grammatical patterns existing in the Kedah Malay dialect in this limited study. As such, only those which are salient to the study are discussed here.

MORPHOLOGICAL PATTERNS

Affixation

The word in the Kedah dialect is either a simple or a complex word or a reduplicative. A simple word is one which occurs only in its root-form (R) without taking any affix, while a complex word is one which has a root and at least an affix (prefix, infix or suffix). In the Kedah dialect, the only type of affix in existence is the prefix (Pre). As such, the complex word in this dialect is one with the structure Pre + R.

The reduplicative is defined as the word which is affected by repetition, partially or wholly. In the Kedah dialect the reduplicative is the type whose root is reduplicated in toto.

As a rule, the Kedah semiotic system consists of simple words. Complex words are used only when specific concepts need to be verbalized and such concepts are embodied in certain affixations. Such affixations generally occur with verbs while with the noun class this process is limited to the pattern with the prefix pe-. The adjectives and the adverbs are not affected by this process.

The verbs are generally used in their root-form. When a verb gets a prefix, it means that a specific concept, such as duration, habituality, causality or such like is incorporated into the meaning already borne by its root. In other words, the verb in the Kedah dialect does not take a prefix merely in relation to its grammatical function. That is to say, verbal prefixes which help to mark a subject-theme or an object-theme sentence are non-existent in this dialect. This is, of course, in contrast to Standard Malay whose prefixes me- and di- serve as theme indicators in sentences.

The verbal prefixes in the Kedah dialect are as follows: me(N)-, ter-, per- and ber-.

1.   me(N)-. As seen from the way it is written, the prefix has nasalized as well as non-nasalized allomorphic realizations, and these are me-, mem-, men-, meny- and meng-.

The non-nasalized allomorph me- occurs before the nasals, the lateral consonant l and the uvular fricative r. As for the other allomorphs, their various nasal components (N) are formed on the basis of a homogenic assimilation between the latent nasalization in me(N)- and the first phoneme of the root or stem: mem- before p and b; men- before t, d, c and j; meny- before s-; and meng- before vowels, k, g and h. If the first phoneme is a voiceless consonant, the nasal component is ellipsed in the process of affixation. Otherwise, it is retained.

The prefix me(N)- in the Kedah dialect denotes habituality or an action done within a certain amount of duration. An action done within a particular time limit does not take this prefix. Hence memotong, mengerat, menanam, memukul, menjahit, etc., do not refer to actions done for a particular moment; rather they refer to actions which have become habitual in one's life, such as one's occupation.

(a)   memotong means "to tap the rubber tree as an occupation". Although the root is potong, "to cut", the verb memotong is never used in a context which refers to the cutting of other things.

(b)   mengerat means "to cut the padi as an occupation". This word has kerat, "to cut into chunks" as its root, but mengerat denotes only the cutting of the padi during harvesting time.

194

(c) menanam only refers to the planting of rice. To convey the concept of the planting of other crops, vegetables or trees, the root-word tanam is used.

(d) memukul (memukoi), means only the threshing of padi during harvesting time to separate the grains from their stalks and their leaves.

(e) menjahit refers to sewing as an occupation. Non-habitual sewing is conveyed only in the root-form jahit.

(f) menjual means "selling for a livelihood". For non-habitual "selling", jual is used.

Verbs with the allomorph mem- in natural discourse usually undergo an elision of me-, leaving m-; hence motong (memokong), and mukul (memukul).

Usually, the habituality verbs do not take an object. This is a feature which places such verbs in contrast with their non-habituality counterparts.

Examples:

(a) (i) Saya nak pi motong

     I   will go   tap-rubber-as-occupation

  = I am going to perform my occupation of rubber tapping.

    (ii) Saya   nak   potong   roti

          I   will   cut   bread

        = I want to cut the bread.

(b) (i) Sudah   mengerat?

         already cut-the-rice-during-harvest

       = Have you harvested your rice?

    (ii) Sudah   kerat   kayu   itu?

         already cut   wood   that

       = Have you already cut the wood?

(c) (i) Dia   ambil   upah   menanam

         she   take   wages plant-rice

       = She plants (somebody's) rice for wages.

    (ii) Dia   ambil   upah   tanam   tembakau

         she   take   wages plant   tobacco

       = She plants (somebody's) tobacco for wages.

(d) (i) Malam   ni,   dia   mukul

         night   this, he   threshes-padi

=   Tonight he threshes the padi.

(ii) <u>Tadi</u>   <u>dia</u>   <u>pukul</u>   <u>budak</u>   <u>itu</u>

     just-now he   beat   child   that

=   Just now he beat the child.

(e) (i)   <u>Kerja</u>   <u>dia</u>   <u>menjahit</u>

     work   he   to-sew

=   He sews for a living.

(ii) <u>Dia</u>   <u>jahit</u>   <u>baju</u>   <u>saya</u>

     she   sew   dress   I

=   She sews my dress.

(f) (i)   <u>Dia</u>   <u>menjual</u>   <u>di</u>   <u>pekan</u>

     he   sell   at   town

=   He is a tradesman in the town.

(ii) <u>Dia</u>   <u>sudah</u>   <u>jual</u>   <u>buah</u>   <u>tu</u>

     he   already   sell   fruit   that

=   He has already sold the fruit.

The <u>me(N)-</u> pattern does not only indicate occupational habituality but may also reflect a characteristic of a particular noun-referent be it human, non-human or inanimate.

Examples:

(a) <u>mengira</u> refers to the business-like attitude of a person. The root-form is <u>kira</u> which means "to count".

    (i) <u>Janganlah</u>   <u>mengira</u>   <u>sangat</u>   <u>dengan</u>   <u>saya</u> <u>ni</u>

         don't   be   business-like   very   with   me this

    =   Don't be too business-like in your dealings with me.

    (ii) <u>Tolong</u>   <u>kira</u>   <u>telur</u>   <u>itu</u>

         help   count   egg   that

    =   Please count the eggs.

(b) <u>menyombong</u> refers to vanity which has become a trait in a person's character. <u>Sombong</u>, the root-word, refers to a single instance of "being vain".

    (i) <u>Dia</u>   <u>tu</u>   <u>menyombong</u>

         she   that   vain-of-character

    =   She is a vain person.

    (ii) <u>Dia</u>   <u>sombong</u>

         she   vain

=   She is vain at the moment.

(c) <u>melawan</u> means having a characteristic which
opposes people all the time. The root <u>lawan</u> means
to oppose at single instances.

(i)   <u>Kerbau   tu   melawan</u>

buffalo   that   having-a   character-which
opposes-others.

=   The buffalo is fierce.

(ii) <u>Dia   lawan   saya</u>

he   oppose   me

=   He opposes me at the moment.

(d) <u>memakai</u> has two meanings:

(i)   Likes   to   wear   beautiful   clothes   and
accessories all the time.

(ii) Uses magic charms on one's body all the time
for a specific purpose.

The   root   <u>pakai</u>   means   "to   wear"   at   single
instances.

(iii) <u>Orang   tu   orang   memakai</u>

person that   person   like-to wear-beautiful-
clothes (or uses magic charms) all-the-time.

199

=   The person is always beautifully dressed (or
         uses magic charms on his body) all the time.

(iv) <u>Dia</u> <u>pakai</u> <u>seluar</u> <u>panjang</u>

      he   wear   pants   long

=   He wears trousers.

Habituality of action may not be related just to particular
"persons" or "actors", but may also refer to habituality as
developed through the community's tradition. Thus, certain verbs
with <u>me(N)-</u> may refer to single instances of action but these
actions have been institutionalized as the community's
traditions. Examples of such verbs are <u>menengok</u>, <u>meminang</u> and
<u>memanggil</u>.

(a) <u>menengok</u> means "to go to a prospective bride's
     house in order to see whether she is suitable as a
     bride (to one's relative or friend)", whereas the
     root <u>tengok</u> means "to look at".

     (i) <u>Dia</u> <u>pergi</u> <u>menengok</u>

          she   go   "menengok" mission.

     =   She goes to the bride's house to check out
              the girl's suitability as a bride.

     (ii) <u>Dia</u> <u>tengok</u> <u>saya</u>

          he   look   I

     =   He looked at me.

200

(Note: menengok also refers to habituality brought
about by occupation, bearing the meaning of "to
prophesy (by palm-reading or some other means) as a
livelihood".)

(b) meminang means "to propose for one's hand in
    marriage". The root is a noun, pinang (betel-nut)
    which is an essential item brought by the
    bridegroom's representatives in the initial
    meeting with the bride's representatives, to
    propose a marriage.

(c) memanggil means "to invite to a feast". The
    root-word is panggil, which means "to call".

    (i) Dia   pergi   menanggil

        he   go   invite-people-to-a feast

    =   He invites people to a feast.

    (ii) Dia   panggil   saya

         he   call   me

    =   He called me.

The pattern me(N) + Verb also means having a quality which
refers to the denotation of the noun which co-occurs with the
verb concerned.

Examples:

(a) melambung (bouncing) from lambung (bounce) refers

to the bouncing objects used in conjunction with the verb concerned.

(b) melekat (sticky) from lekat (to stick) refers to the quality of objects which "stick", for example, glues and gums.

(c) mengusik (inclined to teasing people) from usik (to tease).

(d) merasuk (spirit or ghost inclined to entering someone's body), from rasuk (to enter).

The above examples formed according to the me(N) + Verb pattern, denote that human beings, animals or objects are characterized by certain inherent qualities.

The pattern me(N) + Noun, which generates verbs, may mean "to produce" or "to imitate".

Examples:

(a) menanah (producing puss), from nanah (puss).

(b) mengekor (follow someone physically); literally meaning "imitating the tail", from ekor (tail).

(c) melawak (to joke), literally meaning "imitating the clown", from lawak (a clown).

This pattern indicates that objects are characterized by the ability to produce, while human beings have the ability to imitate.

2.   **ter-**. This prefix **ter-** is a verbal prefix attached to verbs. This pattern denotes non-intention or accidentality of action.

Examples:

(a) **te(r)balik** (fall upside down accidentally), from **balik** (turn over).

(b) **te(r)beresin**   (sneeze   unintentionally),   from **beresin** (sneeze).

(c) **te(r)cabut** (pull out unintentionally), from **cabut** (pull out).

Action is thus seen as being executed without intention or consciousness as opposed to the one done with intention or full consciousness.

3.   **per-**. This prefix provides the speakers of the Kedah dialect with a means for conveying the concept of causality. Attached to adjective-roots, this prefix, realized as **per-** (before vowels) and **pe-** (elsewhere), is found in words such as the following:

(a) **per(h)angat** (to heat), from **hangat** (hot).

(b) **perelok** (to beautify), from **elok** (beautiful).

(c) **pependek** (to shorten), from **pendek** (short).

The morphological pattern per + Adj reflects the world-view of the Kedah dialect speakers in relation to causality, which affects the attribute of (and not the action performed by) a noun-referent.

Causality which is related to action rather that attribute

is conveyed by a syntactical rather than a morphological pattern (cf. discussion on grammatical patterns).

Pe- is a nominal prefix indicating "instrument of action", and is affixed to verb-roots only. In the Kedah dialect, its denotation does not include an agent of action as the case is with Standard Malay.

Examples:

(a) penukul (instrument for hitting 'something'),
    from pukul (to hit).

(b) penumbuk (the fist), from tumbuk (to punch).

(c) penyapu (broom), from sapu (to sweep).

4. ber-. This prefix may occur in the pattern ber + Verb which has two main denotations: reciprocity, and action done without specificity of purpose or target.

(a) Reciprocity

Reciprocity as borne by the pattern ber + Verb is illustrated by the following examples:

(i) bertumbuk (punch one another), from tumbuk (punch).

(ii) berbabil (argue with one another), from babil (argue).

(iii) ber(h)antar (send food to one another): this particularly refers to the custom of exchanging samples of dishes among neighbours in the evenings of the Ramadhan, just before the breaking of fast. The root-word is <u>hantar</u> (send).

(iv) <u>berderau</u> (to take turns to help one another). This word refers specifically to the custom among the padi farmers of helping one another in the various farming chores, from the clearing of land to the harvesting of rice.

In their usage, such verbs are usually followed by the pronominal phrase <u>hang aku</u> (you and I).

Example:

<u>Depa</u>   <u>berbabil</u>   <u>hang aku</u>

they   argue   you and I

= They argue with one another.

(b) <u>Action without specificity of purpose or target</u>

Verbs with this meaning are as follows:

(i) <u>berlari</u> (run), from <u>lari</u> (run).

(ii) <u>berjalan</u> (walk), from <u>jalan</u> (walk).

Both the verbs above refer to the acts of running and walking, for example, in the playing field, without having a specific purpose or target. Such verbs stand in contrast with their non-affixed forms, namely, <u>lari</u> and <u>jalan</u>, which denote the presence of a definite purpose or target.

Examples:

(a) <u>Dia</u> <u>berlari</u> <u>di padang</u> <u>tu</u>

     he   run   the   field   that

=   He runs in the field.

(b) <u>Dia</u> <u>lari</u> <u>dari</u> <u>sana</u> <u>ke</u> <u>sini</u>

     he   run   from   there   to   here

=   He is running here.

The pattern <u>ber</u> + Noun bears the meaning "having, possessing".

Examples:

(a) <u>be(r)daki</u> (having body-dirt), from <u>daki</u> (body-dirt).

(b) <u>be(r)peluh</u> (sweating), from <u>peluh</u> (sweat).

(c) <u>beruban</u> (having grey hair), from <u>uban</u> (grey hair).

The complex prefix <u>berke-</u> denotes commitativity, usually involving more than two subjects:

(a) <u>berketeriak</u> (to cry or weep together), from <u>teriak</u> (cry, weep).

(b) <u>berkelewar</u> (to hang around aimlessly together) from <u>lewar</u>, <u>melewar</u> (to hang around aimlessly).

206

Reduplication

Reduplication in the semiotic system under discussion operates on numerals, verbs, and adjectives. Reduplication of nouns is an innovation resulting from an influence from Standard Malay. Where cardinal numbers are concerned, this pattern indicates succession of events involving noun-referents.

Examples:

(a) satu-satu (one by one), from satu (one).

(b) dua-dua (two by two), from dua (two).

(c) tiga-tiga (three by three), from tiga (three).

Succession of events is a feature of temporal perception. Reduplication of verbs may indicate "casualness of action".

Examples:

(a) tengok-tengok (casually looking at something), from tengok (look at).

(b) cuba-cuba (casually trying to do something), from cuba (try).

(c) sembunyi-sembunyi (casually hiding something or oneself), from sembunyi (hide).

When a reduplicated verb is preceded by the negative word tak, the whole phrase bears the literal meaning "not-action-yet". That is to say, negative + reduplication is equivalent to the verbal aspect "not yet", indicating an unchanging situation through time.

207

Examples:

(a) <u>tak pi-pi</u> (has not yet gone).

(b) <u>tak masak-masak</u> (has not yet cooked or ripened).

(c) <u>tak berenti-berenti</u> (has not yet ceased).

Reduplication of the adjective indicates plurality or extensiveness of the noun-referent which the adjective modifies.

Examples:

(a) <u>putih-putih</u> (white all over, or of many things), from <u>putih</u> (white).

(b) <u>manis-manis</u> (sweet of many things), from <u>manis</u> (sweet).

(c) <u>jahat-jahat</u> (bad of many people), from <u>jahat</u> (bad).

With adjectives describing manner, reduplication indicates intensity. Such adjectives function as exocentric adverbs.

Examples:

(a) <u>pelan-pelan</u> (very slowly), from <u>pelan</u> (slow).

(b) <u>cepat-cepat</u> (very quickly), from <u>cepat</u> (quick).

(c) <u>kuat-kuat</u> (with great strength), from <u>kuat</u> (strong).

208

GRAMMATICAL PATTERNS

The Kedah dialect has nominal, verbal and adverbial categories.
However, number, gender and the verbal aspects are lexical rather
than grammatical categories.

At the sentence level, the pattern that is most frequent and
most significant is the NP-VP pattern, in which NP more often
than not gets eclipsed. That is to say, the Kedah Malay dialect
prefers a verb-theme sentence. The following discourse can
exemplify the point made above.

Speaker A: Nak pi mana?

             will   go   where

         =   Where are you going?

Speaker B: Pi Padang Tok Kesop

             go Padang Tok Kesop

         =   I'm going to the Padang Tok Kesop.

Speaker A: Amboi, lama nu tak jumpa? Dak buat apa?

             dear me long time since met   you   do   what

         =   Dear me, it's a long time since we last met.
             What have you been doing?

Speaker B: Bukan dok sini, dah. Dok di Kodiang nu.
             Pindah lama dah.

209

> =   not live here, already live in Kodiang there
> transfer long-time already
>
> =   I don't live here any more. I now live in
> Kodiang. I moved there some time ago.

Speaker A: <u>Awat, tak serenok ka di sini</u>?

           Why,   not   happy   emph. here

      =   Why, weren't you happy here?

Speaker B: <u>Sajalah</u>. <u>Sana banyak adik beradik</u>

          nothing really there many relatives

      =   It's nothing really. I have many relatives
there.

The thematization of the verb reflects the fact that it is the action or the quality that is overtly signalled. This is not to say that the person or subject is not important but that to make an overt reference to him is unimportant, because this reference is implicated in the action performed by him or the quality attributed to him. As such, we see that in the world-view of the Kedah people, the assertion of the self is not as important as his action and the characteristics attributed to him.

Sentences in the Kedah dialect belong to the simple or the complex co-ordinating type. The hypotactic pattern, consisting of the main clause with one or more subordinate clauses, is non-existent in this dialect. The complex sentences are not like those found in Standard Malay which are marked by the presence of co-ordinating conjunctions. Rather, they are strung together in succession as though they are separate sentences. The only difference between the co-ordinating complex sentences and a string of independent simple sentences lie in the nature of the pause between the component sentences concerned. If the pause is of a short duration then it is a co-ordinating complex sentence. A pause with a longer duration characterizes two independent sentences.

Examples:

Speaker A: <u>Minta</u> <u>maaflah</u>, <u>tak</u> <u>boleh</u> <u>mai</u> <u>kemaren</u>.
<u>Budak</u> <u>hangat</u> <u>badan</u>.

apologies, cannot come yesterday. child had temperature.

= I apologise for not being able to come yesterday. My child had a temperature.

Speaker B: <u>Tu</u> <u>kah</u>? <u>Macam</u> <u>mana</u> <u>la</u> <u>ni</u>? <u>Sehat</u> <u>dah</u>
<u>kut</u>?

that so how now perhaps already well

= Is that so? How is he now? Perhaps he is already well.

Speaker A: <u>Legalah</u> <u>dah</u> <u>sikit</u>. <u>Nak</u> <u>kata</u> <u>sehat</u>
<u>sangat</u> <u>pun</u>, <u>dak</u> <u>juga</u>.

slightly better to say that well not quite true.

= He is slightly better. To say that he is well is not quite true.

211

The juxtaposing of simple sentences, either as independent forms or as forms strung on to one another, is reflective of a type of thinking that is simple and clear. On the other hand, the hypotactic structure reflects a type of thinking that has been intellectualized, that is, one that subordinates related ideas to the matrix. As such, in this type of structure, causality, conditionality, concessionality and so on are subsumed under the matrix sentence. This does not mean that there are no such concepts in languages or dialects which do not have the hypotactic construction. However, such concepts are conveyed in independent simple sentences or clauses rather than subordinated to the matrix. And in the sentence or the clause itself such concepts are either overtly marked by morphemes, for example, per- for causality, or covertly, that is, in terms of the relationship between the meaning borne by this sentence and that of the sentence occurring before or after it, as illustrated by the following examples:

(a) Hujan lebat ni. Habis padi rusak

    rain   heavy this. finished padi destroyed

=   The rain is heavy. The padi is completely destroyed.

In this example, the first sentence Hujan lebat ni provides the cause of the destruction of padi expressed in the second sentence. The causality concept is not embodied by the first sentence alone but by the relationship between both the sentences concerned.

(b) Tak hujan, saya datang

    not rain, I   come.

=   If it doesn't rain, I'll come.

212

The relationship between the two independent clauses in the above example together with the semantics they bear, embody the conditionality concept while the statement of the "conditions for not coming" is borne by the first clause Tak hujan.

(c) Dia tu orang kaya. Dia tak sombong

    He   rich   man.   He   not proud.

=   He is a rich man. He is not proud.

The reference to "concession" is made by the first sentence, but the concessionality concept is found in the relationship between the two sentences concerned.

Grammatical Categories and Semantic Components

Words in the dialect may consist of verbs, adjectives, nouns (inclusive of pronouns), and adverbs.

VERBS

The verbs can be divided into main verbs and auxiliaries.

The latter consist of the modal and the aspect verbs. The modal verbs in the Kedah dialect are buleh, nak and mau while the aspect verbs are dah, dok, tangah, and tak...lagi.

The modal verb buleh may be translated as "can" or "may", depending on the context of its usage.

Examples:

(a) <u>Buleh</u> <u>dak</u>. <u>masuk</u>?

     may   not   enter

=   May I come in?

(b) <u>Dia</u> <u>buleh</u> <u>menanam</u> <u>dah</u>

    he   can   plant   padi already.

=   He can now plant his padi.

Hence, in <u>buleh</u>, the concept of "ability" merges with that of "permissibility".

As for the modal verbs <u>nak</u> "will, want" and <u>mau</u> "will, want", the concepts they bear are not completely identical to one another. That is to say, whilst there is a core concept which is shared by them, there are also areas of divergence which separate the one from the other. Both refer to the modality of desiring or wanting to do or act, but <u>mau</u> suggests a higher degree of desire compared to <u>nak</u>. Moreover, <u>mau</u> can also occur by itself as a full verb, whereas <u>nak</u> cannot.

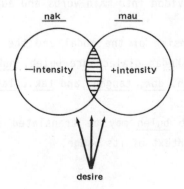

214

The aspect verb <u>dah</u> denotes completion of action or happening. It usually occurs after the main verb.

<u>Dia</u> <u>makan</u> <u>dah</u>

he   eat   already

= He has already had his meal.

Both the aspect verbs <u>dok</u> and <u>tengah</u> denote action in progress.

(i) <u>Dia</u> <u>dok</u> <u>makan</u>

    he   eating

= He is eating

(ii) <u>Dia</u> <u>tengah</u> <u>makan</u>

    he   eating

= He is eating

To convey the concept of action waiting to be done, the dialect makes use of the split phrase <u>tak...lagi</u>.

<u>Dia</u> <u>tak</u> <u>makan</u> <u>lagi</u>

he   not   eat   yet

= He has not eaten yet.

Although the aspect verbs do not stand for the category of tense, they are assuredly related to the concept of time. In

215

other words, they give the action concerned a temporal context in relation to the stage of performance: not yet, in progress or already completed.

The aspect verb <u>dah</u> is related to <u>sudah</u> which in the dialect concerned is a full verb, meaning "have finished", "have completed", but which in Standard Malay is a modal verb for completion of action. In the Kedah dialect, <u>sudah</u> may be followed by <u>dah</u>.

Example:

<u>Baju</u> <u>saya</u> <u>sudah</u> <u>dah</u>

dress I   completed already

=   My dress is already completed.

Hence, it can be deduced that <u>dah</u> is an abridged form of <u>sudah</u> and that in the development of the Kedah dialect the full verb status was reduced to that of an auxiliary, in line with the abridgement of its form.

The phenomenon of the reduction of the full verb to the auxiliary is also seen in the aspect verb <u>tengah,</u> although here there is no phonological abridgement to the form. This particular aspect of the verb can be said to be historically related to the spatial noun <u>tengah</u> (centre, middle). We can say that the temporal concept of this word developed from the original concept pertaining to space. When something is half way from its starting point heading to its destination, it has made a gain in the time spent. Hence the spatial and the temporal seem to merge in the aspect verb <u>tengah.</u>

The lexical verbs may be divided into various semantic

216

categories. A study of them in such detail would need a volume by itself. For the purpose of this study it suffices to discuss action in certain such verbs, particularly in relation to time and space.

All actions and happenings take place within the contexts of space and time. These contexts are expressed in many ways. Time, for instance, is expressed by the aspect verbs, the various morphological patterns, temporal words, and sentence construction.

Certain verbs denote the concept of space within their semantic components without any assistance from the context of the sentence or of another word. Such verbs are action verbs (as opposed to static verbs).

For example:

1. to throw

tauk = throw with arm moving forward

hempas = throw down

baling = throw with arm in full circle

punggai = throw with arm raised upward in back-to-forward movement.

tengalung = throw with arm in full circle but with greater force than baling.

buang = throw away

The various words for "to throw" differ from one another in

the various aspects of space itself. All the words above, with the exception of buang strictly bear the concept of physical distance, such that the degree of distance can be seen in the following ascending order: tauk, hempas, baling, punggai, tengalung. Of these five actions, only hempas denotes the perpendicular movement downwards while the other four denote back-to-forward movements. Furthermore, all the five types of movement also involve the types of force that go with them.

The verb buang represents the merging of the physical and the psychological distance. The physical action of buang means not just the removal of something from one place to another but accompanying this action is the psychological removal of that something, and in this latter sense the word may be used metaphorically with the meaning of "disowning" or "expelling" (someone).

The scheme below shows the diagnostic components of each of the verbs above:

Verbs	Physical Distance	Psychological Distance	Physical Force	Direction of Movements
tauk	1st degree	-	1st degree	⟶
punggai	2nd degree	-	2nd degree	⟶
baling	3rd degree	-	3rd degree	⟶
tengalung	4th degree	-	4th degree	⟶
hempas	all degrees	-	4th degree	↓
buang	all degrees	+	all degrees	all directions

2. <u>to cut</u>

    <u>tebang</u> = cut down (a standing object for example, tree).

    <u>cantas</u> = cut raised objects which are small in size and with rapidity.

    <u>cincang</u> = cut in very small pieces with rapid speed and the knife is wholly lifted perpendicularly.

    <u>hiris</u> = cut into thin pieces as in slicing meat.

    <u>belah</u> = cut into two.

    <u>kerat</u> = cut into big pieces or chunks.

    <u>rincik</u> = cut into very thin pieces with rapid speed with the knife-point hardly leaving the cutting board.

    <u>tetas</u> = cut the seams (in sewing).

    <u>takok</u> = cut on the surface with the knife raised in perpendicular position but it does not go right through; chunks are taken out so that the result is a caved-in impression.

    <u>kelar</u> = cut on the surface with the knife in perpendicular position but it does not go right through the object, such as cutting the surface of the body of the fish before seasoning it.

219

      takek   =   cut on the surface with the knife
                  raised obliquely to the right or left,
                  but it does not go right through; the
                  effect is a caved-in impression.

      tebas   =   cut off low-lying objects with neutral
                  rapidity.

      tebang =   cut off highly raised objects.

      tetak   =   cut on the surface with force and
                  without caved-in impression.

The above paradigm is not exhaustive and can be divided into two sub-paradigms, one consisting of those verbs whose components show the action of cutting right through, and the other consisting of the verbs whose components indicate the type of cutting which affects the surface only. Each of the subgroups above can be divided according to various criteria as given in the diagram. One thing needs be mentioned here, and that is, that there is no general term in the Kedah dialect for "to cut". The verb potong has been a relatively recent addition from Standard Malay. This explains the use of the verb motong for tapping rubber (which was introduced in the late nineteenth century) rather than for the cutting of padi.

The diagram shows that there is a logical order in the relationship between the components of each verb. In the subgroup of "to cut right through", there seems to be a distinction between verbs which are "domestic" and those which are not. That is to say, the verbs tebang, cantas and tebas are those which describe action usually done outside the house. As such, the differentiations on the size and texture of the objects are considered necessary. The verb tebang is usually employed to

220

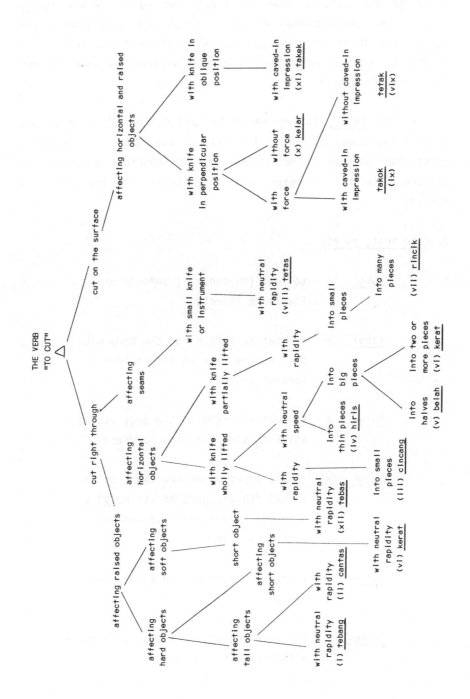

THE VERB
"TO CUT"

cut on the surface

affecting horizontal and raised objects

with knife in perpendicular position

with knife in oblique position

with force

without force (x) kelar

with caved-in impression

without caved-in impression

with caved-in impression

with knife partially lifted

with neutral rapidity (viii) tetas

with rapidity

into small pieces

into many pieces (vii) rincik

into big pieces

into two or more pieces (vi) kerat

into halves (v) belah

with caved-in impression

takok (ix)

tetak (vix)

with caved-in impression (xi) takek

cut right through

affecting seams

affecting horizontal objects

with small knife or instrument

with knife wholly lifted

with neutral speed

into thin pieces (iv) hiris

with rapidity

into small pieces (iii) cincang

affecting raised objects

affecting soft objects

affecting short objects

short object

with neutral rapidity (xii) tebas

with neutral rapidity (vi) kerat

affecting hard objects

affecting tall objects

with rapidity (ii) cantas

with neutral rapidity (i) tebang

with neutral rapidity (vi) kerat

refer to the cutting down of trees and poles, while <u>cantas</u> denotes the cutting down of small trees and undergrowth, and <u>tebas</u> that of cutting the grass. With these three verbs, the number of pieces resulting from the various actions is not considered important.

As for <u>kerat,</u> it may refer to action done both inside and outside the house. In both the milieus the number of resultant pieces may be two or more. All the non-domestic verbs do not differentiate the thinness or the thickness of the resultant pieces.

3. <u>to beat, to hit</u>

<u>pukol</u>   =   to beat (in general) animate or inanimate objects.

<u>tibai</u>   =   to beat (a person) on the body with thin sticks such as sticks from coconut leaves.

<u>balun</u>   =   to beat a person on the body with a stick of some size and hardness.

<u>katok</u>   =   to hit a person on the head, or an animal (on any part of its body) or a thing, with a piece of wood or such-like objects.

<u>tabuh</u>   =   to hit a person on the back with the fist.

<u>tumbuk</u>   =   to hit a person, an animal or a thing with the fist; to pound.

puk   =   to slap a baby gently.

sepak   =   to slap on the face.

tampar =   to slap on any part of the body
            except the face and the head.

luku   =   to hit the head with the knuckles.

jentik =   to hit with the forefinger moving from
            touching the thumb to the target object.

sepak   =   to kick a person, an animal or a thing.

tendang =   to kick a person, an animal or a thing
            with greater force than sepak.

terajang = to kick a person, an animal or a thing
            with greater force than tendang.

sigung =   to hit with the elbow.

sakai   =   same as balun.

sekeh   =   to hit the face with the elbow.

The scheme given indicates these verbs with their various diagnostic components. It shows that the differentiations in the various actions belonging to the paradigm with the general meaning "to beat" or "to hit" result from various factors: types of instrument, type of target and force. Differentiation is made more refined by the details observed in the three factors mentioned above, particularly in the action executed with body-parts and the details of the target-members. All this goes to show the sharpness in the perception of reality among the

THE VERB "TO BEAT", "TO HIT"

	With Object Instrument	With Body Part						Target			Force
	Thickness	Palm	Fist	Knuckle	Elbow	Finger	Foot	Human	Animal	Object	
pukol	-	-	-	-	-	-	-	+	+	+	3rd degree
tibal	+	-	-	-	-	-	-	body	-	-	3rd degree
balun, sakal	+	-	-	-	-	-	-	body	-	-	3rd degree
katok	+	-	+	-	-	-	-	head	head & body	+	2nd degree
tabuh	-	-	-	-	-	-	-	back	-	-	3rd degree
tumbuk - 1	-	-	+	-	-	-	-	body	-	-	+
tumbok - 2	+	+	-	-	-	-	-	-	+	+	+
puk	-	+	-	-	-	-	-	body	-	-	-
sepak (sepak)	-	+	-	+	-	-	-	face	-	-	1st degree
tampar	-	+	-	-	-	-	-	face & body	-	-	2nd degree
luku	-	-	-	-	-	-	-	head	-	-	+
jentik	-	-	-	-	-	+	-	+	+	+	+
sepak	-	-	-	-	-	-	+	+	+	+	1st degree
tendang	-	-	-	-	-	-	+	+	+	+	2nd degree
terajang	-	-	-	-	-	-	+	+	+	+	3rd degree
sigung	-	-	-	-	+	-	-	+	-	+	+
sekeh	-	-	-	+	-	-	-	face	-	-	2nd degree

224

speakers of the dialect under study. Such a paradigm undoubtedly
assists in re-creating a perception that is parallel in
complexity and refinement.

4. to tread

    pijak   =   to tread on someone or something and
                 keeping the foot or feet in position
                 for a certain length of time.

    hindik =   to tread on someone or something with
                 one foot and lifting it up and down,
                 as in pounding padi using the lesung
                 hindik or lesung kaki.

    hirik   =   to tread on someone or something with
                 one foot static and the other moving
                 sideways, as in threshing padi with
                 the feet.

    keretam =   to stamp the feet in succession one
                 after another repeatedly on the floor.

In this paradigm, the most significant correlation existing
between the semantic components of the words is that of space and
time. The spatial and temporal factors appear to be quite
transparent in all the four verbs concerned.

5. to move

    jalan   =   to walk.

    lari   =   to run.

    taktih   =   to toddle.

225

<u>kesot</u>	=	to move on the buttock.
<u>merangkak</u>	=	to move on all fours.
<u>sĕrot</u> (<u>serot</u>)	=	to move backwards.
<u>lompat</u>	=	to jump up or down or both.
<u>terjun</u>	=	to jump down.

Again, in this paradigm there is an obvious correlation between space and time. Space is not only implicit in the physical context of the action concerned but is also linked to two other factors: (1) the direction of the movement be it forward backward or sideways, up or down or both, (2) the manner the action is performed in relation to the body parts, that is, with the movement of the feet, the buttocks, the hands or the knees.

The temporal factor is reflected in the speed of movement. The verbs <u>lari</u>, <u>lompat</u> and <u>terjun</u> may be said to have some degree of speed, while <u>jalan</u> may have a speed that may alternate between fast and slow. On the other hand, <u>taktih</u>, <u>kesot</u>, <u>merangkak</u> and <u>serot</u> are movements characterized by lack of speed.

ADJECTIVES

The adjectives occur only in root-forms. In a comparison the adjective is followed by <u>lagi</u>, such that the comparative degree is conveyed by the structure Adj. + <u>lagi</u> + N.

Example:

<u>Ni</u>   <u>mahal</u>   <u>lagi</u>

    this expensive more

=   This is more expensive.

Intensity of attribute is not conveyed by a morpheme or a structural pattern as such, but by modulation. That is to say, the adjective is uttered with a strong force in the intonation showing a combination of a strong stress and a high-falling pitch.

Example:

<u>Mahal</u>!

=   How expensive!

The adjectives may be subcategorized into adjectives of colour, taste, size, shape, manner, sensation and so on. Some of these will be discussed in their own subsections.

NOUNS

Nouns in the Kedah dialect are viewed from various parameters: animate vs. inanimate, male vs. female; parent vs. off-spring, singular vs. plural, and so on. This is not to say that there are specific morphological features which mark off one category as distinct from the other. Rather, the distinction is realized in phrasal forms; this means that the noun concerned is placed in collocation with words which denote the specific categories mentioned above.

Concept of Animateness Versus Inanimateness, and Human Versus Non-Human

The concept of animate vs. inanimate is manifested in the use of the words which represent the stages of development in a life span. Human beings, animals, plants, and trees and their parts are considered living or animate objects. Human beings and animals are placed in a subcategory different from plants, as recognized from the words they collocate with, which denote the stages of living or being alive.

Human beings and animals are also viewed at from two other parameters: young vs. old and small vs. big.

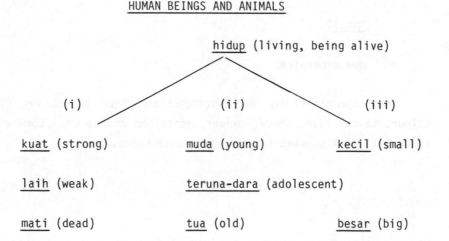

HUMAN BEINGS AND ANIMALS

hidup (living, being alive)

(i)   (ii)   (iii)

kuat (strong)   muda (young)   kecil (small)

laih (weak)   teruna-dara (adolescent)

mati (dead)   tua (old)   besar (big)

All the orders, (i) - (iii), indicate a temporal concept. In (i) this concept is tied with physical energy. In (ii) it is with the normal process of growth in line with a gain in time; here there is a slight differentiation between the male and the female subcategory as seen in the choice of words: teruna for the male and dara for the female. In (iii), there is a merging

228

of the temporal and the spatial: what is small is young, and what is big is old.

With the plants, perception of their temporal progress seems to denote a differentiation according to the parts that are affected: the wood, the leaves, the flowers, and the fruits.

The word hidup for flowers and fruits are generally used in the differentiation between the natural and the artificial ones. With the wood and the leaves, the differentiation is made at a more basic level, namely, in recognizing whether the wood or the leaf is really hidup or otherwise, besides extending the differentiation to distinguish the natural from the artificial. It is interesting to note hence that the wood, the leaves and the fruits, are seen to have a temporal progress from "dead" to "rotten". On the other hand, the flowers are like human beings, as their final stage is "being dead". With the human beings the word reput is applicable only when the remains are no longer identified with a person; they have then assumed the stage of

WOOD	LEAVES
hidup (alive, living)	hidup (alive, living)
↓	↓
muda (young)	pucuk (shoot)
↓	↓
tua (old)	muda (young)
↓	↓
mati (dead)	tua (old)
↓	↓
reput (rotten)	layu (withered)
	↓
	mati (dead)
	↓
	reput (rotten)

229

FLOWERS	FRUITS
hidup (alive, live fresh)	hidup (fresh)
kuntum (budding)	putik (young)
kembang (opening)	mengkar (becoming ripe)
layu (withered)	tua (almost ripe)
mati (dead)	masak (ripe)
	lom (the right stage of ripeness)
	rahum (slightly over-ripe)
	lasu (over-ripe)
	busuk (bad, rotten)

being inanimate. As such, we do not have the collocation between orang (person) and reput but rather between bangkai (the remains of the dead) and reput.

Flowers do not go beyond the mati (dead) stage, presumably due to the fact that in the world-view of the peasants, flowers are supposed to produce fruits; and this means that the fruit is the natural sequence in the development of the flower. The scheme below shows this development:

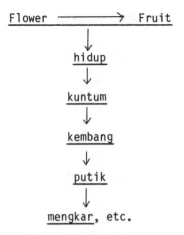

Flower ⟶ Fruit
↓
hidup
↓
kuntum
↓
kembang
↓
putik
↓
mengkar, etc.

The differentiation between the animate and the inanimate, and the human and the non-human is also seen in the use of numeral classifiers. The human noun uses the classifier <u>orang</u>, the non-human the classifier <u>ekor</u>, while the inanimate nouns are given classifiers determined by shapes and sizes.[8]

The stages of development in the padi grain as viewed by the Kedah peasants are undoubtedly based on the gain in time but the differentiation is also linked to the shape and size as well as the colour of the padi grain itself.

The development starts from the swelling of the padi stalks. This stage, known as the <u>padi bunting</u> ("pregnant" padi) stage, is followed by the flowering stage, bearing <u>bunga padi</u> (padi flowers), which in turn is followed by the <u>ringgi</u> stage. What is known as <u>ringgi</u> is the young padi grain which is green both at the husk and in the content. The size of the grain in still very tiny. Then comes the <u>emping</u> stage which shows a development in the colour -- more on the yellow side -- and size of the grain. Then comes <u>padi masak</u> (ripe padi) which is ready for harvesting. Ripe padi grains which are stored for a considerable length of time are known as <u>padi usang</u> (old padi), as opposed to <u>padi baru</u> (newly harvested padi).

231

padi bunting
↓
bunga padi
↓
ringgi
↓
emping
↓
padi masak
↓
padi baru
↓
padi usang

The treatment of plants, especially padi plants, as animate, just like human beings, is not only evident in linguistic data but also in the behaviour of the peasants towards the plants. It has been an age-old practice among the Kedah peasants to handle plants and trees with care, because in their world-view the plants and trees are living things and thus have senses like human beings. People are encouraged to talk to trees and plants so that these living objects will flourish with flowers and fruits. Trees whose capacity to bear fruit seems to be arrested for some reason or other are not only talked to but get "punished" through "suffering" from small scars or dents made on their trunks or branches. If the trees get the message, they will bear fruit the following season.

The padi plant is treated with more "reverence" than any other plant. The padi, inclusive of the grains, is said to have a soul or <u>semangat</u> which has to be "cared for" all the time. Any crudity in the handling of the padi plants or grains may drive the <u>semangat</u> away. This explains the succession of rituals that the padi farmer has to conduct and the taboos that he has to observe from the moment the seeds are sown to the time the padi

232

grains are stored away. But "reverence" for the rice continues to the kitchen and the dining place. Rice has to be handled with care even before being put to the pot and not a single grain should be found lying around on the floor to be trampled by unknowing feet.

Left-over rice also has its share of reverence. However bad and smelly it has become, it cannot be thrown away like any other trash. If it is not given as food to the cat, the chicken or the bird, it is washed clean and dried out in the sun, and this dehydrated product is turned into either human or chicken feed. The consequence of a wasteful handling of rice is god's retribution in the form of poverty. Rice is said to be capable of weeping like human beings, and will take the form of sand to the person who is in need of it but who had mishandled it at a previous point in his life.

Concept of Male versus Female

The concepts of male and female exist in the language of the peasants as manifested in the words jantan and betina/perempuan which are used in collocation with certain nouns: human, non-human and inanimate.

Human beings are differentiated according to their sexes: jantan (male) and perempuan (female). Here the word jantan rather than the Standard Malay laki-laki, is used.

anak jantan	=	male child, or son.
anak perempuan	=	female child, or daughter.
cucu jantan	=	grandson.
cucu perempuan	=	grandchild.

233

In kinship, most of the ranks have their own terms, in which the male or female feature is inherent. That is to say, the overt gender markers in the form of <u>jantan</u> and <u>perempuan</u> are not used.

For example:

<u>tok</u>	=	grandmother
<u>tok wan, wan</u>	=	grandfather
<u>kak</u>	=	elder female sibling
<u>abang</u>	=	elder male sibling
<u>emak</u>	=	mother
<u>pak</u>	=	father

With the non-human nouns the overt markers are <u>jantan</u> (male) and <u>betina</u> (female).

<u>kerbau jantan</u>	=	male buffalo
<u>kerbau betina</u>	=	female buffalo

The kinship terms that are used in collocation with animal names are only <u>ibu</u> (mother) and <u>anak</u> (offspring).

<u>ibu kerbau</u>	=	mother buffalo
<u>anak kerbau</u>	=	young or baby buffalo

Here we see that although <u>ibu</u> and <u>anak</u> are kinship terms, their usage with names of animals does not show a kinship

234

connection; rather this usage identifies the old from the young. Here it is the physical rather than the cultural time that proves significant.

With the plants, the concept of male versus female is identical to that applied to animals.

pokok jantan	=	male tree
pokok betina	=	female tree
petik jantan	=	male papaya
petik betina	=	female papaya

However, while there is anak petik (young papaya plant), anak padi (young padi plant), the concepts of "mother papaya" and "mother padi" do not exist in the speech system under consideration.

The concept of male versus female in inanimate objects is applied to certain objects only.

Examples:

ketupat jantan	=	male ketupat
ketupat betina	=	female ketupat
pongsu jantan	=	male ant-hill
pongsu betina	=	female ant-hill

The paradigm with ketupat refers to the shapes of the ketupat concerned. In this conjunction, it is best to be reminded that the Kedah ketupat is a type of food made from glutinous rice cooked in coconut milk and wrapped in a triangular shape using the palas leaves. The male ketupat differs slightly from the female counterpart; the latter is not liked by housewives because its shape is not as attractive as the former.

The paradigm with pongsu also refers to the size and shape. The male pongsu is bigger and more pointed than the female one.

The world-view that plants are either male or female seems to reflect the attitude of the peasants in their farming practice. As such, however small their padi land is, the peasant finds it imperative to include the glutinous padi or pulut. This is due to the belief that pulut is the male, while ordinary padi is the female. Without pulot, the harvest may not bring about a favourable yield.

Concepts of Shape and Size

Shape and size are spatial concepts. In their perception of the life around them, the Kedah peasants either treat shape and size together or separately. The cases of pongsu jantan and pongsu betina, as well as the stages of the development of the padi grain, exemplify the amalgamation of shape and size, whereas that of the ketupat jantan versus ketupat betina indicates that shape can be separated from size.

Artefacts used by the peasants provide a wealth of examples of the treatment of shape and size, together or separately. The winnowing tray to the Kedah peasant may be represented by the nyiru which is triangular, the badang which is circular, or the pengayak which is circular but perforated. In this paradigm, size is not important.

236

A similar case of shape is seen in the perception of the padi storage place, which is a permanent structure of timber or bamboo. The one made of timber is a replica of a small house, square in shape with a sloping roof. This is known as jelapang. However, if the structure is circular and has a flat cover on top, then it is known as kepok (kĕpok). The jelapang is identified with wealth while the kepok is not; hence the term jelapang padi Malaysia given to Kedah, and not kepok padi Malaysia.

On the other hand, shape and size are inseparable in paradigms for objects like padi containers, cutting instruments, and so on. Padi containers are usually made of mengkuang (pandanus leaves); these containers are given below in an ascending order of size.

kecung = container with tapered top

bakul = container with wide top

Cutting instruments are differentiated according to both shape and size, for example, pisau (small knife), pisau belati (knife bigger than the ordinary one with a curved handle), parang (cleaver), kapak (axe), badek (dagger), lembing (spear).

The importance of size as divorced from shape is seen in the perception of the padi husks, husked padi grains, and measurement terms. Padi husks and padi grains are dichotomized into "bigness" and "minuteness". Hence, the padi husks are either sekam (big in size as a result of little grinding or pounding) or dedak (minute in size as a result of intensive pounding), while the husked padi grains are beras consisting of whole grains or temukut consisting of small broken grains.

Words used for measurement dealt with here are those used in

237

measuring padi and land. The Kedah peasants have their own system of measuring padi, starting from the smallest unit <u>jemput</u> to the largest unit <u>kunca</u>.

<u>jemput</u>	=	quantity that correlates to the five fingers held together.
<u>genggam</u>	=	a handful
<u>kepoi</u>	=	the capacity of a small coconut.
<u>kai</u>	=	consisting of two <u>kepoi</u>.
<u>cupak</u>	=	four <u>kepoi</u> or two <u>kai</u>
<u>gantang</u>	=	four <u>cupak</u>
<u>nalih</u>	=	<u>sixteen gantang</u>
<u>kunca</u>	=	ten <u>nalih</u>

In measuring land, the system consists of the following:

<u>jengkai</u>	=	the span from the tip of the thumb to the tip of the index finger
<u>depa</u>	=	an arm's <u>length</u>
<u>jemba</u>	=	eight <u>depa</u>
<u>rantai</u>	=	four <u>jemba</u>

238

penjuru	=	two rantai
relung	=	four penjuru

More examples of the concepts of shape and size can be seen in the numeral classifiers, particularly the classifiers for inanimate nouns. In such cases, the shape and size, separately or otherwise, determine the classifiers that are permissible.[9]

Colour Terms

There are seven main colour terms in the Kedah dialect and these are putih (white), hitam (black), merah (red), kuning (yellow), hijau (green), biru (blue) and kelabu (grey). Of these, four may be considered to be basic, and these are the colours white, black, red, and green.

The main colours are those which are perceived by the Kedah people in general. Each colour term has various modifications relating to the flora and fauna and objects of nature, to signify its various shades, some of which may have specific terms in other Malay dialects.

(a) putih (white)

putih melepak (extremely white); lepak is an obsolete term for white, cf. nalopak (Batak) = white[10]

(b) hitam (black)

hitam legam (jet black) (legam may represent an absolete term for "black").

239

<u>hitam manis</u> literally means "black sweet", in reference to the brown colour of the Malay skin.

(c) <u>merah</u> (red)

<u>merah darah</u> (blood red).

<u>merah hati</u> (liver red).

<u>merah jambu</u> (guava red), that is, bright red.

<u>merah tua</u> (dark red).

<u>merah muda</u> (light red).

(d) <u>kuning</u> (yellow)

<u>kuning air</u>, literally meaning "water yellow", that is, beige.

<u>kuning langsat</u> (<u>langsat</u> yellow), that is, the colour of the <u>langsat</u> fruit.

<u>kuning kunyit</u> (turmeric yellow).

(e) <u>hijau</u> (green)

<u>hijau telur itik</u> (the colour of the shell of the duck's egg).

<u>hijau daun</u> (leaf green), that is, deep green.

<u>hijau pucuk pisang</u> (the colour of the banana shoot), that is, light green.

240

hijau tua (dark green).

hijau muda (light green).

(f) biru (blue)

biru tua (dark blue).

biru muda (light blue).

(g) kelabu (grey)

kelabu asap (smoke grey).

Besides these seven main colours and their "derivations", there are other references to colour which do not make use of any colour word, but instead relate the concepts directly to particular objects which are characterized by their colours.

For example:

(a) biji remia (dark purple), literally meaning "seed of the remia fruit" which is dark purple.

(b) bunga keduduk (light purple), literally meaning "keduduk flower", which is light purple.

(c) biji asam (dark brown), literally meaning "seed of the tamarind" which is dark brown.

(d) kulit manggis (dark red), literally meaning "skin of the mangosteen", which is dark red.

The four basic colours of white, red, green and black are postulated, due to the overlapping of certain sets of colours in

241

the actual language usage of the peasants and speakers in remote villages. Hence, "red" refers to both red and yellow, "green" to green and blue, "black" to blue, black and grey.

1. white

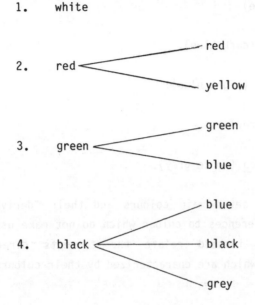

2. red   red
    yellow

3. green   green
    blue

4. black   blue
    black
    grey

As seen in the above diagrams, "red" encompasses the actual colour red (together with its various derivations) and yellow. To the peasants, the colour of the ripe padi is _merah_, not _kuning_; so is the colour of gold and the sun. The term _kuning_ can be said to exist in the speech of those people already in very close contact with speakers of other dialects and of Standard Malay.

There is no word for "brown" in Malay, as the case is with "purple". Besides, the reference to _biji asam_ (brown) is generally referred to as red. Mothers are known to categorize their children as "black-eyed" or "red-eyed".

As the case is with _kuning_, the word _biru_ (blue) could have been an innovation due to contacts with speakers outside the

242

Kedah dialect-area. Previous to this, the Kedah peasants used to refer to the colour of the sky as hijau, or more specifically hijau langit (sky green). However, deep blue or blue black is hitam (black). So is the colour of a bruised skin.

The four basic colours indicate two pairs of polarization: "black" and "white" on the one side, and "red" and "green" on the other. These contrasts relate to the experience of the peasants in their own temporal and spatial milieu. The black and white contrast is related to the contrast between night and day and it influences their way of looking at life in general: whatever is good is white, whilst the opposite is black. This also reflects the Malay preference for light skin girls, although at the same time the hitam manis colour is said to be sweeter than putih kuning when attributed to skin. In historical romances, princesses and ladies of high rank are described as having light coloured skin; those of the middle ranks as hitam manis, while those at the bottom of the social or moral ladder as hitam or hitam legam. This last colour expression is also attributed to the ghost as in the simile hitam legam seperti hantu, or "extremely black like the ghost".

The merah-hijau (red-green) pair also has its origin in the visual contrasts of nature, most probably in the contrast between the redness of the ripening padi and the green colour of its leaves and the surrounding world. Bearing in mind that "brown" is also merah, the milieu that provides the contrast is complete, that is, the Malaysian scenery rich with foliage and undergrowth of fresh green and red.

It was most unlikely that the early speakers of the dialect did not produce the kuning-hijau contrast, because yellow is a constituent of green, besides being a constituent of red. Whether the people are aware of the physical properties of the colour, the facts show that the contrast of hijau-kuning or

243

merah-kuning does not exist in this dialect. The presence of
merah-hijau contrast in the semiotic system of the Kedah people
has influenced the weltanschauung of these people such that they
perceive merah and hijau not as contrasts but as complements.
That is to say, both colours symbolize the good things in life.
Malay wedding ceremonies, for example, are occasions for joy and
celebration, and the colours that abound on such occasions are
those of the red and the green matrices.

It can be concluded from this study, therefore, that the
Kedah dialect started off with a four-colour system and developed
into a seven-colour one. This study also shows that the dialect
makes direct references to objects for their colours and this is
an indication of the way concepts of colour develop in languages
in general.

The main and basic colour ranges occurring in the dialect
indicate that certain colours have multiplicity of meanings.
This goes to show that the minimal differences in the colours and
hence the properties of things described are not perceived by the
speakers concerned. However, the range which associates colours
or various shades of colours to the colour properties of specific
objects such as "water yellow" and "banana shoot green" do on the
other hand show that perception and differentiation are made
possible by a comparison with concrete objects. This colour
terminology is another reflection of the way the Kedah people
perceive space.

However, the terms occurring in the paradigm with muda and
tua such as merah muda, hijau muda, merah tua, hijau tua, and so
on, are indications of temporal perceptions in the dialect
concerned. This is so because the adjectives muda (young) and
tua (old) are temporal words indicating the passage of time
affecting the properties of objects. This perception may have
originated from observations of the local flora which are

244

characterized by the changing of colours into deeper shades with progress in time.

Colour terms, then, offer us an insight into the conception as well as the perception of space and time in the Kedah dialect. Perception is defined as "becoming aware of an impression called forth by the action of an external stimulus on a sensory analyzer".[11] On the other hand, conception is the act of conceiving an idea. The result of this act is a concept, which is defined as "one of the fundamental components of the thinking process; a mental grasp of the essential features of objects or phenomena, the mental equivalent of a name".[12]

Terms for Tastes

There are eleven main terms describing taste in the Kedah dialect and these are : <u>tawar</u> (tasteless), <u>pahit</u> (bitter), <u>kelat</u> (astringent), which usually refers to the taste of the unripe fruit, <u>masam</u> (sour), <u>manis</u> (sweet), <u>pedas</u> (chilli-hot), <u>masin</u> (salty), <u>payaw</u> (a taste that is slightly sour, such as the taste of riverwater), and <u>hayai</u> (a taste between tastelessness and sweetness) such as the taste of an over-ripe fruit, <u>lemak</u> (the taste of milk or coconut-milk) and <u>pedar</u> (the taste of the lemon-rind).

Of the eleven terms, only seven can be considered as referring to basic tastes. These are <u>tawar</u>, <u>pahit</u>, <u>masam</u>, <u>manis</u>, <u>masin</u>, <u>pedas</u> and <u>lemak</u>.

The taste referred to by the term <u>kelat</u> reflects a merging of two types of taste, <u>pahit</u> (bitter) and <u>masam</u> (sour). Likewise, <u>payaw</u> indicates a development from tastelessness to <u>masin</u> combined with <u>kelat</u>, and <u>hayai</u> from sweetness to

245

tastelessness. _Pedar_ describes a combination of the bitter-sour taste that is also astringent.

pahit + masam	= kelat
tawar + masin + kelat	= payaw
manis + tawar	= hayai
pahit + masam + kelat	= pedar

The degrees of intensity of these adjectives may be conveyed not only by the patterns already mentioned but also by collocations with other lexical items, as given below:

Examples:

masam cuak (the latter component is pronounced as _cua_
　　　　　　extremely salty.

manis melecaih	= extremely sweet
pa(h)it bedengung	= extremely bitter
masin pa(h)it	= extremely salty
tawar heber	= really tasteless

Pedas, _kelat_, _hayai_, _payaw_ and _lemak_ do not have collocations parallel to those given in the examples above. An examination of the above phrases one by one at this point would prove most interesting.

In _masam cuak_, the component _cuak_ is presumably an onomatopoeia of a noise when the tastebuds are in contact with

246

sourness. It has no specific meaning on its own and is **never** used except in the context of masam. The word melecaih in manis melecaih is, morphologically speaking, a verb but it does not seem to occur by itself with its own specific meaning. That is to say, melecaih only exists in the collocation with manis, giving the concept "intensity" to the phrase. Phonetically, the word may also be said to be an onomatopoeia referring to the noise made by the tongue in the mouth when involved in extreme sweetness of taste. The word heber in tawar heber may stand on its own referring to people who like to talk without thinking. It can then be deduced that heber originally meant the constant opening of the mouth, and this coincides with the action that comes naturally to a person when something tasteless touches his tastebud.

In pahit berdengung, the modifying component berdengung is a known verb meaning "having resonances" or "resonant", as dengung means "resonance". Hence, the phrase pahit berdengung literally refers to "the bitter taste which echoes in the ears". Again, if one looks closely at the word dengung, it also has its origin in sound symbolism.

Conversely, sound symbolism is not apparent in masin pahit. Here is a case of expressing an extremity of a particular taste by making use of another "taste-word" to modify it. In terms of physical reality, extreme saltiness borders on bitterness of taste.

In their perception of taste, then, the peasants do not resort to similes originating in the flora and fauna of their physical environment; rather, they differentiate the various categories by employing sound symbolism and onomatopoeia that are closely linked with the noises or actions made by the tongue or the lips, as well by juxtaposing two different tastes. It can also be stressed here that the speakers have an awareness of

247

"derived" tastes that result from combinations of different basic tastes as seen in the cases of <u>kelat</u> and <u>payaw</u>. Besides that, they are also able to perceive the changing process from one taste to another as evidenced by <u>hayai</u> and <u>pahit berdengung</u>.

Classification of Padi Grains

There are two main divisions of padi: <u>padi jawi</u> and <u>padi pulut</u>. The former is the non-glutinous type that has become the staple food of the Malays, while the latter is the glutinous type which is used for the making of secondary dishes and cakes. It is therefore clear that the division between <u>jawi</u> and <u>pulut</u> is based on two characteristics: glutinous and staple.

Each of these two categories may be subdivided according to the characteristics pertaining to any or some or all of these characteristics: texture, shape, size, taste and colour of the husk. It is such diagnostic components that give rise to the various nomenclatures for both <u>padi jawi</u> and <u>padi pulut</u>.

There are varieties of <u>padi jawi</u>, such as the following: <u>padi didik</u>, <u>padi mayang sesat</u>, <u>padi mayang tok semai</u>, <u>padi mayang ikal</u>, <u>padi mayang pendek</u>, <u>padi mayang pulau</u>, <u>padi ranggung</u>, <u>padi muda Cik Ali</u>, <u>padi rami hitam</u>, <u>padi jarum emas</u>, <u>padi radin</u>, <u>padi pahit hitam</u>, <u>padi sembilan tangkai</u>, <u>padi mayang bilah</u>, <u>padi pot</u>, <u>padi sesat tok Piah</u> and so on.

Some of the varieties of <u>padi pulut</u> are <u>pulut bunga melung</u>, <u>pulut bunga tebu</u>, <u>pulut sutera</u>, <u>pulut kuku burung</u> and <u>pulut sutera minyak</u>.

It can also be seen that the assigning of nomenclatures to the various grains employs the comparative instrument besides taking note of the diagnostic components already mentioned. The comparison of the characteristics of the grains to other objects of nature reflects an aspect of the perception of the progenitors of those nomenclatures of the world around them. The pulut is realized as being soft of texture, that is, glutinous, and as such, this softness is likened to the delicateness of the flowers, bunga melung (flower of the crinum plant) and bunga tebu (sugar-cane flower) or the softness of silk. It is also a fact that there are varieties of the pulut which are rather hard of texture as exemplified by pulut kuku burung (kuku burung = bird's claws). Besides reflecting the progenitors' perception, those names are able to influence the behaviour of their users in their attitude towards the choice of their grains and their expectancy of their harvest.

As for the jawi varieties, some of them get their labels not only from the features of their grains but also from the characteristics of the stalks that uphold those grains, as evidenced by the nomenclatures padi mayang ikal, padi rami hitam, padi sembilan tangkat, padi mayang bilah, and so on. The concept of time is also interwoven in some of those names, specifically those which incorporate personal names which in all probability refer to persons of yore, who were involved in the cultivation of those varieties, for example, the nomenclatures padi mayang tok semai, padi muda Cik Ali, padi radin and padi sesat tok Piah.

In present-day rice farming in Malaysia, specifically in Kedah, most of the varieties of padi jawi and padi pulut mentioned above are no longer popular strains as they are not adaptable to the short span of time allowed in the annual double-cropping scheme recommended by the government. As such, in terms of economic value, they do not promise prosperity to the farmers although they signal tastiness to the gourmet. In their place are new grains such as Malinja, Mahsuri and A1 which were first conceived in the laboratories and these are the grains that promise more cash for the farmers.

Conclusion

The discussions provide a number of aspects pertaining to the world-view of the Malay (Kedah) peasants and their perception of reality.

Complexity of morphological patterns reflect a semantic superimposition on the already existing diagnostic components of the root-word. This means that a word in complex form creates a weltanschauung different from that invoked by one in simple form.

Grammatical structures are in conformity with the thinking processes, simple and without ostentation. The insignificance of the subject in discourse-sentences is a reflection of a society that de-emphasizes the individual, as the case is with the traditional Malay society in general. A discourse that protrudes the self or the individual is evaded as it is considered to be impolite.

The peasants also appear to possess a sharpness of perception of the reality around them. Conceptualization of actions and attributes and the naming of objects take into account all details perceivable in terms of time, space, direction, shape, size, and so on. An in-depth study of the peasants' conception of space may give an insight into the development of the concept of space from the earlier stages of Malay civilization. To quote Cassirer, "...primitive tribes usually are gifted with an extraordinarily sharp perception of space. A native of these tribes has an eye for all the nicest details of his environment. He is extremely sensitive to every change in the position of the common objects of his surroundings".[13]

250

NOTES

1. Cf. Edward Sapir, "Language and Environment", in David G. Mandelbaum, <u>Selected Writings of Edward Sapir in Language Culture and Personality</u> (University of California Press 1963), pp. 94 -95.

2. Cf. Asmah Haji Omar, "Aspek Kebudayaannya Seperti Yang Terdapat Dalam Sejarah dan Bahasa", <u>Dewan Bahasa</u>, Jilid 22, Bilangan 3 (Mac 1978), p. 150.

3. Witbold Doroszewski, <u>Elements of Lexicology and Semiotics</u> (Mouton & Co., 1973), p. 62.

4. Robert L. Miller, <u>The Linguistic Relativity Principle and Humboldtian Ethnolinguistics</u> (The Hague: Mouton & Co., 1968), p. 10.

5. Edited and introduced by John B. Carroll (M.I.T. Press, twelfth printing, 1976).

6. Ibid., p. 26.

7. Slametmuljana, <u>Srivijaya</u> (Percetaken Arnoldus Ende-Flores, Nusa Tenggara Timur), p. 39.

8. For a more detailed study of this, see Asmah Haji Omar "Numeral Classifiers in Malay and Iban", in <u>Essays On Malaysian Linguistics</u> (Dewan Bahasa dan Pustaka, 1975), pp. 241 - 55.

9. See ibid.

10. Harley Harris Bartlett, <u>Color Nomenclature in Batak and Malay</u>, reprinted from <u>Papers of the Michigan Academy of Science, Arts and Letters</u>, Vol. X (1928), p. 20.

11. Witbold Doroszewski, op. cit., p. 80.

12. Ibid.

13. Ernst Cassirer, <u>An Essay On Man</u> (Yale University Press, 1964), p. 45.

REFERENCES

Asmah Haji Omar. <u>Essays On Malaysian Linguistics</u>, Dewan Bahasa dan Pustaka, Kuala Lumpur, 1975.

_____. "Kedah: Aspek Kebudayaannya Seperti Yang Terdapat Dalam Sejarah dan Bahasa", <u>Dewan Bahasa</u>, Jilid 22, Bilangan 3, Mac 1978, pp. 146-55.

_____. "Numeral Classifiers in Malay and Iban", in <u>Essays On Malaysian Linguistics</u>, Dewan Bahasa dan Pustaka, Kuala Lumpur, 1975, pp. 241-55.

Bartlett, Harley Harris. Color Nomenclature in Batak and Malay, Reprinted from Papers of the Michigan Academy of Science Arts and Letters, Vol. X, 1978.

Bright, Jane O and William Bright. "Semantic Structures in North-western California and the Sapir - Whorf Hypothesis", American Anthropologist 67, No. 5, Part 2 (October 1965): 249-58.

Brown, Roger Langham. Wilhelm von Humboldt's Conception of Linguistic Relativity, Mouton & Co., The Hague, 1967.

Carroll, John B, ed., Language, Thought and Reality: Selected Writings of Benjamin Lee Whorf, The M.I.T. Press, Cambridge, Massachusetts, twelfth printing, January 1976.

Cassirer, Ernst. An Essay On Man: An Introduction to a Philosophy of Human Culture, Yale University Press, Twelfth Printing, July 1964.

Doroszewski, Witbold. Elements of Lexicology and Semiotics, Mouton, The Hague, 1973.

Esland, Geoffrey. Language and Social Reality, The Open University Press, 1973.

Henle, Paul, ed., Language, Thought and Culture, The University of Michigan Press, Ann Arbor, Second Printing 1959.

Kenny, Anthony. Wittgenstein, Pelican Books, 1973.

Leech, Geoffrey. Semantics, A Pelican Original, Penguin Books, 1974.

Lyons, John. Semantics, Vols. 1 and 2, Cambridge University Press, 1977.

Mandelbaum, David G., ed., Selected Writings of Edward Sapir in Language, Culture and Personality, University of California Press, 1963.

Miller, Robert L. The Linguistic Relativity Principle and Humboldtian Ethnolinguistics: A History and Appraisal, Mouton, The Hague, 1968.

Nida, Eugene A. Componential Analysis of Meaning, Mouton, The Hague, 1975.

Sagle, Unian Von. Language, Thought and Perception: A Proposed Theory of Meaning, Janua Linguarum, Mouton, The Hague, 1974.

Sapir, Edward. Culture, Language And Personality: Selected Essays, University of California Press, 1960.

_____. Language: An Introduction to the study of Speech, A Harvest Book, Harcourt, Brace and World, Inc., New York, 1949.

Slametmuljana. Srivijaya, Percetakan Arnoldus Enda-Flores, Nusta Tenggara Timur.

UNESCO. Cultures and Times, The Unesco Press, Paris, 1976.

THE WORLD-VIEW OF PENINSULAR MALAYSIAN FOLK-TALES AND FOLK DRAMAS

MD. SALLEH YASPAR

Introduction

"World-view" is one of those terms used in socio-cultural studies to conceptualize a people's view of themselves and the realities around them. Other terms such as "cognitive pattern", "cognitive orientation", "culture pattern" or "configuration" are often used to describe the same thing. To date various definitions have been used to explain both the term as well as the concept. Robert Redfield (1966, p. 85), for example, defines "world-view" as "the way people characteristically look outward upon the universe", whereas Clifford Geertz (in Dundes 1968, p. 303) explains it as a people's "picture of the way things in sheer actuality are, their concept of nature, of self, and of society". And quite recently, Jones (1972, p. 83), after a lengthy discourse, defines "world-view" as a set of wide ranging vectors or attitudes in an individual's belief. These attitudes are learnt early in an individual's life, so that they determine his behaviour and they are not usually conveyed in the referential mode but in the expressive one.

From the above definitions it is clear that the term "world-view", first of all, recognizes the distinction between man and his surrounding or universe, and refers to a certain aspect of the relationship between the two. The aspect or issue focused on in this relationship is how man looks on his universe,

253

that is, what does he think of himself, of his surrounding, and what pattern of relationship he sees between them. Thus, "world-view", ultimately, concerns the set of ideas man has, firstly about the universe that confronts him. The universe comprises mainly of the human, that is, society, and the non-human which is made up of both natural and supernatural objects and beings.

A "world-view" study, then, is an attempt to study how a group of people view themselves, their society, nature and the supernatural.

The present study attempts a descriptive analysis of the folk-tales and folk dramas found in Peninsular Malaysia. Specifically it will try to examine, identify and describe the salient aspects and elements of the world-view as expressed or projected in the folk-tales and folk dramas. The scope, however, will be limited to the following: (i) it will deal with only three main issues, namely the relationship between man and society, between man and nature, and between man and the supernatural; (ii) the term "Peninsular Malaysian" will be used to refer to the indigenous groups in the Peninsula: the Malays and the Orang Asli, including the Negritoes, the Senois and the Proto-Malays or Orang Melayu Asli (Carey 1976, p. 6); (iii) with regard to the data used, only the much documented Marchen type of folk-tales will be considered for the Malay world-view, and for the Orang Asli, legends and myths will be included because of the lack of documented Marchen in the corpus of their literature (see Appendix). However, with regard to the latest Malay dramatic texts of wayang kulit, mak yong, manora, jike and mek mulung will also be included as data[1] (see Appendix). To date, Orang Asli folk drama texts have not been substantially brought to light, and thus no attempt can be made to understand the people's world-view from such materials.

In order to arrive at a fair deduction of the traditional Peninsular Malaysian world-view, the data stated above will be examined and analysed primarily to answer the following questions. What does the Peninsular Malaysian tend to focus on; what does he think of the objects of his focus, and what is the relationship he sees between himself and those objects; and is the relationship affective, reactional or merely cognitive in nature? With this basis of enquiry the data will also be utilized to provide answers to the following groups of questions:

1. The question of the relationship between man and society which involves:

   i) the inward look, including the origin of man, the concept of human nature and the man-woman and youth-age differences;

   ii) the concept of social entity, including kinship, origin of settlement, social values and social relationship.

2. The question of the relationship between man and nature, including:

   i) the origin and classification of natural features;

   ii) man's control and exploitation of nature.

3. The question of the relationship between man and the supernatural which involves:

   i) the nature and classification of supernatural beings and powers;

ii) man's attitude and reactions to these beings
and powers.

The World-View

Peninsular Malaysian folk-tales and folk drama stories of the
Marchen type may not yield a complete picture of the people's
world-view. Enough deduction can nonetheless be made from them
so as to obtain a fairly clear outline of the subject concerned,
one that may complement findings and deductions made from other
narrative forms, such as myths and legends.

Generally, these folk-tales and folk drama stories present a
typically primitive universe which may be defined as both
non-differentiated and interrelated. In this universe it is not
only man and animals that are animate, that is, having spirits or
souls and powers, but plants and other objects also share these
attributes. Consequently, not only is man able to conduct
personal communication within himself, but also with natural
objects and supernatural beings that surround him. In other
words, in this universe of Peninsular Malaysian folk-tales and
folk dramas, the modes of existence of the various objects and
beings are not always completely differentiated; instead, they
are often considered as similar to that of man.

This non-differentiated and rather man-centred universe is
marked by yet another reality, that is, the interrelatedness of
the unity of the various types of existence, natural or
otherwise. As may be seen in the following discussions, man, for
instance, is at times related to earthbound animals and
creatures, as he is occasionally linked to heavenly spirits and
deities. Certain artefacts too could be his kinsmen as some

mountains and rocks are his direct transformations. This ideology of relationships, in a way, generates the sense of mutual belonging among friends and relatives and similarly generates mutual distrust and hatred among enemies. Besides, it also limits the extent of the universe only to those realms within the reach of man, that is, _pulau buah_, the land of the dead; _tasik pauh janggi_, the middle of the ocean; _kayangan_, the skyworld; and the underworld, _dunia_, which is man's habitation, is conceived as the centre.

Man and Society

In Peninsular Malaysian folk-tales and folk dramas, man is often viewed either as a creature of direct divine origin or as one of divine creation. The idea of divine origin of man is especially true of Malay folk-tales and dramas which generally stress on the related phenomena of virgin-birth, transformation and reincarnation. The belief in the divine creation of man is largely reflected in Orang Asli legends or myths.

Malay tales such as Aa 1, 3, 5, and 7 and Malay folk dramas such as B20 in the Appendix tell various stories of virgin-birth when describing the origin and nature of their respective protagonists. Awang Lutung in tale Aa7, for example, is a monkey-hero conceived and born after his mother has drunk some water collected in an elephant's footstep. Likewise, Wong Singrat in folk drama B20 is born after his mother, a mermaid, drinks the urine of a certain Buddhist priest. In tale Aa5 the hero, Awang Burung Bayan, is born in the form of a cucumber, also without a paternal father. And similarly, in tale Aa7, Anak Nakhoda Anjing's mother becomes pregnant and then gives birth to him just after she has said a prayer to God. As may be observed, the central theme in most of these stories of virgin-birth is the

257

receiving or partaking of a fertile foreign element such as strange urine, betel leaf, and pomegranate respectively, by a woman destined to be the hero's mother. This element is more often than not ascribed to, or associated with, some higher beings like mysterious elephants, priests and deities. The fertile nature of the element and its association with those beings of higher status certainly indicates that it is not ordinary urine, or betel leaf, or any other object. Instead it may be viewed more as an object with a supernatural soul or spirit intended for future development in the human womb. In other words, it is really a transformation of an immortal soul which is sent down from kayangan to dunia wherein, by way of a woman, it will be reincarnated as a mortal. This notion of divine origin, however, may be seen more clearly later in stories of overt transformation and reincarnation.

As a rule, once on earth these elements would initially assume a lowly existence in the forms of either animals such as the monkey, vegetables such as the cucumber, objects such as cooking-pots or whatever, until such time when they find it necessary to transform themselves into handsome and charming princes. Later, in their dealing with other mortals, including kings, they would always be in the position whereby they could display their superiority. And, in times of emergency they would usually perform the yang-yang (magical incantation) to invoke their parents or ancestors in the kayangan for assistance. Indeed, as a testimony to their divine origins, their requests are often immediately granted. Upon his invocation, Awang Burung Bayan, for example, receives divine help in the forms of Awang Mendung Daki, a warrior, and Muda Hijau Isma Dewa, a supernatural horse. Similarly, upon his request, Awang Belanga of tale Aa3 is immediately provided with a host of supernatural armies by his ancestors to combat his adversaries. Of course, in the case of Awang Belanga, the divine descent is clear, for it is overtly stated that his mother, Mak Siti Galing, is a creature from kayangan. The ideology of the divine origin of man as manifested in stories of virgin-birth is made clear in other tales wherein the heroes, after their earthly sojourn, often return for good to kayangan. Such, for instance, is the case of Anak Haja Bacang in tale Aa2.

Besides stories of virgin-birth, there are also Malay tales which tell of overt transformation and reincarnation and which directly or more clearly point to the notion of the divine origin of man. These are the stories found, for example, in folk drama B2, "Bentara Keripan", and B6, "Cerita Maharaja Wana". In B2, a wayang kulit story of Javanese origin, the major characters are either descendants of dewa-dewa or reincarnations of them. The princes of Karipan, Daha, Gegalang and Singgasari, for example, are all descendants of dewa-dewa. The lowly and comical Semar or Pak Dogoh is really the reincarnation of Sang Yang Tunggal, the sperm of the dewa of kayangan. And as for the prince of Bentara Keripan and the princess of Sentara Daha, it is stated that they are reincarnations of Dewa Kerma Jaya and Bidadari Lela Kesokma, respectively. Both are sent down at the request of their prospective earthly parents. As the story has it, the male, Dewa Kerma Jaya, is first transformed to buah lonan, custard apple, and then thrown down to earth into the garden of Bentara Keripan. When the fruit is eaten by the queen she consequently gives virgin-birth to a prince. Bidadari Lela Kesokma, the goddess, undergoes the same process too, only in her case, she is transformed into a promegranate, eaten by the queen of Daha and reincarnated as a princess.

The above idea of transformation and reincarnation pointing to the divine origin of man is similarly manifested in B6, a wayang kulit story of Indian derivation. In this story, it is stated that the principal characters, Raja Seri Rama, Siti Dewi, Maharaja Wana, are all reincarnations of their previous existences in heaven. In their previous lives, they were all identified respectively as Dewa Berembun and Serajuk. Besides them, Hanuman, the monkey lord who defeated the evil Maharaja Wana, is also of divine origin. For he is, in actuality, the son of Dewa Berembun conceived by Dewa Angin, the queen of the wind, when she accidentally swallowed some airborne sperm of the dewa.

Next to the idea of the divine origin of man is the idea of the divine creation, which maintains that man is either directly or indirectly created by god, often out of earthly elements. This idea may be deduced largely from legendary and mythological tales of the Orang Asli. In the Negrito tale Ab11, for example, man is said to have been created by the god Ple, and is given life by the latter's brother, Kari. Similarly, a Jakun tale, Ab3, maintains that the original couple was created by the god Perman, who later set them afloat in a perahu (boat). Another Jakun tale (Joo 1976) claims that the first couple was created by the god Tuhan out of some earth. Yet another version (Skeat 1906, vol. II, p. 184) says that the first men, Mertang and Blo, were created by god from a lump of earth and a drop of water. The Mah Meri tale, Ab6, however, offers a different view of the creation, saying that man was first moulded out of clay by the prophet Nabi, and only then was he given the semangat (soul) by Tuhan. This is rather similar to the one offered by a Besese version (Ayampillay 1976), which ascribes the creation of man to Tun Fatimah, the prophetess, who performed her duty on the instruction of Tuhan.

Varied as it is, this Orang Asli belief in divine creation has a lot of similarities with the Quranic or Islamic world-view of creation -- that man was created by Allah out of a lump of earth. Such an idea must have made an impact on the Orang Asli especially after their contact with their Muslim Malay neighbours. Interestingly, the Malays themselves do not seem to reflect such an idea in their own folk-tales, but instead, they still maintain the Hindu idea of the divine origin of man.

Besides the general belief in divine creation, there exists too in the Orang Asli tales a rather unique idea about the origin of man, that of his being descended from the apes. This idea, however, is limited to certain tales of the Mantra group, which in various ways, recount the story of man's descendence from ungka putih, the white ape (Skeat 1906, vol. II, p. 185).

In Peninsular Malaysian folk-tales and folk dramas, whether man is thought of as a divine creation or of divine origin, he is always viewed as a creature made up of body and soul, two different elements with different modes of existence. This notion is best seen in the Negrito tale cited which describes how man's body or physical existence is first brought about by Ple, and then given soul or spirit by Kari. In Malay folk-tales and folk dramas, the idea may be seen in stories such as those of Aa16 and Aa25 in which certain characters often remove their souls from their bodies and deposit them in safety objects like cembul, or small jar. As may be seen, these stories do not only differentiate man's soul from his body, that is, the spiritual from the physical, but also suggest that the former may be separated from the latter, and may lead an independent existence. It may be significant to note that among the Negritoes there is a belief that a man's soul exists even before he is born. It exists in the form of a bird called chim-ini. In Malay folklore this recognition of the possible independent existence of the soul may be deduced from the fact that in curing the sick the pawang or medicine man often coaxes the wandering soul to return to its body, referring to it as pingai or kur, a bird. As opposed to the soul, the body is not capable of independent existence. In fact, it will disintegrate or cease to exist the moment it is left by the soul. The sick man, for example, would die if his semanagat or soul refuses to return to his body. And, as shown in tale Aa16 and Aa25 and in folk drama B6, a man would die when his soul, kept somewhere in safety, is finally destroyed.

261

Regarding stages in man's life, Peninsular Malaysian folk-tales and folk dramas seem to view youth as the most eventful and significant stage. Childhood is often associated with immaturity, while adulthood is viewed as incapability. Different from both childhood and adulthood, youth is a stage seen as full of vitality and interesting adventures, and one that offers a lot of promises too. That is why the focus in all the stories is on youth. Indeed, all heroes in these folk-tales and folk dramas are pictured as young people with lots of passion and will-power. They would be engaged in eventful and interesting adventures as soon as they emerge from childhood, when things are still not fully understood by them. And then, as a rule, they would all cease any further adventures the moment they reach adulthood because by then they would be less ambitious and physically unfit, and would prefer to settle on their thrones and live peacefully ever after. The weaker ones would even abdicate abruptly in favour of younger and stronger successors, and thus would slowly, but surely, fade away from a vigorous and eventful life.

Between the young, however, there is a difference too. For in Peninsular Malaysian folk-tales and folk dramas there is always the notion that the youngest of brothers or sisters, usually referred to as bungsu, is always the smartest. Kheruddin, the youngest child in tale Aa24, for instance, is presented as the smartest of the seven brothers mentioned in the story. Likewise, Puteri Bungsu in folk drama B13 who is the youngest of the twelve sisters, is the smartest of them all. This "youngest-smartest" idea is so widespread that it can be found in many other folk-tales and folk dramas of both the Malays and Orang Asli, such as Aa2, Aa5, Ab16 and B15 in the Appendix. It would be rather difficult to account for this idea in these folk-tales and folk dramas, but, as Melville Jacobs (1971, p. 226-27) suggests regarding the American-Indian tales, it may be connected with the rivalry between siblings. It may be a form of psychological device employed in fiction to promote self-esteem in the youngest sibling, who, in reality might find life to be less advantageous in terms of physical strength and social position.

With regard to sexual differences, generally, the folk-tales and folk dramas seem to view the male as superior in various ways to the female. Firstly, this is obvious from the fact that all stories are centred around the hero, the male protagonist. The heroine has her place too, but never in the middle, so as to overshadow the hero. In fact, all stories are structured in such a way that they may be regarded as biographies of their respective heroes, and not heroines. As the central figure, the hero is always pictured as ambitious, brave, adventurous and industrious. In fact, it is always his passions and desires that lead to the ultimate meeting with the heroine, thus leading to their mutual happiness. On the contrary, the heroine is often viewed as one who is on the waiting end. She does not have to go through adventures and battlefields to attain her dreams and desires; instead she may just remain in her royal abode and wait for the hero to come to her.

The notion of the inferiority of the female may be viewed in intellectual terms too. For, as the folk-tales and folk dramas have it, she is often easily tricked by the villain, or even by the hero himself. A typical example of her naivette may be seen in the popular Malay folk drama B6, "Cerita Maharaja Wana". In this story Siti Dewi, the heroine is twice cheated by Maharaja Wana into having intercourse with him. Embarassed, she promises herself that she would take her revenge. But this she fails to fulfil even in her present existence. Instead, she again falls into Maharaja Wana's trickery and finally lands in his island-state, Langkapuri. She would have remained there forever had it not been for Hanuman, the witty and resourceful male monkey.

Aside from the origin and nature of man, the concept of social entity may also be deduced from the Peninsular Malaysian folk-tales and folk dramas. This includes the ideas of kinship, social relationship, social values and, to a certain extent, the origin of settlements. The idea regarding the origin of settlements is almost absent in the Malay folk-tales and folk dramas consulted. But this is to be expected of the Marchen type. The idea, however, may be found in certain Proto-Malay tales of a mythological and legendary nature. In these tales of origin, the stress is always on two related phenomena: migration and land formation.

As may be understood from the Mah Meri tale, Ab7, the Proto-Malays view themselves as a group of people who originated either from China or Indochina. They crossed over to the Peninsula in ships or boats a long time ago. In doing so they were guided by the god Tuhan who instructed them to close their eyes while sailing. However, after some time, and when they were somewhere around the Peninsula, some people became restless. They started to disobey the instruction by opening their eyes, only to see that the ships had begun to run aground and eventually petrified as hills and mountains, some of which can still be seen today (Ayampillay 1976, p. 174). As for the people, they could not proceed any more, and thus, they remained in the newly formed hills and jungles.

From the above Mah Meri tale at least two related ideas may be gleaned regarding the origin of settlements. Firstly, the original Proto-Malay settlers of the Peninsula were those primordial people who migrated either from China or Indochina under the guidance of god. And, secondly, the original settlements of the Proto-Malays, that is, certain areas in the Peninsula, are really petrifications or transformations of their ancestral ships.

264

Regarding kinship, there are several patterns of relationship that may be discerned from both Malay and Orang Asli folk-tales and folk dramas. These are the sibling relationship, the marital relationship, and the relationship between children and parents. An aspect of the sibling relationship has actually been pointed out earlier when discussing the nature of man. This concerns the idea that the youngest sibling is always the smartest. Another aspect is the notion that the youngest sibling is always envied by the older ones. This is actually an extension of the "youngest-smartest" idea. As may be understood, siblings like outsiders, can also be sensitive to qualitative differences. They can sense who among them is the smartest. And, consequently they can also entertain rivalry among themselves. This being the case, it is only natural that the youngest sibling is always envied by the rest, since he or she is always the smartest of them all. This is exactly the position of Melor in folk drama B15 and Anak Raja Bacang in tale Aa2. Both of them are envied and consequently given the treatment deemed fit for them by their elder sisters and brothers. But, like the rest of the youngest protagonists or bungsu in the tale, they are not easily beaten. For, after all, each of them is the smartest of his or her siblings.

On marital relationship there is an interesting aspect which is often featured in the folk-tales and folk dramas. This is the relationship between co-wives. Like the pattern of relationship between siblings, this relationship is also often viewed as one marked by ill-feelings, jealousy and cruelty. As may be observed, a good number of the heroes in these folk-tales and folk dramas are princes or kings with polygamous tendencies. Some of them are motivated in this respect by a natural need and desire to maintain their lines of descent, while others are simply too capricious to limit themselves to only one woman. Whatever the case may be, once a hero takes to polygamy there is bound to be disharmony in his household or life. For ill-

265

feelings and jealousy or even cruelty will arise whenever there is even a slight disparity between the wives, either in terms of existing positions or future prospects. This is in view of the fact that from then on the wife with the child would gain more of the king's favour and, therefore, would rise higher in position in the royal household, whereas the childless ones would slowly but surely be neglected and pushed to the background. The child would also grow up as a royalty, and, in the case of a boy, would be the successor to the throne, thus putting an end to the aspirations of the childless wives to have one of their own children in such a position. Of the relationship between children and parents there are two types which are significant in the folk-tales and folk dramas. These are the relationship between the step-mother and her step-daughter and the relationship between the unfilial son and his parents. As viewed in the folk-tales, the relationship between the step-mother and her step-daughter is always strained and bloody. The step-daughter is always presented as beautiful, good-mannered and industrious. But the step-mother is often viewed as a woman devoid of affection and sympathy. She is the real image of the self-centred and unfeeling lady of terror. As portrayed in folk-tale Aa20, "Puding Emas Fuding Perak", she is usually the second wife who would do everything to oust her rival, the first wife, so that she could keep their common husband for herself. Having ousted her, often by resorting to killing, she would then dominate the husband to gain his full co-operation in ill-treating her step-daughter. Thus, the step-daughter would be ridiculed, made to starve and forced to do hard work, including serving her ugly, lazy and arrogant step-sister. Often the step-mother and step-sister would deny her existence in order to further their own ends. They would, for example, keep her away from a charming prince so that the prince would have his eyes only for her step-sister. The poor girl, however, survives all this on account her own virtues and her dead mother's spirit, which constantly keeps returning to comfort and guide her through difficult times. And, as expected, in the end she would triumph over them, for the prince would finally discover her and take her away as his bride. As for the step-mother and her daughter, they would in due course be properly punished for all their crimes. Such is the end of the relationship where the good is always rewarded and the bad punished.

Regarding the relationship between the unfilial son and his parents, Malay folk-tales and folk dramas have it that the son usually becomes unfilial when he gets wealthy and climbs up a higher social ladder. For his unfilial acts he would ultimately be killed or destroyed by higher forces. Folk drama B12, for example, tells of how a son of a poor man gets his wealth and high position by marrying a widowed queen. When the man hears of his son's good fortune he immediately asks for aid. But the son has by then become too proud of himself to recognize his poor father's needs to provide him food and clothing. This unfilial son is justly punished when shortly afterwards a robber enters his house and robs him of all his wealth. Consequently, he has to work as a captain of a ship in order to survive. Before long his ship is wrecked and he loses his life.

Folk drama B5, "Cempakieo Campaton", offers a more or less similar view of the relationship between the unfilial son and his parents. In this case, however, the son goes a step further so as to beat his father. And for this the old man, in turn, curses him so that he will suffer an immediate death. The significant point in these two folk dramas is the outcome of the son's attitude or behaviour towards his father or parents. In the world-view of the folk-tale, a son would ultimately meet with destruction when, having succeeded in life, he refuses to recognize or turns against his father or parents. Significant too, in this context, is the image of the father or parents which has a remarkable aura of power and dignity around it.

Besides the world-view on kinship ties, the folk-tales and folk dramas also abound in the world-view of social relations and social values. What is significant in the social relationship is what may be termed as "we-they" relationship, while the social values have for their central focus "Good" versus "Evil". The "we-they" relationship may be seen in at least two separate contexts. Firstly, it may be seen in the context of the difference between mortals and immortals or men and gods. Men are always viewed as beings that are created by, and inferior to, gods. Thus, they do not usually go against the latter. Those Malay folk heroes, such as Terong Pipit and Malin Deman of folk-tale Ab15, who venture to kayangan either to seek aid from, or fight against some dewas are really not ordinary men, but men of divine origin, immortals among mortals. That is why, in spite of their lowly appearance such as that of Awang Lutung, they always triumph over their adversaries who are mere men. These heroes are also always conscious of their position. They realise that they are different from other men, and that they belong to the family of immortals. Thus, they would usually invoke their parents or ancestors in the kayangan whenever they are in trouble.

Secondly, the "we-they" relationship may be seen in the perception by one ethnic group of another. In Malay folk dramas, the Orang Asli are often viewed as both lowly and esoteric. Generally, they are considered inferior to the Malays, but in some respect they are looked upon as good-natured, wise and even mystical. Thus, there exists a sort of ambivalence -- that of awe, respect and even fear -- towards them, especially the old and the hermits. Similarly, the Orang Asli have their own view of the Malays. In a Negrito tale, Ab20, for example, the Malays are viewed as a group of people from whom wild pigs get their origin. Wild pigs, it may be noted, are among the favourite trophies in the Orang Asli hunting trips. Their world-view of the Malays is, therefore, value-charged and as a sort of wish-fulfilment, they tend to infer that the Malays are a sort of inferior people who ought to be subjugated.

Regarding social values, particularly that of Good versus Evil, the folk-tales and folk dramas uphold the universal notions of justice: that Good must finally triumph over Evil, and Good is rewarded while Evil is punished. These ideas of justice run through nearly every folk-tale and folk drama of both the Malays and the Orang Asli. The Malay tale of "Puding Emas Puding Perak", which is similar to the "Cinderalla" motif, is a very good example of this because the tale concerns itself mainly with the Good versus Evil conflict.

Man and Nature

Peninsular Malaysian folk-tales and folk dramas, like most other folk-tales and folk dramas, view the relationship between man and nature as one that is closely bound together or one that is undifferentiated. The view is also true of the relationship within nature itself. This general outlook may be inferred from the more specific ideas regarding the origin and classification of nature, from the relationship between man and nature, and from man's manipulation of nature. Generally, the folk-tales and folk dramas present the idea that animals have their origin or ancestry in man. The Orang Asli folk-tale regarding the wild pigs which was previously cited is a case in point. Another tale, Ab13, holds that muntjac and goat-antelopes, or for that matter all animals, were once man. Besides animals some objects and plants too are thought to have their origin in man. This is especially true of rocks, hills and mountains. Nature, in the world-view of the folk-tales and folk dramas, falls under three main categories: animals, plants and objects. Animals possess legs and wings and, thus, are mobile, while plants and objects

269

are essentially stationary. Animals and plants feed and grow, but objects are devoid of these characteristics, although, like them, objects are subject to decay too. The division into the three categories, however, does not affect the basic notion that the three have one thing in common, that is they are all animate. According to this idea, animals, plants as well as objects are said to have semangat (spirits) and supernatural powers. In the Malay folk-tales Aa9, Aa20, and Aa24, objects such as rocks, rings and plants have to be treated with care, for semangat is believed to live in them. Likewise, in the dramatic performances of mak yong and wayang kulit, objects like the stage, gong, gendang (drums) and puppet are also thought to possess semangat. Hence, they are usually handled with great care, lest their spirits get hurt and cause nasty incidents during the performance. To ensure that all will be well, a special opening ceremony is held before every performance so as to invoke the spirits connnected with the wayang as well as the local spirits. And should any spirit get offended later in the course of the performance, a special offering is then quickly made to appease it.

The above notion of pan-animism is actually closely related to another idea, that of universal kinship. Kinship ties between man on the one hand, and animal and object on the other, have been suggested earlier, especially in connection with Orang Asli folk-tales. In Malay folk-tales, kinship between man and objects may be further seen in birth stories of various heroes. In the tale of Raja Donan (Aa21) for instance, it is said that the hero is born with magical objects in his arms. These objects, a sword and a gun, remain with him until he grows up, seeing him through all his adventures. The idea of kinship between man and nature may also be seen in another context, that of man's ability to transform himself, or be transformed, into elements of nature. In "Puding Emas Puding Perak", for example, when the heroine's mother is pushed into the sea, she is transformed into a turtle.

The turtle is always present to comfort the girl whenever she faces a problem. And when the turtle is in turn killed it is again transformed, this time into a brinjal plant. Later on in the story, the brinjal plant is again transformed into a puding plant which finally helps the heroine to meet her charming prince.

This concept of relationship is actually related to the idea of geographical ties. It is in crux the notion that man, animal, plant and object are co-inhabitants of one common part of the universe, the dunia. Within this dunia, man as a creature dominates the central part which is called negeri or the populated regions, like the towns and villages, while the plants and animals occupy the jungles and the waters which are unpopulated. Objects are everywhere because potentially they will be used by man. This territorial division, however, is not clear-cut and does not mean that the three groups do not mix with one another. Man, for instance, is free to trudge the jungle or sail the sea if he so wishes, although he has to be mindful of the fact that he is actually in the territories of other living souls, and therefore cannot wantonly misbehave himself. Animals too often leave their natural domains to be with man, either with good or bad intentions. Some of them have even been domesticated by man and remain peacefully in the negeri.

Besides being the inhabitant of the central part of the dunia, and therefore at the centre of all happenings, man is also viewed as being more intelligent than nature. He is often seen as a force capable of manipulating the different elements of nature in order to live a peaceful existence with them. Two situations may be cited as examples of the harmonious contact between man and nature and how it can be manipulated to the advantage of man. In an everyday situation, man, by virtue of his intellectual superiority, is able to use his natural environment to his own advantage. Man fashions items such as arrows and boats from the wood of the forests and utilizes other natural elements such as rivers or animals. The other situation is when man is confronted by the forces of nature which in ordinary circumstances can destroy him. In such a situation, man, using his intelligence and reasoning would avoid the impending confrontation and come to terms with those forces, which are often in the world-view of man transformed into supernatural beings. Thus, a prayer supplicating the supernatural forces looking after the waterways is said by man before he dares to sail an unfamiliar sea or river. Before a strange tree is felled, or before shooting an arrow at an unfamiliar object, man will offer an invocation to the relevant spirits in nature so that his deeds are not construed as harming nature but blended into it. Even after bringing harm to an element of nature, man can still restore the harmonious relationship by holding a ritual and making an offering to the injured party.

Man and The Supernatural

As seen in the Peninsular Malaysian folk-tales and folk dramas, besides nature, man also shares the dunia or benua with various forms of supernatural beings. As is the case with nature, the relationship between man and these beings is also close and intimate, for the latter generally have a keen interest in human affairs. The supernatural may be generally classified as follows. The highest type or form are the Malay Dewa Sang Tunggal and/or Tuhan and the Orang Asli Ta' Pern and/or Perman. These gods either give birth to men or create them together with the universe. Their domain is the kayangan or heaven situated above the dunia. Next to them in the hierarchy and sharing the same abode are the rest of the Malay dewas and some of the Orang Asli chenois or special ancestral spirits. These beings are closer to man and, as in the case of the chenois, often act as intermediaries between man and the higher gods or deities. Third in line are the various forms of spirits, including the penunggu or local guardian spirits and the spirits of the dead. These creatures inhabit the dunia and are very much involved in the day-to-day affairs of man. The fourth and last group belonging to the supernatural are really animals with monstrous looks and supernatural powers. To this category belong the gergasi or the giant, the naga or the dragon, the garuda or the giant eagle, and gajah putih or the white elephant. Generally, they occupy two different parts of the universe which are very far removed from the negeri, the habitat of man: one part is known as pusat tasik pauh janggi, which is a great whirlpool somewhere in the middle of the ocean, and the other part is known as padang jauh, and sometimes known as puncak gunung, situated at the far end of the jungle. These places, including dasar laut (ocean bed) which is connected with the great whirlpool, are normally beyond the reach of mere mortals.

As suggested earlier, the supernatural beings have keen interest in human affairs and they often get involved in them. This is true of all categories of supernatural creatures, whose interest in and involvement with human life may be seen in various forms. Sang Yang Tunggal, the supreme lord of kayangan himself, descends to dunia just to observe the deeds of mankind. Other dewa give a helping hand to certain heroes whenever their aid is needed. Some others, like the one in folk-tale Aa17, even take mortals as their wives. And, in some cases, they even fight man to settle disputes over these females. Among the lower inhabitants of the supernatural world especially the local spirits, interest in human activities is manifested in quite a different way. Generally, these spirits are more concerned about their rights in life. That is why they always see to it that man in his quest for life does not encroach upon their rights. However, like humans, they would feel more comfortable if, prior

273

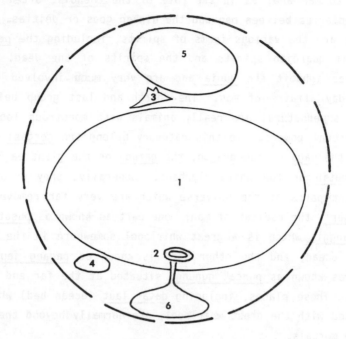

	REGION	INHABITANTS
1.	Dunia or benua	Man, animals, plants, objects, spirits.
2.	Pusat tasik pauh janggi	Nagas, jins, garuda
3.	Padang jauh dan puncak gunung	Giants, jins.
4.	Pulau buah	Ancestral spirits (Orang Asli)
5.	Kayangan	Dewa, Perman
6.	Dasar laut	Raja Lebis

to an act of encroachment, a proper notice is served and an approval sought. This is often done through rituals where an offering or sacrifice is offered to the spirits. Hence, in the world-view of the indigenous folks in Peninsular Malaysia, expressed both in their folk-tales and folk dramas and in their folk beliefs, constant and harmonious relationship is maintained with the local spirits around them.

The interest and involvement of the supernatural beings in the daily affairs of man consequently develops a corresponding attitude in the latter. This attitude generally reflects man's desire to maintain a harmonious relationship to protect his own well-being and security. Aware of the fact that the gods and spirits always keep a watchful eye on him, man continuously strives to observe taboos and constraints in life so that he can avoid all the pitfalls and misfortunes that may befall him. For his own well-being he, therefore, makes offerings to appease the gods and spirits. However, there are situations when, in order to advance his cause, man may venture to distant regions like pusat tasik pauh janggi, dasar laut and even kayangan to combat adversaries, including naga and dewa or to win his betrothed. In the folk-tales or in folk dramas, there are instances when the protagonist has to venture into these mysterious domains in pursuit of his inhabitant of kayangan. Such a hero may be a semi-mortal himself or, if he is not, he gets the supernatural to help him in his quest.

Conclusion

The discussion above has attempted to picture some aspects of the world-view as manifested in the Peninsular Malaysian folk-tales and folk dramas. The salient points to be noted are as follows. The world-view seems to uphold and confirm the traditional belief

275

in the division of the universe into three entities, that of man, nature and the supernatural, with man playing the dominant role. However, man as the dominant entity, has his origin in the supernatural because he is either a creation or a descendant of the latter. As for man himself, folklore places more importance on the male of the species and portrays the stage of youth as the most forceful. Although man, nature and the supernatural overtly demonstrate a rather different mode of existence, they are actually interrelated as they are not completely separated or differentiated. This is mainly due to the ideas of "pan-animism" and "universal kinship" prevalent in the world-view of the people. According to these ideas, plants and objects may be different from man in physical structure, but they share with the latter a common internal element, the semangat. In another respect, man too cannot be completely differentiated from the gods, for he has his origin in them. And neither can he be totally differentiated from nature, since some natural elements are actually in his direct transformation. Finally, the universe, as viewed in the folk-tales and folk dramas, is essentially a man-centred one. Events take place mostly around man, in the dunia, especially, his part of it, the negeri. In this context, man's relationship with nature and the supernatural is both cognitive and reactional in form. He recognizes the fact that he shares the dunia with the latter too. He knows too that to promote his cause and to ensure his survival he has to live with them harmoniously. While on the one hand he would utilize them to serve his own ends, on the other he respects them for their influences, because his life and theirs, in the world-view of the indigenous people of Peninsular Malaysia, at least as expressed in their folk-tales and folk dramas, are intertwined.

APPENDIX

Folk-tales and Folk Dramas Consulted

A. Folk-tales

(a) Malay

1. "Anak Nakhoda Anjing", comp. Mokhtar Yassin. Typescript (HLN 232/USM), 1978.

2. "Anak Raja Bacang", comp. Mohd Basir Haji Noor. Typescript (HLN 232/USM), 1978.

3. Awang Belanga. Kuala Lumpur: Dewan Bahasa Dan Pustaka, 1972.

4. "Awang Betoi", comp. Amri Lah. Typescript (HLN 232/USM), 1978.

5. "Awang Burung Bayan", Cerita-cerita Rakyat I, ed. Siti Aishah Mat Ali. Kota Bahru: Percitakan Al-Ahliyah Sdn. Bhd., 1976.

6. "Awang Golok Besar", comp. Abu Bakar bin Ismail. Typescript (HLN 232/USM), 1978.

7. "Awang Lutung", Cerita-cerita Rakyat I, ed. Siti Aishah Mat Ali. Kota Bahru: Percitakan Al-Ahliyah Sdn. Bhd., 1976.

8. "Awang Sulung Merah Muda", ed. R. O. Winstedt. JSBRAS, 52 (March, 1909), 31-95.

9. "Batu Belah Batu Bertangkup", comp. Timah binti Chek. Typescript (HLN 232/USM), 1978.

10. "Burung Ketitir", Cerita-cerita Rakyat I, ed. Siti Aishah Mat Ali. Kota Bahru: Percitakan Al-Ahliyah Sdn. Bhd., 1976.

11. "Ceciwi", comp. Noriah Taslim. Typescript (HLN 232/USM), 1978.

12. "Cerita Raja Serkat Dewa", Cerita-cerita Rakyat I, ed. Siti Aishah Mat Ali. Kota Bahru: Percitakan Al-Ahliyah Sdn. Bhd., 1976.

13. Cerita Sulung Jawa, ed. Jamilah Ahmad. Kuala Lumpur: Dewan Bahasa Dan Pustaka, 1978.

277

14. Hikayat Anggun Che Tunggal, ed. R. O. Winstedt. Singapura: Malaya Publishing House Ltd., 1960.

15. Hikayat Malim Deman, ed. R. O. Winstedt. Singapura: Malaya Publishing House Ltd., 1960.

16. Hikayat Terang Pipit, narr. Panglima Ali Mudin bin Panglima Hasan. Kuala Lumpur: Oxford University Press, 1964.

17. Jambul Emas. Kuala Lumpur: Dewan Bahasa Dan Pustaka, 1972.

18. Malim Sakti. Kuala Lumpur: Dewan Bahasa Dan Pustaka, 1973.

19. "Mok Sekin", comp. Abdul Ghafar Taib. Typescript (HLN 232/USM), 1978.

20. "Puding Emas Puding Perak", comp. Yahya Ismail. Typescript (HLN 232/USM), 1978.

21. "Raja Donan; Malay Fairy Tale Told By A Malay Rhapsodist", ed. W. E. Maxwell. JSBRAS 18 (December 1886): 241-69.

22. "Sri Rama; A Malay Fairy Tale", ed. W. E. Maxwell. JSBRAS 17 (June 1886): 87-115.

23. Tambi Hitam. Kuala Lumpur: Dewan Bahasa Dan Pustaka, 1974.

24. "The Story of Kheruddin", ed. G. M. Laidlaw. JSBRAS 46 (December 1906): 27-57.

25. "Tok Taja Rom", Cerita-cerita Rakyat I, ed. Siti Aishah Mat Ali. Kota Bahru: Percitakan Al-Ahliyah Sdn. Bhd., 1976.

26. "Tuan Puteri Menora Dan Kenapa Daun Nyok Carek", comp. Shaari Omar. Typescript (HLN 232/USM), 1978.

(b) Orang Asli

1. "A Menik Kaien Legend", Studies in Religion, Folklore and Custom in British North Borneo and the Malay Peninsula, J. H. N. Evans. London: Frank Cass & Co. Ltd., 1970.

2. "A Tiger Story", Studies in Religion, Folklore and Custom in British North Borneo and the Malay Peninsula, J. H. N. Evans. London: Frank Cass & Co. Ltd., 1970.

3. "A Trip to Gunung Blumut", comp. D.F.A. Harvey. JSBRAS 3 (July 1879): 85-115.

4. "Bonsu and Tak Kemoit", Studies in Religion, Folklore and Custom in British North Borneo and the Malay Peninsula, J.H.N. Evans. London: Frank Cass & Co. Ltd., 1970.

5. "Budak Yoid Intoie", <u>Studies in Religion, Folklore and Custom in British North Borneo and the Malay Peninsula</u>, J.H.N. Evans. London: Frank Cass & Co. Ltd., 1970.

6. "Cerita Asal Dunia Zaman Dahulu", <u>Mah Meri Art and Culture</u>, R. Werner. Kuala Lumpur: Muzium Negara, 1973.

7. "Cerita Asal Melayu Zaman Dahulu", <u>Mah Meri Art and Culture</u>, R. Werner. Kuala Lumpur: Muzium Negara, 1973.

8. "Cerita Moyang Kapis dan Moyang Bertam Berasal Batu Hunjo Kelang", <u>Mah Meri Art and Culture</u>, R. Werner. Kuala Lumpur: Muzium Negara, 1973.

9. "Hantu Jin Bulu Makan Manusia Zaman Dahulu", <u>Mah Meri Art and Culture</u>, R. Werner. Kuala Lumpur: Muzium Negara, 1973.

10. "Legend of Kari the Thunder-God", <u>Pagan Races of the Malay Peninsula</u>, Vol II, W.W. Skeat and C.O. Blagden. London: Frank Cass & Co. Ltd., (new impression), 1966.

11. "Legend of Ple", <u>Pagan Races of the Malay Peninsula Vol II</u>, W.W. Skeat and C.O. Blagden. London: Frank Cass & Co. Ltd. (new impression), 1966.

12. "Legend of the Origin of the Negritos", <u>Studies in Religion, Folklore and Custom in British North Borneo and the Malay Peninsula</u>, J.H.N. Evans. London: Frank Cass & Co. Ltd., 1970.

13. "Mempes", <u>Studies in Religion, Folklore and Custom in British North Borneo and the Malay Peninsula</u>, J.H.N. Evans. London: Frank Cass & Co. Ltd., 1970.

14. "Si Nibong", <u>Pagan Races of the Malay Peninsula Vol II</u>, W.W. Skeat and C.O. Blagden. London: Frank Cass & Co. Ltd. (new impression), 1966.

15. "Tak Chemempes", <u>Studies in Religion, Folklore and Custom in British North Borneo and the Malay Peninsula</u>, J.H.N. Evans. London: Frank Cass & Co. Ltd., 1970.

16. "The Cockroaches' Village", <u>Studies in Religion, Folklore and Custom in British North Borneo and the Malay Peninsula</u>, J.H.N. Evans. London: Frank Cass & Co. Ltd., 1970.

17. "The Creation of Man", <u>Pagan Races of the Malay Peninsula</u>, Vol II, W.W. Skeat and C.O. Blagden. London: Frank Cass & Co. Ltd. (new impression), 1966.

18. "The Legend of the Peopling of the Peninsula", <u>Pagan Races of the Malay Peninsula Vol II</u>, W.W. Skeat and C.O. Blagden, London: Frank Cass & Co. Ltd. (new impression), 1966.

19. "The Mai Mensud", Studies in Religion, Folklore and Custom in British North Borneo and the Malay Peninsula, J.H.N. Evans. London: Frank Cass & Co. Ltd., 1970.

20. "Wild Pigs", Studies in Religion, Folklore and Custom in British North Borneo and the Malay Peninsula, J.H.N. Evans. London: Frank Cass & Co. Ltd., 1970.

21. "Yak Kampeh and Piagok", Studies in Religion, Folklore and Custom in British North Borneo and the Malay Peninsula, J.H.N. Evans. London: Frank Cass & Co. Ltd., 1970.

B. Malay Folk Drama

1. "Andrea Dewa", The Magic Kite and Other Ma'yong Stories, ed. Mubin Sheppard. Singapore: Federal Publications, 1960.

2. "Bentara Keripan, Wayang Kulit Stories from Trengganu", A.H. Hill. JMBRAS, XXII, III (1949).

3. "Bungsu Sakti", The Magic Kite and Other Ma'yong Stories, ed. Mubin Sheppard. Singapore: Federal Publications, 1960.

4. "Cahaya Bulan, Permainan Mek Mulung", Zaleha Hamid. Graduation Exercise. Universiti Kebangsaan Malaysia, 1974/75.

5. "Cempakieo Campaton, Jikey - Tradisi Rakyat Melayu Kedah", Mohd. Shuib Abu Bakar. Typescript (HDR 391/USM), 1977/78.

6. "Cerita Maharaja Wana", Malay Shadow Puppets, Amin Sweeney. London: Trustees of the British Museum, 1972.

7. "Dewa Muda", The Magic Kite and Other Ma'yong Stories, ed. Mubin Sheppard. Singapore: Federal Publications, 1960.

8. "Hikayat Melayu Burma, Jikey - Tradisi Rakyat Melayu Kedah", Mohd. Shuib Abu Bakar. Typescript (HDR 391/USM), 1977/78.

9. "Kera Emas, Wayang Kulit Stories from Trengganu", A.H. Hill. JMBRAS, XXII, III (1949).

10. "Malim Bungsu, Permainan Mek Mulung", Zaleha Hamid. Graduation Exercise. Universiti Kebangsaan Malaysia. 1974/5.

11. "Menora", comp., Shaari Ahmad. Typescript (HLN 232/USM), 1978.

12. "Phai Yat Tat, Satu Penyiasatan Ringkas Tentang Drama Tradisional Jike", Mustafa Md. Isa. Typescript (AH 221/UM), 1972.

13. "Puteri Dua Belas or Lakun Aperot, Permainan Mek Mulung", Zaleha Hamid. Graduation Exercise. Universiti Kebangsaan Malaysia, 1974/75.

14. "Puteri Timun Muda", The Magic Kite and Other Ma'yong Stories, ed. Mubin Sheppard. Singapore: Federal Publications, 1960.

15. "Raja Gondang", The Magic Kite and Other Ma'yong Stories, ed. Mubin Sheppard. Singapore: Federal Publications, 1960.

16. "Raja Muda La'leng", The Magic Kite and Other Ma'yong Stories, ed. Mubin Sheppard. Singapore: Federal Publications, 1960.

17. "Raja Muda Lembek", The Magic Kite and Other Ma'yong Stories, ed. Mubin Sheppard. Singapore: Federal Publications, 1960.

18. "Raja Muda Serupa", The Magic Kite and Other Ma'yong Stories, ed. Mubin Sheppard. Singapore: Federal Publications, 1960.

19. "Raja Tangkai Hati", The Magic Kite and Other Ma'yong Stories, ed. Mubin Sheppard. Singapore: Federal Publications, 1960.

20. "Wong Singrat, Seni Jike Mesti Ada Keling", Omar Abdullah. Mastika 2, 34th year (February 1974): 129-35.

NOTES

1. <u>Wayang kulit</u> is the Malay shadow play already much written about; <u>mak yong</u> is a dramatic form popular in Kelantan; <u>manora</u> is popular in Kelantan and known in Kedah and Perlis; <u>jike</u> is found in both Kedah and Perlis; and <u>mek mulung</u> is performed only in and around Wang Tepus, Jitra, Kedah.

REFERENCES

Ayampillay, S.D. <u>Kampung Tanjung Sepat: A Besese Community of Coastal Selangor.</u> Provisional Research Report No. 6. Social Anthropology Section, School of Comparative Social Sciences, Universiti Sains Malaysia, Penang, 1976.

Denton, Robert Knox. <u>The Semai: A Non-violent People of Malaya.</u> New York: Holt, Rinehart and Winston, 1968.

Endicott, Kirk Michael. <u>An Analysis of Malay Magic.</u> Oxford Clarendon Press, 1970.

Evans, Ivor H. N. <u>Studies of Religion, Folklore and Customs in British North Borneo and the Malay Peninsula.</u> London: Frank Cass & Co. Ltd., 1970.

Geertz, Clifford. "Ethos, World-View and the Analysis of Sacred Symbols". <u>Every Man His Day,</u> edited by Alan Dundes. New Jersey: Prentice-Hall, Inc., 1968.

Hill, A.H. "Wayang Kulit Stories From Trengganu". <u>Journal of the Malayan Branch of the Royal Asiatic Society</u> (<u>JMBRAS</u>), XXII, III (1949).

Jacobs, Melville. <u>The Content and Style of An Oral Literature.</u> Chicago: The University of Chicago Press, 1971.

Jones, W.T. "World Views: Their Nature and Their Functions", <u>Current Anthropology</u> 13, 1 (February 1972): 79-91.

Joo, Lee Kok. "Kampung Lubok Bandung: A Temuan Community of Malacca State". Provisional Research Report No. 5. Social Anthropology Section, School of Comparative Social Sciences, Universiti Sains Malaysia, Penang, 1976.

Ku Zam Zam Ku Idris. "Muzik Tradisional Di Kedah Utara: Ensembel-ensembel Wayang Kulit, Mek Mulung dan Gendang Keling Dengan Tumpuan Kepada Alat-alat, Pemuzik-pemuzik Dan Fungsi". M.A. thesis, Universiti Malaya, Kuala Lumpur, 1978.

Lee, Dorothy. "Codifications of Reality: Lineal and Nonlineal". <u>Every Man His Day,</u> edited by Alan Dundes. New Jersey: Prentice-Hall Inc., 1968.

Maxwell, W.E. "Folklore of the Malays", <u>JSBRAS</u> 7 (June 1881), 11-29.

Mohd. Shuib Abu Bakar. "Jikey -- Tradisi Rakyat Melayu Kedah". Typescript (HDR
391/USM), 1977/79.

Mohd. Taib Osman. "Myths, Legends and Folk-tales in Malay Culture", Asian
Pacific Quarterly II, 2 (1970): 54-62.

Muhammad Affandi Ismail. "Mak Yong: Sebuah Tinjauan Dari Sudut Persembahan".
Graduation exercise, University Malaya, 1973.

Mustafa Md. Isa. "Awang Belanga, Penglipun Lara Dari Perlis". M.A. thesis,
Universiti Sains Malaysia (in preparation).

_____. "Satu Penyiasatan Ringkas Tentang Drama Tradisional Jike". Typescript
(AH 221/USM), 1972.

Nelson, Cynthia. "Analysis of World View in A Mexican Peasant Village: An
Illustration", Social Forces.

Omar Abdul. "The Orang Kanaq of Southeastern Johor: A Preliminary Ethnography".
Provisional Research Report No. 7. Social Anthropology Section, School of
Comparative Social Sciences, Universiti Sains Malaysia, Penang, 1978.

_____. "Seni Jike Mesti Ada Keling". Mastika, 2, Yr. 34 (February 1974):
129-35.

Radin, Paul. Primitive Man As Philosopher. New York: Dover Publications, Inc.,
1957.

Rahmah Bujang. "The Menora/Nora/Menora Siam". Typescript, 1978.

Redfield, Robert. The Primitive World and its Transformations. Ithaca: Cornell
University Press, 1966.

Rentse, Anker. "The Kelantan Shadow-Play", JMBRAS XIV (1936): 284-301.

Robertson, Roland, ed. Sociology of Religion: Penguin Education. Baltimore:
Penguin Books Inc., 1972.

Safian Mohd Nazir. "Kampung Temakah: A Temiar Community in Perak". Provisional
Research Report No. 4. Social Anthropology Section, School of Comparative
Social Sciences, University Sains Malaysia, Penang, 1976.

Saleha Ishak. "Persembahan Jikey di Pulau Langkawi dan di Kangar, Perlis: Satu
Pengenalan", mimeographed. Jabatan Persuratan Melayu, Universiti Kebangsaan
Malaysia, 1977.

Sheppard, Mubin. "Manora, The Ballet of Ligor". Straits Times Annual (1959),
pp. 12-15.

Skeat, Walter William. Malay Magic. London: Frank Cass & Co. Ltd., 1965.

Skeat, Walter William and Blagden, Charles Otto. Pagan Races of the Malay
Peninsula , Vol. I & II. London: MacMillan and Co. Limited, 1906.

Sweeney, Amin. Malay Shadow Puppets. London: Trustees of the British Museum, 1972.

_____. "Professional Malay Story-Telling: Part One: Some Questions of Style and Presentation", JMBRAS XLVI, 2 (1973).

_____. Ramayana and the Malay Shadow Play. Kuala Lumpur: Penerbit Universiti Kebangsaan Malaysia, 1972.

Winstedt, Richard Olof. The Malays: A Cultural History. London: Routledge & Kegan Paul Limited, 1953.

Zaleha Hamid. "Permainan Mek Mulung". Graduation exercise, Universiti Kebangsaan Malaysia, 1974/75.